THE EMPLOYMENT CONTRACT IN TRANSFO

THE EMPLOYMENT CONTRACT IN TRANSFORMING LABOUR RELATIONS

Edited by

LAMMY BETTEN

With contributions by

Lammy Betten
Marco Biagi
Breen Creighton
Reinhold Fahlbeck
Matthew Finkin
Mark Freedland
Richard Mitchell
Manfred Weiss
Ryuichi Yamakawa

KLUWER LAW INTERNATIONAL
THE HAGUE / LONDON / BOSTON

A C.I.P. Catalogue record for this book is available from the Library of Congress.

ISBN 90-411-0149-7

Published by Kluwer Law International,
P.O. Box 85889, 2508 CN The Hague, The Netherlands.

Sold and distributed in the U.S.A. and Canada
by Kluwer Law International,
675 Massachusetts Avenue, Cambridge, MA 02139, U.S.A.

In all other countries, sold and distributed
by Kluwer Law International,
P.O. Box 85889, 2508 CN The Hague, The Netherlands.

Printed on acid-free paper

Printed in the Netherlands

CONTENTS

FOREWORD

This book is the follow-up of a Colloquium on the Future of the Contract of Employment, held on the 29th of April, 1995, in The Hague. The Colloquium, organised by Kluwer International, The Hague Institute for Socio-Legal Studies and the Europa Institute of the University of Utrecht was in celebration of the 10th anniversary of the International Journal for Comparative Labour Law and Industrial Relations. Although the papers presented at the colloquium form the core of this book, not all contributions included here were presented at the Colloquium. Due to a stay in Sapporo, Japan, Professor Reinhold Fahlbeck was unable to present his contribution. So was professor Manfred Weiss; Rudolf Buschmann, editor of *Recht und Arbeit,* was so kind to take Professor Weiss' place at the Colloquium.

This book could not have been produced without the assistance of many people, to whom I would like to express my gratitude. First of all, my gratitude goes to the authors for their kind and enthusiastic co-operation; to professor Alan Neal, founding editor of the International Journal, for drafting the questionnaire, which provided the cement for this book.

Delma Mac Devitt of The Hague Institute for Socio-Legal Studies assisted in the language editing. The assistance of Marieke Klap-Vreugdenhil, secretary at the Europa Institute in Utrecht, was pivotal in making the typescripts camera-ready. Michel Trietsch and Sheila Faessen were very helpful in the final, as usual hectic, stages of the editing.

I would also like to thank Gwen de Vries of Kluwer International for her continuous co-operation in organising the colloquium and producing the book.

Last but not least, my thanks go to my colleagues of the Department of Labour Law and Social Security of the Europa Institute for their support.

Utrecht/The Hague, August 1995
Lammy Betten

THE ROLE OF THE CONTRACT IN TRANSFORMING LABOUR RELATIONS

Lammy BETTEN

1. Introduction

"Flexibilisation", "deregulation" and "globalisation of the economy" have become key words in the area of labour law and industrial relations of the 1990's. All three have become central concepts for the advocates of new employment strategies and practices aimed at a more liberal and flexible labour market with a minimum of government interference. This tendency to return to the philosophy of "laissez-faire, laissez aller" is alleged to be necessary to be able to compete on a market which is becoming increasingly "global" with new countries acquiring a competitive position on the world market by a combination of high-technology and low wages. This process is usually referred to as the "globalisation of economy".

One of the interesting aspects of these developments is that when, about a century ago, communications, trade and commerce were becoming increasingly international, employers in particular called for (binding) regulation of working conditions at national and international level. At the international level, this resulted in the establishment of the International Labour Organisation (ILO) which, according to its Constitution as laid down in the Peace Treaty of Versailles, was to become a promoter of more social justice without which "universal and lasting peace" would be an untenable goal. Even though history has demonstrated that, in spite of the adherence to internationally agreed labour standards, universal and lasting peace still proved to be an impossible mission while social justice proved to be equally idealistic, the ILO's work is most certainly very valuable.

The point to be made here, however, is that at present internationalisation (globalisation of economy) is used as an argument to deregulate at the national as well as international levels. Employers in particular are showing more and more resistance to regulation of labour relations at any level.

On the other hand, the resistance against giving the "marketeers" free reigns is growing, too. The nefarious effects on societies as a whole of a

1

L. Betten (ed.), The Employment Contract in Transforming Labour Relations, 1-15.
© 1995 *Kluwer Law International. Printed in the Netherlands.*

return to a free market are aptly described by various authors.[1] Others emphasise the importance of the protection of workers' rights as an essential part of the struggle for long term economic prosperity.[2]

There is wide agreement, however, that, as we approach the millenium, the concept of the "Welfare State" needs thorough reconsideration. Some aspects of welfare originated in a unique period of economic prosperity in the capitalist countries and a rigidly organised centrally planned economy in the socialist states. Both have come to an end. In the capitalist countries, the years of economic prosperity which marked the era of the 1970's[3] have been followed by economic crises at worst and periods of precarious recovery at the best. The dissolution of the socialist system was followed by boundless glorification of the free market.

In this book, the emphasis is on developments in capitalist countries which all have problems with coping with the specific demands of a new era. It is increasingly accepted that some aspects of the social systems built up in the seventies in these countries have to be critically assessed, simply because they no longer provide the solutions for the problems that face present day societies of which the most outstanding are high levels of unemployment in general and structural unemployment in particular.

Some submit that the fight against unemployment would be more successful if governments stopped interfering in the labour market and left it to market forces. This is another way of saying that measures which protect the weaker party (*i.e.* the workers) stand in the way of full economic recovery with, allegedly, full(er) employment. European employers (and the British government) like to point to American society which has much lower unemployment levels and much less protection through employment contract. Their argument is that there is a correlation between the level of unemployment and the protection offered by public measures, through, for instance, legal regulation of the employment contract. It is undisputed that protection afforded to workers by public measures as well as the costs of the unemployed is an enormous financial burden for the society as a whole. At

---

1   See e.g. Will Hutton, *The State We're In*, London. 1995; John Kenneth Galbraith, *The Culture of Contentment*, Boston/New York/London, 1992.

2   See, for example, Simon Deakin and Frank Wilkinson *Rights vs Efficiency? The Economic Case for Transnational Labour Standards,* Industrial Law Journal, Vol. 23, December 1994, at pp. 289 - 310.

3   See Ajit Singh, *Global Economic Changes, Skills and International Competitiveness,* International Labour Reviw, Vol. 133, 1994, No. 2, pp. 166 - 184, at p. 168.

the same time,   subjecting (the division of) employment entirely to market forces, without further government interference, causes other effects which are a good deal less desirable.[4]

It may be seriously questioned that this is the way European societies ought to go. There are not many, outside the British government, who take an optimistic view of the effects of the emphasis on the importance of market forces in the United Kingdom for the past sixteen years.[5]

Moreover, there is growing evidence that the correlation between labour costs, rigidity and economic prosperity is far less clear than suggested and that there is no single response to increased market competitions because of significant differences in employment relations and practices between and even within in countries.[6]

Even though there is no sound argument for alleging that a free market is the answer to all our problems, it is undeniably true that the reality of the late 19th centruy concept of the "Welfare State" which emerged in the 1950s has to be adjusted to the demands of the present and future time. This affects no doubt the labour market and the regulation (or protection) of employment and employment relations. The difficult question which faces all is *how* to adapt to the tranformation of industrial relations.

A central role in changing industrial relations is played by the contract of employment which is seen as an instrument to protect part of the working population against, in general terms, unfair treatment. One of the central issues in this context is that, in most capitalist countries, the contract of employment offers protection against unfair dismissal and even when there is no such protection, employers must respect a certain period of notice when

---

4   Galbraith gives an interesting analysis of the future of the American society divided in contented "upperclasses" concentrating on short term self-satisfying economic success and an underclass, denied support to change their situation. Galbraith, *op. cit.* footnote 1.

5   Hill discusses the results of the relentless emphasis on the values of the market economy by the British conservative governments. According to him, sixty per cent of the British population are now either belonging or on the virge of belonging to the people out of work and no hope to get back into employment. The other forty per cent do not represent a rich elite, he includes also lower class people, who are fortunate enough to have a relatively safe employment situation. Will Hutton, *The State we're in, op. cit.* footnote 1, at p. 14 and pp. 105 - 110.

6   See Richard Locke, Thomas Kochan and Michael Piore, *Reconcenptualizing comparative industrial relations: Lessons from international research,* International Labour Review, 1995/2, pp. 139 - 161.

they want to terminate the contract. In the context of flexibilisation this is a central issue, because employers allege that this protection is one of the aspects causing rigidity on the labour market (fixed minimum wages being another, important one). In the view employers, flexibility means that labour is hired and fired on conditions created by the market and not fixed by regulation. In many countries, this would mean that the contract of employment should be abolished. But this is painting the picture in black and white, while, in reality, there are many shades. Most employers are well aware that complete dictation of labour conditions by "the market" is not desireable. Most employers are well aware of the advantages of the values of social protection.

The question is not the abolition of the contract of employment, but of rethinking its role and function in the context of transforming labour relations.

Should the traditional, full time, indefinite employment contract be given up in favour of more flexible conditions? If so, how are the negative effects of insecurity and instability be avoided? Should a regular income be guaranteed so that workers receive some form of basic income in the periods between work and, if so, who is going to pick up the bill? How can it be ensured that categories of persons who are less attractive for employers are not completely neglected and that a tension between those who have regular jobs and those who have not is avoided? Is flexibility of the labour market an economic answer only? Is it socially justifiable, too? What is the role of trade unions in this context?

There is an infinite number of questions which can be asked in this context. They make clear that the social consequences of an increased flexibility should at least be investigated before governments retreat entirely from the labour market. It is far too optimistic and simplistic to suggest that flexibility is a *conditio sine qua non* for reducing the high unemployment figure. There is increasing evidence that part of these figures concern structural unemployment; that is a huge problem which needs other answers than a *laissez faire laissez aller* attitude towards the labour market. There is also increasing evidence that there is no clear-cut correlation between the increase in the use of "atypical" working contracts and a decrease of unemployment figures.[7]

---

7   See, for instance, L. Delsen, *Atypical Employment, an International Perspective*, Groningen, 1995, *passim*.

2. The Role of the Employment Contract in Domestic Systems

The answers to all these questions are not, of course, to be found in this book. The intention is to show developments in the role and function of the contract of employment in various parts of the world. The authors were asked to look at all the elements that influence and/or determine the role of the contract of employment and to consider its future. They have provided a series of outstanding contributions which show some interesting deviations as well as common trends.

The authors have examined a variety of questions such as the relation between legislation and employment relations, between the role of the individual contract of employment and (the normative effect of) collective agreements, and the significance of the difference in conceptions between the contract of employment and the contract of rendering services. The analyses of these questions have been carried out in a framework of other developments within the domestic systems, that is to say most authors have focused on the changes occurring in employment relations and on the effects these have on the role of the contract of employment.

The central question is where developments in post-industrial society leaves the individual contract of employment. Two important question arise here; one is the the position of the individual contract of employment as opposed to collective agreements and the other is the role of the contract of employment as opposed to contracts of services.

Is it still true, as Kahn Freund and Wedderburn pointed out, that the contract of employment represents a fiction of real agreement, based on meaningful negotiation between the employer and the worker or that the employment contract is a satisfactory vehicle for the normative outcomes of collective agreements?[8]

Is it time to reconsider the "monolithic conceptions"[9] of the employment contract on the one hand and the contract of services on the other?

An interesting aspect is, as most authors note, that nowhere is the notion of the "contract of employment" defined. As WEISS points out, the central aspect of a contract of employment seems to be the notion of "subordination" as opposed to the contract of services of which "personal freedom", *i.e.* the freedom of the individual to organise his/her own work and working time is

---

8   Freedland, *infra,* at p. 19.

9   *Ibid.*

an essential feature.[10]   As he explains, the notion of subordination has become far less useful in recent decades. Other authors also note that it is much more the contents of the contract to which courts now refer to determine whether the employment relations can be defined as an employment contract. BIAGI refers in particular to the growing practice of "self employment", work relationships, which, upon closer analysis, show strong elements of personal subordination instead of freedom.[11]

Whereas, in Europe, it is generally assumed that one of the central issues of the importance of labelling an employment relationship is the protection against arbitrary termination (or unfair dismissal), this is not at all the case in Australia and the United States of America. As CREIGHTON and MITCHELL put it: "provided the employer gives the proper amount of notice to terminate the contract, the common law has not traditionally concerned itself with either the motive for, or manner of, termination".[12] FINKIN explains that in the USA employment is basically held "at will", although the relationship is nevertheless contactual - either party is free to terminate at any time, thereby creating a maximum of flexibility, which is however, subject to certain modifications. This author, too, points out the increasing role of the judiciary in the interpretation of the employment contract.[13]

The limited role of the individual employer and worker in determining the contents of the employment relationship is particularly clear in the Swedish system, where, as FAHLBECK notes "[T]he substance of the employment contract is derived from other sources".[14] In Germany and Japan, too, collective agreements have considerable influence on the individual employment contract. As YAMAKAWA explains, however, although the Japanese system is based on the German system, it differs in various aspects, in particular with regard to the doctrine that the most favourable provision

---

10   Weiss, *infra*, at pp. 31-34.

11   Biagi, *infra*, at pp. 65-66.

12   Creighton and Mitchell, *infra*, at pp. 141-142.

13   Finkin, *infra*, at pp. 171-178.

14   Fahlbeck, *infra*, at p. 91.

should apply (*Günstigheids-* or *Begünstigungsprinzip*).[15]

The two outstanding conclusions emerging from these contributions are, thus, that the concept of "personal subordination" may no longer be satisfactory as the determinant for affording persons in an employment relationship with a certain protection against e.g. unfair termination of the contract. In view of the character of new employment relationships, the time may have come to replace this notion with that of "economic dependency". That would cover the situation of the so-called "self-employed" who are, in effect, dependent on one labour hirer; it would also cover the highly ranked, specialist white collar workers, who, although economically dependent, can hardly said to be "personally subordinated" to the employer.

A second aspect which emerges very clearly from nearly all contributions (with the possible exception of the USA) is that the influence on the contents of the employment contract by the individual parties involved is very minor. In spite of an over-all decline in trade union membership, the effect of working conditions agreed to at a collective level remains predominant. The methods by which this is achieved differ significantly but the effect is the similar.

3. The Future Role of the Contract of Employment

As to the future role of the employment contract, there is a number of elements which emerge from the contributions to this book.

First, although the earlier mentioned decline in union membership does not necessarily lead to less collective regulation of employment relations, because of, for instance, the normative effect of collective agreements, it must, as the Australian authors put it, "inevitably compromise the efficacy of the system as a regulatory mechanism".[16]

Added to this, the emphasis on human resource management focuses on the individual worker rather than the collective work force. In the words of BIAGI, "[I]f labour in the past was aimed primarily at protecting values such as job security, a new law of human resources is emerging which promotes employment opportunities (...)".[17]

This would point to an increased role for the individual employment

---

15   Yamakawa, *infra,* at pp. 122-123.

16   Creighton and Mitchell, *infra,* at p. 157.

17   Biagi, *infra,* at p. 70.

contract in the future. WEISS and YAMAKAWA also indicate the instrument of the work(place) agreement (or work rules) as a mechanism for shaping working conditions within an undertaking.[18]

The second aspect is that the employment contract in itself should be reconsidered in that it is no longer the element of personal subordination which plays a predominant role as a *conditio sine qua non* the worker will not be protected against unfair treatment. FREEDLAND in particular pays attention to the theoretical implications of rethinking the dichotomy between the contract of employment and the contract of services.

It seems that the aspect of personal subordination, mentioned by most authors as the determinant for assuming a need for workers to be protected, is on its way out. It is consistent with the changing trends in employment relations that it is no longer personal subordination, but economic dependency which should be emphasised in individual employment relations.

Whether or not the employment contract is an appropriate instrument for dealing with the problems of a changing pattern of industrial relations depends, in other words, on the rethinking of the concept in order to find a balance between efficiency on the labour market and protection of the weaker parties on that market.

4. The Role of Contract in the Perspective of International Standard Setting

One of the interesting aspects of this comparative exercise is that hardly any reference are made to developments at the international level. This may be due to the fact that there are no such developments, that they are of no importance to the developments at the national levels, or that there is very little awareness at the domestic levels of international standards as to the employment contract.

Yet, as was submitted above, there are trends caused by socio-economic developments at the international level which influence the role of the employment contract at all national levels. The recent trends towards deregulation and flexibilisation, which are a direct result of the globalisation of the economy, form an obvious example of this. Logically, this could be an incentive for agreements at the international level as to the role of the employment contract.

To some extent, such agreements are being discussed at present, for

18   See also Weis, *infra* at pp. 39-41 and Yamakawa at pp. 108-109.

instance in relation to social clauses in international trade contracts. These social clauses call mainly, however, for the guarantee of minimum conditions for the labour side of industrial production in developing countries. They do not seek any regulation of the protection of employment conditions in the western world. A negative view of this call for social clauses is that there is a contradiction between this demand and what western employers want for themselves: deregulation and flexibility for themselves, regulation and some kind of rigid regulation for others. A more positive view is that they aim at convergence: more flexibility in countries where the labour market is highly regulated (and considered to be too inflexible), more regulation in countries with very flexible labour markets. As social clauses in trade contracts aim at regulating employment contracts in developing countries, this issue falls largely outside the scope of this book.

BIAGI notes that the real risks for labour law is not so much individualisation and flexibilisation of employment contracts, but labour costs and the consequent increase of social dumping on a global scale. He argues that, to avoid that risk, the two sides of industry should jointly pursue the goal of exploiting the only competitive advantage left to industrialised countries: the development of human capital.[19]

At the same time, it is the rigidity of contractual regulation which is at the core of the problem of labour costs. Therefore, the question of whether this problem can be solved at national level, or whether industry should turn to the international level to find solutions should be addressed. Here again, I would refer to the reason for the emergence of international regulation of labour law at the beginning of this century. It was exactly the argument of costs which played a predominant role. At that time, the problem was the improvement of working (and living) conditions. The subsequent rise in the cost of labour and thus in the cost of the product was a major obstacle which could be overcome only if conditions were changed in all industrial countries, hence the call for regulation at international level. Concerted action was also the device for re-establishing the European economies after World War II. Can the two organisations which emerged in these two periods, i.e. the International Labour Organisation and the European Community play a role in the regulation of the employment contract? More specifically, are these international fora an appropriate place in discussing of flexibility and the future role of the contract of employment?

---

19   Biagi, at pp. 68-69 *infra*.

4.1 THE INTERNATIONAL LABOUR ORGANISATION (ILO)

As recalled above, the ILO emerged as the result of a call - which started about the middle of the 19th century - for international regulation of employment conditions, based on the argument that improvement of working conditions should be achieved at the international level to avoid distortion of competition, which would be caused by unilateral improvement of employment conditions.[20] This is not to say that once it was agreed that international standards would be adopted, the problem of the delicate balance between protecting workers' rights and profit making industries at world wide level was solved. The functioning of the ILO since 1919 gives ample evidence of the difficulties involved, in international standard setting itself, but even more in implementing these standards at the national levels. Moreover, where the call for deregulation and flexibility at the national levels has become stronger, this is also true for international standardsetting. Employers within the ILO have insisted recently that the Organisation should no longer aim at setting out detailed standards - which has always been the characteristic of ILO Conventions - for all areas of industrial relations, but should, instead concentrate on the protection of the more basic rights of workers only.[21]

The more than 170 ILO Conventions cover nearly all areas of employment and social security. Since 1919, the ILO has set standards for working hours, minimum wages, paid holidays, health and safety, etc. etc. After the Second World War, more emphasis was put on the protection of fundamental rights such as freedom of association, equal treatment and prohibition of forced labour.[22]

ILO Conventions are concerned with setting minimum standards for just

---

20   Of course, it will forever be open to debate whether the last step towards international standardsetting would indeed have been taken if the Russian Revolution had not demonstrated the extremes to which popular dissatisfaction with working and living conditions can lead.

21   This question was discussed in the ILO Director-General's General Report ("Defending Values, promoting Change") to the 81st Session of the International Labour Conference in 1994. See on this issue also, L. Betten, *75 Years of the International Labour Organisation: Looking Towards the Future,* Netherlands Quarterly of Human Rights, 6, 1994, at pp. 413 - 431.

22   Between the First and the Second World War, one Convention on the Prohibition of Forced Labour (Convention No. 29, 1930) and one on the Right of Association in Agriculture (Convention No.11, 1921) had been adopted.

and fair conditions of employment. The protection offered by the employment contract as such has, so far, not played a major role. There are no general Conventions on the demand for a written employment contract, on terms of hiring and firing, or on flexible working conditions. There are, however, some more recent Conventions which are relevant to this such as Convention No. 158 on the Termination of Employment (1982)[23] and Convention No.175 on Part-Time Workers (1994).[24]

4.1.1 Protection Against Unfair Dismissal

The 1982 ILO-Convention No. 158 includes standards on the protection against unfair dismissal. It offers as a basic principle that the employment of a worker shall not be terminated unless there is a valid reason for such termination connected with the capacity or conduct of the worker or based on the operational requirements of the undertaking.(Art. 4). It prescribes a reasonable period of notice or compensation in lieu thereof (unless the worker is guilty of serious misconduct), the possibility of appeal against the termination, severance allowance or other separation benefits or benefits from unemployment insurance or other social security benefits.

This Convention has all the signs of a compromise reached with some difficulty. The inclusion of the term "a reasonable period [of notice]", is a classic sign of dissent between the negotiating parties. In earlier Conventions, exact periods were laid down in the texts, which then could

---

23   Ratified by Australia, Bosnia and Herzegowina, Cameroon, Cyprus, Etheopia, Finland, France, Gabon, Malawi, Morocco,Niger, Slovenia, Spain, Sweden, Uganda, Venezuela, Yemen, Yugoslavia, Zaire and Zambia.

24   The Employment Policy and Protection Against Unemployment Conventions (No. 122, 1964 and No. 168, 1988) bear no relevance to the subject. The Employment Policy Conventions belong to the category of declaratory documents, that is to say that general principles and aims of such policies are declared without leading to many specified obligations. The 1964 Employment Policy Convention declares, for instance, that "an active policy, designed to promote full, productive and freely chosen employment" should be pursued, without specifying how this should be achieved. The Convention specifies that workers' and employers' representatives should be consulted, analytical studies be undertaken, young workers should be assisted, but there are no concrete, well specified, obligations, which can be reviewed by the ILO's supervisory bodies. The 1988 Convention does not go much further. There is no reference to the employment contract *in se* as an instrument of protection against unemployment in either Convention.

serve as a landmark for countries adopting (new) legislation on the subject.[25] In this respect, therefore, the 1982 Convention does not demand much extra effort from the ILO Member States. This is also clear from a 1995 Report on the protection against fair dismissal which recognises that "[O]ff all the rights enjoyed by workers in connection with termination of employment, the right to a period of notice is widespread. In countries where no reason is required for termination of employment, the right to a period of notice is the main form of protection afforded to the worker when employment is terminated".[26] It is recognised that the period of notice varies considerably from one country to another, and even within the same country from one sector of industry to another, or from one category of workers to another. This difference in the length of the period it takes to dismiss a worker is, it is submitted, forms a substantial part of the arguments for employers in countries with the longer periods, which are usually the same countries in which the procedural safeguards against unfair dismissal are the most cumbersome, to demand more flexibility. By not specifying this period , even in relative terms, the Convention offers no useful international landmark.

4.1.2 Part-Time Workers
At its 1994 Meeting celebrating the 75th anniversary of the Organisation, the International Labour Conference adopted the first Convention explicitly dealing with flexible working conditions: the Convention concerning Part-Time Work. The employers were, not surprisingly, against the regulation of flexible working relations which, in their view, would have adverse effects on employment opportunities.[27] Basically, the Convention obliges States Parties to afford part-time workers the same protection as full-time workers with regard to employment conditions and social security schemes. It refers in particular to the right to organise, collective bargaining, the right to act as workers' representatives, occupational health and safety, discrimination in

---

25   For instance, the 1919 Maternity Leave Convention set a standard e (at least) twelve weeks maternity leave; the 1921 Weekly Rest (Industry) Convention prescribed a weekly period of uninterupted rest of 24 hours in every seven days; the 1936 Holidays with pay Convention laid down the entitlement of a paid holiday of six days per annum (for workers under 16 years of age twelve days).

26   Protection Against Unjustified Dismissal, General Survey on the Termination of Employment Convention (No. 158) and Recommendation (No. 166), 1982, International Labour Office, Geneva 1995, at p.89.

27   ILC, Records of Proceedings 1994, at p. 24.

employment and occupation (Art. 4) as well as to the areas of maternity protection, termination of employment, paid annual leave and paid public holidays and sick leave (Art. 7). Although it includes no explicit reference to the employment contract as such, it is clear from the text of the Convention that it excludes the possibility of allowing situations in which contractual obligations, in existence with regard to full-time workers, either on the basis of legislation of collective agreements, can be waived with regard to part-time workers.

4.2 THE EUROPEAN COMMUNITY

There is no need to set out here the role of the European Community in the area of employment conditions. The resistance to interference from "Brussels" in social policy in general is equally widely known. Yet, the legislative activities of the Community in this area are more important because of their effect than because of their quantity. There are, outside the area of health and safety, very few E(E)C Directives affecting employment conditions,[28] but the upheaval caused mainly by the Equal Treatment Directives and the Court of Justice's interpretation of these, have made Member States very weary of the EU Commission's attempts to approximate employment conditions. It is the obligation of Member States to incorporate the contents of Directives into the body of national law (Art. 189 EC Treaty), the direct effect given by the Court of Justice to certain provisions of Directives, the threat of an infringment procedure (Art. 169 ECT) in case of non or inadequate implementation of Community legislation as well as the general doctrines of preemption, superiority etc., which make Member States' obligations under Community law far more stringent than obligations under international law in general in the area of labour law and social policy.

4.2.1 Part Time Work and Flexible Contracts
The 1989 Community Charter on Fundamental Social Rights of Workers calls for European intiatives in the area of atypical work. The Commission's 1989 Social Action programme, based on the Charter, promised proposals for EC legislation on contracts of employment relationships "other than full-time opend-ended contracts".

In 1990, the Commission issued three proposals for Directives on issues

---

28   For a survey of existing E(E)C legislation and case law, see: Angela Byre, *EC Social Policy and 1992*, Deventer 1992 (new edition forthcoming). See also: Roger Blanpain and Chris Engels, *European Labour Law*, 3rd ed. 1995.

regarding flexible employment contracts: a proposal for a Directive on certain emploment relationships with regard to working conditions[29]; a proposal for a Directive on certain employment relationships with regard to distorsion of competition[30] and a proposal for a Directive supplementing the measures to encourage improvements in the safety and health at work of workers with a fixed duration employment relationship or a temporary employment relationship.[31]

All three proposals basically represent the idea that atypical employees should be offered protection in all areas of work similar to full-time employees. The first two met with severe criticism from various quarters, mainly due to the legal bases the Commission had chosen for these Directives.[32] This, of course, has to be considered in the context of a period in which the development of Community social policy as a whole came to a halt. The conflict between advocates of regulation on the one hand and deregulation on the other halted in an impasse in social legislation activities. This impasse still exists and is likely to continue to do so for a while. The 1994 White Paper on Social Policy[33] speaks of consolidating existing policies rather than actively undertaking new initiatives outside a few restricted areas such as cross-border work.

The third proposal regarding health and safety of atypical workers has been adopted by the Council in June 1991. Later that year, the Council adopted the Directive on the employer's obligation to inform employees on the conditions applicable to the contract of employment.[34] The Directive applies to all paid employees having an employment contract or employment relationship as defined by the national laws of the Member States.

Although the above mentioned proposals for Directives on flexible working arrangements have not been adopted, it is clear that the direction which the (proposed) Community legislation takes is towards setting the boundaries for flexible employment arrangements.

---

29   COM(90)228 final of 13 August 1990.

30   COM(90)228 final of 13 August 1990.

31   Council Directive 1991 91/383/EEC of 25 June 1991.

32   Angela Byre, *op.cit.* footnote 28 *supra*, at pp. 24-25.

33   COM 94/333/fin.

34   Directive 91/553 EEC.

In conclusion, it is submitted that the ILO as well as the European Community is undertaking attempts to come to some form of international regulation of flexibility on the labour market. There is, however, a marked difference between the situation now and that at the beginning of this century. At that time, the call for international standard setting in order to improve working conditions, came, mainly, from employers. There was a clear shift away from the *laissez-faire, laissez aller*. Now, it seems that employers are advocating a move back to free market forces and away from regulations of employment relations. Yet, in view of strong arguments for the value of a good social policy as a guarantee for economic prosperity in the long term, set in the context of the globalisation of economy, there is more value than ever in increasing the awareness of the benefits of international standard setting in this area.

Experiences at the domestic level and the analysis of good and bad practice provide a good basis for the preparation of international standards, if these are desired by the two sides of industry. It is, however, not only in this context that the authors in this book have contributed to the process of rethinking the role of the contract of employment in industrial relations. Their contributions provide essential reading for anyone who, at national level, is involved in restructuring labour relations in order to meet the demands of a newly emerging (post)-industrial society.

THE ROLE OF THE CONTRACT OF EMPLOYMENT IN MODERN LABOUR LAW

Mark FREEDLAND

1. Introduction

The purpose of this paper is to suggest that it is time for those concerned with the exposition of Labour Law to take a fresh look at the role of the contract of employment; some ideas will be advanced about the ways in which the law of the contract of employment might usefully be developed in a rapidly changing employment environment. The paper is concerned mainly with English law, but is intended to provoke comparative discussion of the points which it makes. The central theme is to propose a new form of questioning of what we mean and should mean by the category which we label as the contract of employment, and the dichotomy which we make between the contract of employment and the contract made with an independent contractor. We have to clear some ground before we can satisfactorily explore that theme.

The first point to be made in this respect is that, at least in English law, it is important to think about the common (*i.e.* judge-made, precedent-based) law of the contract of employment as a system of regulation of the employment relationship. The point might appear too obvious to be regarded as important, or even as worth making at all. However, as we shall now seek to show, labour lawyers seem to have taken up positions which conflict with or deny that apparently obvious statement.

One such position became a commonplace one in the 1970s, and was a reaction to the immense increase in the scope and intensiveness of statutory regulation of the individual employment relationship, especially though not solely the termination of that relationship. One thinks here of the contracts of employment and redundancy payments legislation of the 1960s, and the unfair dismissal and other employment protection legislation of the 1970s, not to mention the equal pay and anti-discrimination (both as to gender and race) legislation of that period. Labour lawyers tended to conclude that statute law had almost comprehensively superseded the common law as the regulatory structure for the individual employment relationship, largely reducing the law of the contract of employment to the status of an interpretative jurisprudence for

17

L. Betten (ed.), The Employment Contract in Transforming Labour Relations, 17-27.
© 1995 *Kluwer Law International. Printed in the Netherlands.*

the relevant statute law. From that perspective, the main role of the law of the contract of employment had become that of telling you to which workers the statutory regulations applied and what meaning to attach to concepts such as that of dismissal which were defined by reference to the contract of employment.

Another such position, not unrelated to that one, tended to be taken up by labour lawyers in the 1980s and 1990s in response to the trend of reducing the scope and extent of statutory employment protection, for example by increasing the qualifying period for unfair dismissal rights to a period of two years. This process was described as one of de-regulation; those who advocated its reversal by further legislation would, equally, speak about re-regulation. At one level, of course, this terminology is appropriate; one is talking about decreasing or increasing the level of legislative regulation. But at another level, that terminology implies that the reduction of legislative regulation creates a regulatory vacuum, an area of non-regulation or *anomie*. In fact, the law of the contract of employment retained some of its importance as a regulatory system in its own right even in the heyday of statutory regulation of the individual employment relationship; and to the extent that statutory regulation was rolled back, it gave way to the law of the contract of employment, and, so far from revealing a state of *anomie*, placed the law of the contract of employment in a new position of prominence.

Of course, those who speak of de-regulation have not simply overlooked the point that the pulling back of the curtain of statutory regulation reveals the common law of the contract of employment rather than a totally empty and bare regulatory stage. Rather, they have consciously or unconsciously concluded that the common law of contract of employment is simply a specific manifestation of a general idea of freedom of contract, at best no more than a series of default settings which the parties - in practice the employers - are free to override as and when they will.

However, it will be one of the main purposes of this contribution to argue that such views greatly understate the importance of the common law of the contract of employment as a regulatory system in its own right. This is true if only because employers and workers do so often in practice rest on the default settings, and may in some situations have no effective choice but to do so. In fact, the legal framework of the individual employment relationship is to a significant extent determined by the common law of the contract of employment rather than by the private drafting of terms, whether at an individual or a collective level. This central fact makes it very important to consider the modern role of the common law of the contract of employment as a regulatory system; the remainder of this contribution is in effect devoted to that discussion.

2. Existing Scepticism about the Role of the Contract of Employment

In the previous section we referred to perceptions of the law of the contract of employment, especially in the 1970s and 1980s, as a marginal and if anything decreasingly important phenomenon. It is important for our present purpose to realise that labour lawyers, as well as recently stressing this marginality, have also over a longer period of time engaged in criticism, sometimes fierce criticism, of the social adequacy of the law of the contract of employment. The present paper lies within that sceptical discourse about the role of the contract of employment but offers a rather different critique from those which have previously been advanced. So we begin by describing the existing critical discourse in order to locate within it or alongside it the particular thesis which is advanced in this paper.

As with so much of the discourse of English labour law, one finds the main starting points in the writings of Kahn-Freund. He was concerned about the way in which the contract of employment represented what was almost invariably a fiction of real agreement, based on meaningful negotiation, between the employer and the worker.[1] Moreover he was also troubled about the way in which some workers were allocated to the independent contractor category by reference to antiquated notions of the extent to which subordination of the worker to the detailed managerial control of the employer was regarded as a pre-condition to acknowledging the existence of a contract of employment.[2]

In a similar vein, Wedderburn cast doubt on the notion that the contract of employment provided a satisfactory legal vehicle for the normative outcomes of collective.[3] He showed how the doctrines which governed the incorporation of the results of collective bargaining into the individual contract of employment could easily distort those outcomes, for example by treating some of those outcomes as aspirational rather than normative, or as being intended to be informal understandings rather than prescriptive undertakings. He showed, in other words, how the stereotyping of employment relationships as individual contracts could enable the common law judges to marginalise collective bargaining if they felt so disposed.

---

1   He provides a highly complex and subtle exploration of his position vis-a-vis the contract of employment in O. Kahn-Freund, *Blackstone's Neglected Child: the Contract of Employment*, 1977 Law Quarterly Review, p. 508 *et seq.*

2   See O. Kahn-Freund, *Servants and Independent Contractors*, 1951 Modern Law Review, p. 504 *et seq.*

3   See Wedderburn, *The Worker and the Law*, 3rd. ed. 1986, pp 326-343.

Looking at the impact of the law of the contract of employment from a rather different perspective, Davies and the present author sought to show how in the UK that body of law helped to sustain, until the mid-1960s, a fairly minimalist approach to employment protection rights - a state of individual laissez-faire which matched or sometimes prevailed over the collective laissez-faire which was much lauded as the dominant characteristic of British labour law at that period.[4]

Attacks on the law of the contract of employment which were both more direct and more closely connected with our present purpose have been made by Collins and by Hepple. Collins attacked on two fronts. First he argued that the law of the contract of employment offered a conceptual apparatus which was inherently ill-suited to the regulation of the employment relationship.[5] This was because the law of the contract of employment did not recognise that the power of the employer over the employee was essentially bureaucratic power which has, as such, to be interpreted and controlled by the reasoning of public rather than private law if it is to be adequately regulated.

Collins' second line of attack was along a path which Hepple had opened up somewhat earlier. Hepple argued that it was basically unsatisfactory to attempt to construct a system of statutory employment rights upon the foundation of the common law contract of employment.[6] This was because that common law foundation was too technically complex and uncertain, too much committed to the favouring of the interests of employers, and too exclusive of important categories of workers, to provide an adequate set of pillars on which the statutory superstructure could be rested.

Collins pressed this argument further by showing that, even to the extent that the contract of employment had ever offered a satisfactory basis for gathering the workers upon whom statutory employment rights should be conferred, it had done so on the basis of assumptions about the vertical integration of industrial production which were now being falsified by vertical disintegration.[7] That is

---

4   See Davies and Freedland, *Labour Legislation and Public Policy*, Oxford 1993, pp. 15-20, 24-26, 48-54.

5   See H. Collins, *Market Power, Bureaucratie Power and the Contract of Employment*, 1986, Industrial Law Journal, p. 1 *et seq.*

6   See B. Hepple, *Restructuring Employment Rights*, 1986 Industrial Law Journal, p. 69 *et seq.*

7   See H. Collins, *Independent Contractors and the Challenge of Vertical Disintegration to Employment Protection Laws*, 1990 Oxford Journal of Legal Studies, p. 353 *et seq.*

to say, employing organisations were previously tending to be concentrated into larger units but are now being disaggregated by phenomena such as contracting out.

3. A New Challenge to the Law of the Contract of Employment

The discourse about the contract of employment in British labour law is thus a highly sceptical one, and often tends to the position that we ought to re-construct individual employment law on some radically different basis which made it largely or wholly independent of the law of the contract of employment, especially so far as the criteria for inclusion within statutory employment rights are concerned. This paper, while not rejecting that sceptical discourse, seeks to suggest ways of re-conceptualising the law of the contract of employment rather than discarding it.

The law of the contract of employment tends to be perceived and expounded in unitary terms. The contract of employment is seen as a monolith. The monolith has been erected on one side of a dichotomy, on the other side of which sits another monolithic conception, namely the contract for services between the employer and the independent contractor. The law of work relationships thus acquires a bare, indeed arid, landscape consisting of two uniform land masses on either side of a deep and largely unbridged gorge. It is the existence of this gulf which makes the territory on either side seem compact and undifferentiated. In this landscape, other legal relations such as that of agency or office-holding are located in the far distance, relegated to the status of distant and alien territories.

The suggestion which is urged in this contribution is that it is time to try to re-design that map. The law of the contract of employment ought to cover the territory of work relationships more broadly, and with fewer and less formidable internal and external boundaries. The law of the contract of employment has hitherto engaged in a sort of regulation by typecasting. It has designated a certain large sub-set of work relationships as conforming to a particular contract-type, and has been committed to maintaining a series of contrasts between that contract-type and other contract types, above all the contract for services. Within each type, or at least within the particular type of the contract of employment, a high degree of homogeneity is achieved by the formulation of implied terms, which even if they are displaceable nevertheless establish a norm and a normative framework.

The purpose of this contribution is certainly not that of arguing that no such normative framework is required. It is rather one of trying to free the existing normative framework from a certain conceptual rigidity. We need to recognise that work relationships lie along a very broad spectrum of integration or dependency, and that there is no sound basis for confining the contract of employment to one precise part of that spectrum - nor any really satisfactory criteria for so doing even if there were good reason to do so. If this is recognised, it becomes easier to adapt the law of the contract of employment to the changing state of the labour market, and to up-date that body of law not just in its role as a criterion for the application of statutory employment rights but also in its role as a regulatory system for the individual employment relationship.

4. The Contract of Employment and the Spectrum of Dependency

We could perhaps think again along the following lines about the place of the contract of employment in a spectrum of dependency of work relationships. We have, as indicated earlier, maintained two stereotypes for work relationships - the dependent one, identified with the contract of employment, and the independent one, identified with the contract for services. There are in fact a large number of types of work relationship which are not easily or sharply differentiated; and the spectrum of dependency on which they sit is not a simple monolinear one.

At the independent end of the spectrum, the theoretical stereotype seems to be that of the individual worker making a large number of simple task contracts with a large number of distinct employers. That sort of straightforwardly independent worker must now be rather rare, for even the jobbing gardener or window-cleaner or taxicab driver who might once have been in that situation is now much more likely to be part of or be employed by a firm or a company.

The reality at that end of the spectrum of dependency is a much more complex one, in which work relationships shade off into arrangements for the sale or supply of a combination and goods and services, and in which the links between human and legal persons form a web of contracts and obligations rather than a single bi-partite contract. Such might be the case where a house-owner employs a small firm of builders to construct an extension to a house, and the building firm provides the building materials, employs other firms to erect scaffolding or instal a heating system, provides the building labour partly from its partners and partly from its employed workers and so on.

Also at or towards that end of the spectrum, we may find arrangements which are presented as independent business relationships rather than work relationships, but which are in reality not only work relationships, but semi-dependent or wholly dependent relationships. This may be the appropriate analysis of certain franchising arrangements, agency arrangements, consultancy arrangements, or arrangements for the leasing and working of vehicles or of premises or catering facilities.

At the other end of the spectrum of dependency, we find a similar realm of complexity, in which workers become so highly integrated into the employing enterprise that their relationships take on the attributes of incorporation into the enterprise, or in other words start to place them in a proprietary role towards the enterprise. This may be true of the salaried partner in a firm of solicitors, or of a senior managerial employee of a company; and in another sense it is the issue at the heart of the supposed distinction between the employee and the "office-holder".

In this rather complex universe, it seems rather simplistic to attempt to operate with two exclusive stereotypes. A more adequate response to these complexities would be to regard the law of the contract of employment as much more broadly applicable across the spectrum of work relationships, and as containing a wide variety of sub-species, between which it would be unnecessary to draw hard and fast lines. It would be necessary to identify a category of dependent employment relationships for the purposes of various statutory regimes; this could, however, be achieved without the disfunctionality which is involved in attempting to bend the whole of the law of the contract of employment to this purpose.

5. The Law of the Contract of Employment - Re-formulating the Regulatory Regime

That disfunctionality arises in this way. The view of the contract of employment as lying on one side of a dichotomy between it and the contract for services encourages, as we have said, the notion of the law of the contract of employment as uniformly applicable to all work relationships coming within its scope, so that all such contracts can be uniformly contrasted with contracts for services. By according to the contract of employment a broader more loosely defined scope across a wider spectrum of work relationships, we might make it easier to break through that sense of uniformity.

That might be a useful move in that it might permit a more constructive development of the common law regulatory structure which exists in and around the contract of employment. That regulatory structure has as its core content the common law implied terms of the contract of employment. Those implied terms are for the most part displaceable by express agreement; but in so far as not displaceable or not displaced, they are assumed to be applicable to all or almost all contracts of employment and to no or hardly any contracts for services. Both the positive and negative aspects of that assumption deserve to be questioned, and are placed in question by the argument which is sought to be developed in this paper.

It helps to clarify this argument if we distinguish between two levels at which contracting or norm-making takes place within work relationships. At the first level, we are concerned with the exchange of services for remuneration. In the general law of contract, we think about this as the area of executory contracting. At the second level, we are concerned with the creation of obligations concerned with the security of expectations. For the worker, these are expectations about security of income, security of employment, and regard for health, safety and well being. For the employer, these\are expectations about how the worker will affect the realisation of the employer's goals either positively by making and implementing commitments going beyond the rendering of particular services, or negatively by refraining from competition. The contract of employment/contract for services dichotomy encourages the view that these two levels are separable, with the contract for services operating only at the first level and the contract of employment operating mainly at the second level. Employment arrangements need to be recognised as operating in a more fluid and complex way between the two levels. We might hope to achieve this if we regarded the law of the contract of employment as extending across a wider range of work relationships, but as doing on the basis of a more variable approach to implied terms than we seem to have in the present structure.

A significant outcome of, or at least a significant way of high-lighting, that argument is its message about the place of the contract of employment in the discourse about relational contracts. It is all too easy to assume that the contract of employment is quintessentially a relational contract while the contract for services is, equally quintessentially, a non-relational contract. In trying to enforce that dichotomy on our thinking about contracts of employment, we may be missing a number of subtleties about the way in which the law of the contract of employment in fact regulates employment relationships; and we may also be missing some possibilities for reform of the law of the contract of employment from within the contractual discourse rather than from outside it.

6. Some Concluding Illustrations from Recent Case-Law

There are some quite vivid illustrations of these developments, and of the potential for future development, in recent and on-going British case-law. A brief account will be given of one case where the courts did transcend the service/services dichotomy, and of another case which shows the magnitude of the problems which may have to be confronted in this area.

The case which transcended the division between types of work contract was that of *Spring v Guardian Assurance plc*,[8] which concerned the question of whether a duty of care was owed to a worker by an employer to give an employment reference which would not cause damage by negligence to the worker's prospects of obtaining employment. The House of Lords held that such a duty did arise, and that there had been an actionable breach of that duty, which could be viewed either as a delictual duty or a duty implied into the relevant contractual relationship. The interesting point for our present purpose is that the work relationship which gave rise to that duty was a complex one arising in that uncertain area of territory between the dependent and the independent work relationship with which we are specially concerned in this paper. It was also a multi-partite rather than a bilateral relationship. The worker had been employed as a sales director and office manager in the office of a firm of estate agents, from which base he had acted as an agent for Guardian Assurance, selling their insurance policies on a commission basis. The insurance company took over the estate agency business in which the worker was employed, but it was with respect to his work as a selling agent for them that they wrote a job reference about him to another insurance company for which he wished to act as a company representative.

The judges in the House of Lords were uncertain, and even to some degree at variance with each other, as to the question of whether a contract of employment existed between the worker and the insurance company; but they were agreed that the doubt about this did not prevent them from holding the insurance company to the standard of obligation appropriate to an employment relationship. It was important that this could be viewed as either a delictual liability or a contractual one; the House of Lords was unwilling to allow technical niceties of contractual classification to limit a liability which could be discussed in delictual terms without any such technical limitations.

A contrast with that analysis is presented by the case of *Walker v Northumberland County Council*, which at the time of writing has been heard in the High Court[9] but is due to be heard on appeal in the Court of Appeal. The case concerned the question of liability for negligently caused injury to health resulting from stress due to overwork, in the circumstances that the plaintiff was employed by the defendant local authority as the manager of their social services, and that he suffered successive mental breakdowns as the result of pressure of work, the second breakdown being a predictable consequence of

---

8   [1994] Industrial Cases Reports 596 (House of Lords).

9   [1995] All England Law Reports 737 (Queen's Bench Division).

renewed work pressure following his return to work after the first such occurrence.

The contrast with the previous case consists in the fact that, while the liability in this case could, as in the first case, be regarded as arising either on a delictual or a contractual basis, that liability was identified more easily and straightforwardly as arising from an implied term of the contract of employment than as arising in delict, because the employer's implied contractual duty to provide a safe system of work yielded a clearer result than the corresponding body of tort (delict) law, where the award of damages for mental injury is still rather constrained by technicalities.

One can welcome this evidence of potential for creative development of the law of the contract of employment while at the same time feeling some concern at the prospect that such a development would be narrowly confined to the contract of employment as traditionally defined, and would not extent into the larger territory we have been exploring. It would obviously be difficult to extend a duty of care for the mental health of the worker too far into the realm of non-dependent employment; and the determining of the scope and level of such a duty is in any case a matter of public policy which cannot ultimately be wholly controlled by judicial law-making. However, the common law of the contract of employment would be in danger of seriously distorting the working of the labour market if, by drawing far ahead of the law of the contract for services in its development of duties of this kind, it put a colossal premium for employers upon the constituting of employment relationships in the latter form.

The conclusion which it is suggested that we can draw from the foregoing analysis of recent shifts in the role of the contract of employment would seem to be as follows. It is at the second, relational, level of contracting that most of the concerns which labour law has developed for social values come into play. The shift to short fixed-term or task-defined contracting threatens to move the contracting process towards the first level, leaving the relational issues to be resolved, if at all, by other parts of the common law - tort of negligence, fiduciary law - or by statute law - *e.g.* pensions law. So the role of contract law is in danger of being re-defined not just in terms of an enhanced or re-asserted freedom of contract, but in terms of a rudimentary conception of contractual employment relationships - a conception in which collective and associative considerations are marginalised. It is that syndrome which labour lawyers now have to take seriously; this paper has tried to suggest one way of doing so.

Sources

Hugh Collins, *Market Power, Bureaucratic Power, and the Contract of Employment*, (1986) 15 Industrial Law Journal 1.

Hugh Collins, *Independent Contractors and the Challenge of Vertical Disintegration to Employment Protection Laws* (1990) 10 Oxford Journal of Legal Studies 353.

Paul Davies and Mark Freedland, *Labour Legislation and Public Policy*, (Oxford, 1993).

Bob Hepple, *Restructuring Employment Rights* (1986) 15 Industrial Law Journal 69.

O. Kahn-Freund, *Servants and Independent Contractors*, (1951) 14 Modern Law Review 504.

Sir Otto Kahn-Freund, *Blackstone's Neglected Child: the Contract of Employment* (1977) 93 Law Quarterly Review 508.

Lord Wedderburn, *The Worker and the Law*, 3rd ed., (London, 1986).

THE FUTURE OF THE INDIVIDUAL EMPLOYMENT CONTRACT IN GERMANY

Manfred WEISS

1. The Instruments to Regulate Working Conditions

In Germany, the individual employment relationship may be shaped by four different instruments of regulation: legislation; a collective agreement as concluded either between a trade union and an employers' association or between a trade union and an individual employer; a work agreement as concluded between works council and individual employer; and finally an individual employment contract as concluded between an individual employee and an individual employer.

Legislation containing minimum standards affects all employment relationships whether the prospective employee is unionised or not. There is a comprehensive range of such minimum standards covering practically all kinds of working conditions. There is, however, no statutory minimum wage. As far as working conditions are concerned, where statutory minimum rules exist collective agreements, work agreements and individual employment contracts only have the function to improve these minimum standards in favour of the employees whereas, in the wage area, the minimum standard is usually set by collective agreements.

The normative part of collective agreements affects the individual employment relationship directly. In other words, if rights embedded in normative clauses of collective agreements are violated the individual employee, or the employer to whom these clauses apply, has recourse to court assistance.[1] But it should be kept in mind that, at least according to the law, such clauses only cover trade union members employed by an employer who is a member of the employers' association or is a party to the collective agreement. Since

---

1 See M. Weiss, *Labour Dispute Settlement by Labour Courts in Germany* (1994) Industrial Law Journal 1 (5)

L. Betten (ed.), The Employment Contract in Transforming Labour Relations, 29-42.

only slightly less than forty percent of the workforce are unionised,[2] this means that only this proportion is affected by the normative part of collective agreements. This assumption, however, would be highly misleading. In practice, the normative part of collective agreements is extended to non-unionised employees (even those who are employed by an employer who does not belong to the employers' association) by way of individual employment contracts. Employers do not want to give workers an incentive to join trade unions by giving worse working conditions to those who are unionised. Hence it may be fair to say that, in practice and in spite of the law, collective agreements define the overall pattern of minimum working conditions.

Work agreements as concluded between works council and an individual employer also may contain normative clauses, which have basically the same effect on the individual employment relationship as normative clauses of collective agreements.[3] Work agreements, however, always cover all employees falling within the scope of the agreement, whether they are unionised or not. This effect is not merely the result of practice but is an implication of statutory law. This basic disparity creates enormous problems of harmonisation between collective agreements and work agreements. The relationship between collective agreements and work agreements is, therefore, for this and many other reasons, one of the most difficult problems of German labour law.[4]

2. Definition and Development of the Employment Contract

In Germany, the employment contract is not defined by statute. The Civil Code (§ 611) only provides rules for the contract for services, according to which a party supplying services undertakes to perform the agreed services and the party commissioning services undertakes to pay the agreed compensation. The contract for services is the basic form of contract for the "sale" of services. It was out of the contract for services that the contract of employment was developed by doctrine and by the courts in the first decades

2   See M. Weiss, *Labour Law and Industrial Relations in Germany*, 2nd ed., (1995), at p. 126.

3   See M. Weiss, *op. cit.* footnote 2, at p. 186

4   See for example the controversial positions as represented by O.E.Kempen, *Betriebsverfassung und Tarifvertrag* (1994) Recht der Arbeit 140 on the one hand and by D.Reuter, *Betriebsverfassung und Tarifvertrag* (1994) Recht der Arbeit 152 on the other hand.

of this century.[5]

It is commonly understood that the parties to a contract for services remain "self-employed". This is the criterion for distinguishing between contract for services and an employment contract. There is a statutory definition of "self-employed" in § 84 of the Commercial Code. According to this definition, a person who is essentially free to organise his or her work and to determine his or her working time is presumed to be self-employed." Thus, personal freedom is the main characteristic of being self-employed. Therefore, the traditional definition of employee implies just the opposite of personal freedom, *i.e.* personal subordination. According to this still current definition, an employee is a person who is obliged to work for somebody else on the basis of a private contract in a relationship of subordination.[6] One key element of this formula has become personal subordination. The other key element is the private contract which excludes all relationships which are not voluntarily agreed upon but where the individual is forced to work (for example a prisoner in prison), and/or where the relationship is based on instruments of public law (for example civil servants or judges).

2.1 THE NOTION OF "PERSONAL SUBORDINATION"

For a considerable time, the notion of "personal subordination" was accepted as a helpful and valid criterion for defining an employment relationship. Personal subordination was always understood to differ from mere economic dependency on the employer. The question of whether a person is an employee or not has, therefore, nothing to do with the amount of remuneration the individual worker earns. This difference between personal subordination and economic dependence is still valid. The problem is that the meaning of the notion personal subordination now has become subject of controversy. The traditional view of an individual simply obeying his or her employer's orders with regard to the organisation of his or her work, or his or her working time, does not correspond to the fact that more and more highly skilled individuals enjoy more or less significant freedom in deciding how and when they carry out their work. Thus, in the early sixties the problem arose about whether a leading medical doctor in a hospital should be considered an employee, even if he or she had the exclusive power to decide what medical treatment was to be given and how and when it was to be

---

5   See A. Söllner, *Grundriß des Arbeitsrechts,* (1994) 11th edition, p. 241 *et seq.*

6   See W.Zöllner/ G.Loritz, *Arbeitsrecht,* (1992) 4th edition, p. 43 *et seq.*

carried out. The choice was either to exclude such a medical doctor from labour law or to include him or her and thereby to redefine the notion of personal subordination. The Federal Labour Court[7] chose the latter alternative, basing its decision mainly on the fact that the medical doctor's working capacity was almost totally absorbed by the hospital and was, therefore, to be considered as a relationship of "personal subordination". This case not only showed up the inadequacy of the traditional notion but it also marked the beginning of a debate on the notion of "employee" which is still going on.

The above-mentioned debate has intensified and accelerated since the mid-seventies because of the activities of a specific group on the labour market, the so-called free collaborators of the mass-media. These individuals had contracts for services with newspaper enterprises, radio stations etc. to work for them as journalists, musicians etc. As parties to contracts for services they were, evidently, considered to be self-employed. When the economic crisis started to affect the budgets of the mass-media, and when these so-called free collaborators thus had to face the fact that, without the protection of labour law, their position on the labour market was very precarious (especially as regards protection against dismissal), many of them claimed that, in reality, they were employees. Thus, the Labour Court had no choice but to define their status. The result of this Court activity shows a very important tendency with regard to the future of the employment contract and even to the future of labour law as a whole. The notion of employee is extended in order to cover as many people as possible, thereby providing them with the protection laid down by labour law.

First of all, the Federal Labour Court made perfectly clear that it is not up to the parties to the individual contract to define the legal character of the relationship. Whether labour law is applicable or not depends exclusively on the content of such a relationship. In other words, there is no possibility of escaping the constraints of labour law simply by mutual agreement.[8] This view evidently implies that the real content of a relationship is to be evaluated. And here again the question arises of what "personal subordination", as a criterion for distinguishing an employee relationship from a self-employed relationship, could possibly mean. It must be said that, even today, clarity in this respect has not yet been reached. This will be a main task of the future.

The Federal Labour Court, in the meantime, has turned the notion of

---

7   Federal Labour Court, Judgement of 27 July 1961 = Arbeitsrechtliche Praxis, § 611 BGB Ärzte, Gehaltsansprüche Nr. 24

8   See Federal Labour Court, Judgement of 3 October 1975 = Entscheidungssammlung zum Arbeitsrecht, § 611 BGB Abhängigkeit Nr. 3

personal subordination into a very complex structure consisting of a wide range of elements which have to be combined and evaluated as an entity.[9] Thus, it is always up to the Courts to determine, whether, in a particular case, the combination of factors indicating the status of an "employee" is sufficient or not. Factors which, among others, serve as indicators for the employee-status are: the enterprise expects the individual to be always ready to accept new tasks; the individual is not free to refuse to carry out tasks requested by the enterprise; the individual is, to a certain extent, integrated into the organisational structure of the enterprise; the time required by the individual for performing the tasks for an enterprise uses up a significant part of his or her working capacity. The main criterion underlying of all these and additional factors is the following: to what extent does the situation of such an individual correspond to those whose status as employee is not questioned? The real decisive criterion, therefore, is no longer that of personal subordination but the generally shared and accepted view of what an employee is supposed to be. Since this understanding is not defined at all, and since the factors indicating the status of an employee are numerous, it is, in fact, up to the courts to draw the new borderlines. And here it must be repeated that there is a tendency to extend the scope of labour law as far as possible. It has to be pointed out that this strategy is not uncontested. It is opposed by a significant section of employers in the name of flexibility.[10]

The final outcome of the ongoing debate cannot be predicted. How difficult things still are, may be illustrated by the fact that, a draft Code of Employment Contract Law drawn up by a group of labour law professors in 1992, contained no definition of "employee" or "employment contract".[11]   No agreement on this topic could be reached.

It has to be stressed that the protective standards of labour law apply not only to employees who are employed full time for an indefinite time, but also, at least in principle, to so-called atypical work (employees on contracts of fixed duration, temporary workers or part-time workers). Of course, in a contractual relationship of fixed duration, the statutory rules for protection

---

9   For all the details see M.L. Hilger, *Zum "Arbeitnehmer-Begriff"*, (1989) Recht der Arbeit 1.

10   As an illustrative example of such a critical approach see B.Rüthers, *Rundfunkfreiheit und Arbeitsrechtsschutz*, (1985) Recht der Arbeit p. 129 *et seq.* (especially at p. 131).

11   See Arbeitskreis Deutsche Rechtseinheit im Arbeitsrecht, *Welche wesentlichen Inhalte sollte ein nach Art. 30 des Einigungsvertrages zu schaffendes Arbeitsvertragsgesetz haben ?*, (1992) Gutachten D zum 59. Deutschen Juristentag, pp. 19 and 84 *et seq.*

against unfair dismissal lose their relevance: a contract of fixed duration automatically ends when the agreed period expires. Therefore, since the twenties of this century the courts have been engaged in an ongoing attempt to establish obstacles to the conclusion of contracts of fixed duration.[12] In 1985, this trend was reversed by an Act on the Improvement of Employment Opportunities. According to this statute it is now possible, without any preconditions, to conclude a contract of fixed duration with a new employee or, if, immediately after an apprenticeship, an employment relationship is established in the same enterprise. Such a contract for a definite period can only be concluded once for a maximum period of 18 months: it cannot be renewed.[13] This statutory intervention which was intended to offer an instrument to fight unemployment by providing an attractive employment pattern for employers is highly controversial. It is strongly opposed by the trade unions[14] whose main objection is the instability of such employment relationships. There is, however, no indication that this pattern will change in the near future. The effect of this statutory intervention is rather significant. In the second half of the 1980s, every third newly hired employee was engaged first on a basis of fixed duration.[15] In the territory of the former GDR, this percentage is even higher in some branches of industry: there, every second hiring is, first, on the basis of fixed duration.[16] Unfortunately there are no reliable statistics on how many new recruits are transferred into a steady employment relationship. The effect of this measure on the unemployment situation is, therefore, still unclear.

---

12   For this development see the comprehensive survey by S.Frohner/R.Pieper, *Befristete Arbeitsverhältnisse*, (1992) Arbeit und Recht 97

13   This Act originally was supposed to automatically expire after five years. In the meantime it has been extended twice, each time for another five years. At the turn of the century the next examination will take place in order to decide whether further extension will be necessary.

14   As an example of such trade union opposition see R.Buschmann/L.Schwegler, *Fördert das Beschäftigungsförderungsgesetz die Beschäftigung?* (1986) Betriebs-Berater 1355

15   See C.F.Büchtemann/A.Höland, *Befristete Arbeitsverträge nach dem Beschäftigungsförderungsgesetz* (BeschFG 1985), (1989) p. 54 *et seq.*

16   See H.Bielenski/J.Enderle/B.v.Rosenbladt, *Arbeitnhmer Monitor für die neuen Bundesländer,* (1992) BeitrAB 148.4 and 148.5

3. Change of the Content of the Employment Contract

The original concept of the individual employment relationship consisted in two corresponding duties: the employee's duty to work and the employer's duty to pay remuneration. In this concept, a duty to actually employ the employee did not exist. The employer was considered to fulfil the contractual obligations simply by paying the remuneration, whether or not he or she gave the employee actually an opportunity to work.

3.1 THE DUTY TO EMPLOY

This traditional approach was viewed increasingly as incompatible with the basic values expressed in articles 1 and 2 (human dignity and guarantee of free development of one's personality) of the Federal Constitution. The actual possibility to work is nowadays understood to be a basic precondition for self-fulfilment. And it is also considered to be the only way to prevent deskilling and the implied effects this has on the employee's position on the labour market. For all these reasons, the Federal Labour Court has strengthened the duty to employ the worker and elevated it to be the second of the main duties of the employer. At first, the duty to employ was accepted only for certain occupations,[17] now it is a general and uncontested rule.

Under certain very restricted conditions (for example if the employee is suspected of grave misconduct he or she may be suspended until the suspicion is confirmed or has been proved wrong) the employer can unilaterally declare a suspension and is thereby and exceptionally exonerated from the duty to employ. In such a case of unilateral suspension, of course, the duty to pay the remuneration still remains.

3.1.1 *The Duty to Work and the Freedom of Conscience*
Another important change in the concept of individual employment relationship refers to the employer's power to give orders specifying the vague notions describing the employee's duty to work in the contract. This power to give orders is also interpreted in the light of the basic values contained in the Federal Constitution. There the fundamental right guaranteeing each individual the freedom of conscience, for example, plays an important role. This implies that an employer is not allowed to give orders which would be incompatible with the employee's conscience. In such a case the employee

---

17   See Federal Labour Court, Judgement of 10 November 1955 = Entscheidungssammlung
      zum Arbeitsrecht, § 611 BGB Nr. 1

would be entitled to refuse to do the work he or she is supposed to do. And it has to be stressed that there is no objective criterion on what the content of conscience may be. This is not subject to examination by the courts. It is exclusively up to the individual employee to define his or her conscience. This, therefore, places far-reaching limits of the employer's power to execute the contract.[18] Many other examples of how recourse to the basic values as embedded in the Federal Constitution shapes the structure of the individual employment relationship could be given. The example chosen here may be sufficient to indicate the trend.

4. The Function of the Individual Employment Contract

The idea that the individual employment contract is the result of real negotiation between employer and employee in most cases has nothing to do with reality. Negotiations leading to a compromise between the different interests may occur in specific circumstances: contracts with members of the executive staff (where, next to statutory minimum provisions, the individual employment contract is the only instrument to regulate working conditions); contracts with high level white-collar employees whose remuneration is above the level covered by collective agreements (for whom, in addition to statutory provisions and individual labour contract, work agreements may also play a role) or contracts with employees offering specific skills not generally available on the labour market. In other words, in most cases the individual employment contract has not much to do with individual arrangements. On the contrary: the individual employment contract is normally characterised by unilaterally preformulated terms, by standardisation and by uniformity. Most of the time, the content of the contractual relationships defined with reference to the existing collective agreements or work agreements. Clauses referring to the specific condition of the individual play only a marginal role.[19]

The fact that, most of the time, the only choice the employee has is to agree to a preformulated text or to forget about the job has led the courts to

---

18   The Federal Labour Court, Judgement of 24 May 1989 = Entscheidungssammlung zum Arbeitsrecht, § 611 BGB Direktionsrecht Nr. 3; For a careful and illuminating analysis of the problems related with such and similar situations see U.WENDELING-SCHRÖDER, Autonomie im Arbeitsrecht,(1994)

19   For the factual situation see U.Preis, *Grundfragen der Vertragsgestaltung im Arbeitsrecht*,(1993) p. 51 *et seq.*

feel that it is within their ambit to check that the terms and conditions as stated in the individual employment contract are in line not only with the relevant statutes, collective agreements and work agreements but also with the basic values as expressed in the Federal Constitution. In this way, the courts have laid down another whole set of limitations on contractual freedom based on the list of fundamental rights contained in the Constitution.[20]

5. The Relationship Between Individual Employment Contract and Collective Agreement

The relationship between individual employment contracts and collective agreements is governed by the principle of the most favourable provision (*Günstigkeitsprinzip*).[21] This principle offers the possibility of departing from the regulations laid down in the collective agreement by improving on them in the employee's favour. It is a consequence of the fact that in Germany the parties to collective agreements are entitled only to fix minimum conditions.

5.1 THE PRINCIPLE THAT THE MOST FAVOURABLE PROVISION SHOULD APPLY

The question of whether a condition in an individual employment contract is more favourable than a norm in a collective agreement is determined by means of a procedure of comparison which, in principle, is confined to the condition in question. If, for example, the question to be resolved is whether a certain wage is more or less favourable, the only reference point is the section on wages in the collective agreement. It is not possible to take a comprehensive approach and compare the individual employment contract and the collective agreement as a whole. Such a comparison would allow to worsen some items and improve others if only in cumulation those in the individual employment contract could be evaluated as on the whole being better for the employee. Such an approach, however, would be very dangerous: it would be very intransparent and it would open the door to wide-ranging manipulation. Unfortunately, the courts have not adhered strictly enough to the original approach according to which each item is to be

---

20   See the comprehensive survey in U.Preis, *Ibid.*, at p. 147 *et seq.*

21   See M.Weiss, *European Employment and Industrial Relations Glossary: Germany*, (1992) at p. 171

compared in isolation. They have allowed small sets of interrelated items to be considered in combination.[22] It is, however, very difficult to develop clear-cut criteria on what this may mean. Hence it is more or less up to the courts to establish the boundaries.

5.2 THE QUESTION OF WHAT IS MORE FAVOURABLE

There is another - perhaps even more important - problem. The more the parties to collective agreements focus on topics beyond the area of wage negotiations, the more difficult it becomes to evaluate what is more favourable for the employee. If, for example, a collective agreement fixes a certain weekly working-time, the question arises whether it is more favourable for the employee to work more or less hours, given that longer working time means of necessity a bigger salary. Here the question of what should be taken as the reference point arises: is it the declared interest of the individual employees, what generally is to be considered to be in the best interest of the employees or the intention of the parties to the collective agreement when they decided to determine the weekly working time. There is an ongoing heated debate on this issue but there are no indications that a consensus could be reached in the near future.[23]

It should be stressed that, in actual practice, the working conditions as agreed upon in individual employment contracts, especially with reference to wages or fringe benefits, differ quite often from those determined in the collective agreements. During the boom times of the fifties and sixties the wage drift was, of course, significantly bigger than it is now. Nevertheless, payment above the level fixed by collective agreements is the rule rather than the exception.

6. The Relationship Between Individual Employment Contract and Work Agreement

The relationship between the work agreement and the individual employment contract is also governed by the principle that the most favourable provision

---

22   For this development see the survey and the critical remarks by W.Däubler, *Tarifvertragsrecht,* (1993) 3rd edition, p. 143

23   For a detailed analysis of this problem see U.Schweibert, *Die Verkürzung der Wochenarbeitszeit durch Tarifvertrag,* (1994) and the impressive number of references provided there.

should apply and is subject to the same conditions as the relationship between the individual contract and collective agreements. Since, however, work agreements take account of the specific circumstances of the establishment for which they are concluded unlike collective agreements which are usually concluded for a whole branch of industry or at least a regional part of it, they normally specify the actual working conditions. Deviations by individual employment contract are the exception rather than the rule.

6.1 THE INSTRUMENT OF DISMISSAL FOR "VARIATION OF CONTRACT"

Quite often, a portion of employees' wages (benefits, bonuses etc.) are paid on the basis of uniform individual contracts concluded with all employees or at least a group of them. If an employer wants to reduce labour costs by reducing the level of these payments, he or she has access to an instrument that is available in employment law just for such a purpose: dismissal for variation of the contract.[24] In practice, however, this turns out to be very difficult. According to German dismissal law, the case of each individual worker has to be examined to see whether such a modification is socially justified. If they get involved, the Labour courts have to check whether the justification offered by the employer is valid. All this is extremely time-consuming and burdensome. In view of the fact that the employer's cost reduction strategy in such a case is focused not on the individual employee but on all of them as a collective, the instrument of dismissal for variation of the contract turns out to be very impractical.

6.2 THE ROLE OF WORK AGREEMENTS

In searching for a more appropriate instrument to modify working conditions in such a case, the question of whether this could be achieved by work agreements as concluded between works council and employer arose. However, the principle that the most favourable provision should apply makes this very problematic: standards set by individual contracts cannot be worsened by work agreements. Nevertheless, for a long period, the Federal Labour Court adopted a perspective to overcome this obstacle: uniform conditions based on uniform contracts were no longer understood as belonging to the category of individual contract but as being quasi-collective. They were, therefore, put on the same level as a work agreement and,

---

24   For this instrument see M. Weiss, *op. cit.* footnote 2 *supra*.

consequently, could be worsened by work agreements. The courts, however, were, at the same time, given the power to examine whether the modification remained within tolerable limits.[25] This approach came increasingly under attack on the grounds that it mixed up individual and collective categories in an unpermitted way.

In 1987, the Federal Labour Court developed a new pattern.[26] First it corrected the former approach by stating that, in cases of uniform conditions and contracts, the above mentioned principle of the most favourable provision should also be applied. Secondly, it changed the meaning of the principle as it applies to these cases: the comparison to be made is not between the individual's position in the work agreement and in the individual contract but between the total spent on remuneration by work agreement and by the uniform individual contracts. According to this amendment, the work agreement may reduce standards for the individual employee, if only the total sum of money to be spent on the basis of the uniform contracts is not reduced. This means that it is possible to restructure the distribution between the different employees by work agreement, but not to reduce labour costs as a whole. This, in effect, means that the position of the individual contract was strengthened. But, at the same time, the employers' ability to reduce labour costs was taken away: the mere possibility of redistribution does not save money. It is no surprise, therefore, that this new approach by the Federal Labour Court has become the subject of controversy.[27] It should be added that this "collective" principle applies only if monetary questions are at stake. As far as non-monetary issues are concerned, the "individual" principle is now strictly applied.[28]

In discussing the relationship between individual and work agreements, it should be stressed that matters for which the works council has a right of co-determination are no longer at the discretion of the individual employer and employees. To give an example: neither the employer nor the employee is

---

25   Federal Labour Court, Judgement of 30 January 1970 = Entscheidungssammlung zum Arbeitsrecht, § 242 BGB Nr. 31

26   Federal Labour Court, Judgement of 16 September 1986 = Entscheidungssammlung zum Arbeitsrecht, § 77 BetrVG 1972 Nr. 17

27   See for Example R.Richardi, *Der Beschluß des Großen Senats des Bundesarbeitsgerichts zur ablösenden Betriebsvereinbarung*, (1987) Neue Zeitschrift für Arbeitsrecht 185

28   Federal Labour Court, Judgement of 7 November 1989 = Entscheidungssammlung zum Arbeitsrecht, § 77 BetrVG 1972 Nr. 34

free to agree overtime by contract. This is a matter to be agreed by the works council in the context of co-determination. Here, the work agreement substitutes the individual agreement. And this is only one of many examples of the same kind.

7. Perspective

In Germany, there is no Code containing all the regulations concerning the individual employment contract. Already in the 1920s,[29] in the 1930s[30] and in the 1970s[31] attempts were made to elaborate such a Code and thereby to overcome the situation of having scattered statutes on specified issues. These attempts, however, turned out to be unsuccessful. German reunification gave new impetus to the idea of codification. The former GDR had a comprehensive Labour Code containing all labour law regulations. When the unification treaty was negotiated, the GDR delegation insisted on transferring this tradition into the newly unified Germany. This, however, was opposed by the delegation from the former FRG: the FRG law was extended to the territory of the former GDR as it was and the GDR law was abolished. But, as a gesture towards compromise, an article was inserted into the unification treaty according to which the Parliament of the unified Germany was to codify "the law on the individual employment relationship" as soon as possible.[32] However, it is extremely doubtful whether such a codification will ever take place.[33] Recently, a draft elaborated by an individual State (Land) was presented in the Federal Council and thereby brought into the

---

29   Molitor/Hueck/Riezler, *Der Arbeitsvertrag und der Entwurf eines allgemeinen Arbeitsvertragsgesetzes* (1925)

30   See A.Hueck, *Der Entwurf eines Gesetzes über das Arbeitsverhältnis*, (1938) Zeitschrift der Akademie für Deutsches Recht, p. 298

31   See P.Hanau, *Der Kommissionsentwurf eines Arbeitsvertragsgesetzes*, (1978) Zeitschrift für Rechtspolitik, p. 215

32   See M.Weiss, *The Transition of Labor Law and Industrial Relations: The Case of German Unification - A Preliminary Perspective*, (1991) Comparative Labor Law Journal, p. 1 *et. seq.* at p. .

33   See the minutes of the discussion Deutscher Juristentag, *Verhandlungen des 59.Deutschen Juristentages Hannover 1992*, vol. II, Sitzungsberichte, (1992) part P

legislative machinery[34]. It is, nevertheless, very unlikely that this effort will be successful, even if there are indications that other States *(Länder)* will follow this example.

The individual employment contract will continue to be important. But it will also be increasingly in the shadow of the work agreement. The instrument of flexibility in Germany is not primarily the individual employment contract but the work agreement. The focus is not on the individual employee but on the pattern of working conditions for the establishment. Only where the work agreement does not play a role (for executive staff and for employees in small and medium-sized enterprises where a works council often does not exist) the individual employment contract remains the dominant factor.

---

34   See *Gesetzantrag des Freistaates Sachsen, Entwurf eines Arbeitsvertragsgesetzes, Bundesrat, Druchsache 293/95* of 23 May 1995.

PAINFUL REBIRTH FROM ASHES: THE FUTURE OF THE INDIVIDUAL EMPLOYMENT CONTRACT IN ITALY

Marco BIAGI

1. Introduction

The aim of this paper is to discuss the role of the individual employment contract in the Italian legal system. In order to offer a comprehensive overview of this issue - which is the issue of extensive debate in Italy at the moment - a historical perspective covering three different phases has been adopted.

First, the recent past will be discussed. This is the period from the late 1940s to the mid 1970s which is commonly classified as one of legislative (statutory) and collective (bargaining) interventionism, characterised by a juridification process leading to guaranteeism. The hegemonic role of the subordinate employment contract has led to a marginalisation of atypical working practices, leaving limited room for negotiation to contracting parties, individual as well as collective. Nevertheless, it will be demonstrated that, even in this heavily legalised context, the consensual nature of the employment contract did not completely disappear.

Secondly, the present situation from the mid 1970s to the present will be described. This period is characterised by a clear trend towards more flexibility in the regulation of working activity performed in a subordinate status. After the repeal of the numerical recruitment system, the consensual nature of the agreement made between the employer and the employee was re-discovered. The title of this paper ("painful rebirth from ashes") refers to the fact that, in the last ten-fifteen years, a variety of new employment arrangements has been introduced and this has been accompanied by a more open attitude on the part of the labour courts. But this process has been highly controversial and has given rise to frequent, painful social and political clashes between the social partners and in their relationship with the Government. Having briefly described this legislative evolution, attention will be paid to the process of privatisation of employment relationships in the

43

L. Betten (ed.), The Employment Contract in Transforming Labour Relations, 43-75.
© 1995 *Kluwer Law International. Printed in the Netherlands.*

public sector; a process which is at an early stage but which is indicative of future trends in the Italian system as a whole.

The final part of the paper is dedicated to some increasingly widespread working practices (*e.g.* selfemployment) which are changing traditional concepts of Italian labour law and to the impact that new human resource management techniques are likely to have on the legal framework of employer-employee relationships. In this light, the declining role of trade unions and the individualisation of industrial relations will be analysed, taking into account special working contexts (*e.g.* small businesses) and new frontiers in our field (participatory management). The concluding remarks will emphasize the role of ethical principles in regulating working life and the increasing importance of contractual arrangements negotiated on an individual basis in the context of collective agreements between employers and employees.

2. The Past. Legislative and Collective Interventionism: Subordinate Employment Status vs. Contractual Freedom

The Italian legal system does not provide any statutory definition of what constitutes an employment contract. Employment status as an employee is defined by art. 2094 of the Civil Code as working activity performed in a situation of subordination in favour and under the direction of another person (the employer) who hires one or more people in order to carry out an economic, though not necessarily entrepreneurial, activity. For this purpose, a contract of employment is stipulated and this gives rise to an employment relationship.

Unless otherwise specified by collective agreements (or by law as in the case of part-time work), there is no obligation to put an agreement in writing. As a result, more disputes arise over the existence of an employment relationship, than over alleged infringements of rights and duties laid down in the contract itself. Disputes over whether labour law is applicable to a specific situation are more common than those over violations of labour legislation.

2.1 THE NON-CONTRACTUAL THEORY

This kind of legal regulation has led some theorists to affirm that the employment relationship is based more on a status than on a contract.[1] This "non-contractual" theory bases itself on the rule (stated by art. 2126 of the Civil Code) that the mere performance of work (which is not rejected by the employer) is sufficient to establish an employment relationship. But this approach raises the problem of the apparent contradiction[2] between the existence of legislative and collectively agreed rules which, particularly in the past, placed considerable limits on the freedom of contracting parties, on the one hand, and the presumed inexistence of any contractual basis, on the other.

It is undeniable that, traditionally, since most terms and conditions of employment were pre-established either by statutory law or through collective bargaining, the only options open to the prospective employee were simply to accept or reject the employer's offer.[3] For a long time in the post-War period (up to the mid-1970s), Italian labour law was based on the almost unanimously accepted social model of the employee as the weaker part of the employment relationship. By far the dominant conception saw the worker as an underprotected citizen, whose activity had to be carried out on a full time basis, because of the continuous, open-ended nature of the employment contract.[4] It is in this light, that the traditionally favourable attitude of the Italian system towards employment relationships of which the expiry dates were not fixed in advance, can be understood.

The original purpose of social legislation in Italy and elsewhere was to redress the balance between two contracting parties who differed considerably in terms of economic and social power. State intervention, aimed at limiting private negotiating autonomy in the relationships between capital and labour was legitimated, in the Constitution of 1948 and

---

1   S. Anderman, *Labour Law. Management decisions and Workers' Rights*, London 1992, at p. 31; W. Streeck, *Status e contratto nella teoria delle relazioni industriali* in Giornale di Diritto del Lavoro e Relazioni industriali, p. 673 *et seq.*

2   M. D'Antona, *L'Autonomia individuale e le fonti del diritto del lavoro,* in Giornale di Diritto del Lavoro e Relazioni Industriali, 1991, N. 51, at p. 466.

3   L. Montuschi, *Il contratto di lavoro fra pregiudizio ed orgoglio giuslavoristico*, in Lavoro e Diritto, 1993, N. 1, at p. 29.

4   U. Carabelli, Italy, in B. Veneziani (ed.), *Law, Collective Bargaining and Labour Flexibility in E.C. Countries*, Rome, 1992, at p. 379.

elsewhere, by the perceived need to protect the employee as the weaker party to the contract. Historically this made possible the separation of the individual employment contract from ordinary contracts, restricted the influence of private market forces and granted positive rights to individual workers regardless of their union affiliation.[5]

2.1.1 The Role of Collective Bargaining

In this respect it is also worth stressing the key-role played by collective bargaining. Traditionally, collectively agreed minimum terms and conditions of employment apply to those workers (the vast majority) covered by industry-wide agreements. These sectoral agreements are legally binding on employers who are members of the signatory employers' organisation. Since art. 39 of the Italian Constitution has never been implemented, the unions having always refused to accept a procedure of registration which involves a check of their internal democratic organisation, no specific legal provision is in force that allows agreements to be extended to cover employers in the same sector who are not affiliated with any bargaining organisation. But case law has always stated that collective agreements are binding on those employers who behave in such a way as to induce acceptance, albeit implicitly. Furthermore, the labour courts have established that minimum pay rates set out in industry-wide agreements must be applied by non-affiliated companies, since these minima are deemed to correspond to the principle of proportional and sufficient wages laid down in art. 36 of the Constitution. As a result, apart from very small businesses and the informal economy, almost all employees, unionised or not, are legally covered by collective agreements.

The individual labour contract for an indefinite period, which originates from a contractual convergence and is based on the autonomy of negotiating parties, has been traditionally regulated extensively by either statutory law or collective bargaining. This model of legislative and collective interventionism has created a uniform protection for employees who are assumed to belong to a homogeneous group of adult males, performing a specific task for an unspecified length of time. The assumption (which differentiated Italian post-war labour law from the original nineteenth century *droit ouvrier*)[6] was that the protection of the weaker party in the employment relationship had to

---

5   M. Vranken, *Autonomy and individual labour law: a comparative analysis*, in the International Journal of Comparative Labour Law and Industrial Relations, Vol. 5, 1989, at p. 108.

6   L. Castelvetri, *Il diritto del lavoro delle origini,* Milano, 1994.

be extended to all forms of subordinate work. Consequently, Italian labour law developed, particularly in the late 1960s and in the first half of the 1970s, as a system for regulating the treatment of employees which was based on the classic model of the individual employment relationship, *i.e.* a stable, lasting relationship of unspecified duration, with one employer, on a full-time basis.[7]

Certainly, in the Italian legal system as based on the 1948 Constitution (and also on the Civil Code of 1942), traces of a neoclassical economic model are almost non-existent. The idea of contractual freedom between equal negotiating parties (part of the liberal ideology of the 19th century), and of the wage-work agreement seen as a voluntary exchange between individuals, has been rejected due to various doctrines including social Catholicism and Marxist socialism. The conception of labour as a commodity has been replaced with the idea of the worker as a person involved in the employment relationship. This was an inevitable evolution, since, historically, the promise of contractual freedom has never been fully achieved mainly because of the social condition, *i.e.* the status, of the employee. In fact, the idea of the contract of employment has been defined, in the author's opinion rightly, as the history of a false arbitration.[8]

Nevertheless, the contractual nature of the employment relationship has survived in spite of severe limitations that were imposed between the late 1940s and the mid-1970s on the choice of the employee to be hired by the employer and on the determination of the content of the contract. Let us discuss these two points.

2.2 THE PRINCIPLE OF NUMERICAL RECRUITMENT

For a long time, from 1949 (Act N. 264) up to the early 1990s (see para. 3 *infra*), hiring procedures in Italy were governed by the general principle of numerical recruitment. This meant that requests to take on workers had to be submitted to the local public employment office. Employers were allowed to specify only the number, category and skill level of the workers needed. The identification of employees to be placed with the employer was made on the basis of order of precedence. This system of mediation between labour

---

7   B. Veneziani, *Labour Law Research in Italy*, in Edlung S. (ed.), *Labour Law Research in Twelve Countries*, Stockolm, 1986, at p. 177.

8   B. Veneziani, *The Evolution of the Contract of Employment*, in B. Hepple (ed.), *The Making of Labour Law in Europe. A Comparative Study of Nine Countries up to 1945*, London/New York, 1986, at p. 170.

supply and demand carried out by public bodies (State employment offices) was traditionally supported by the trade unions in order to avoid any form of discrimination in hiring.

According to a minority of labour law scholars, the stipulation of the employment contract was - at least in part - due to the role of public employment service. The worker had to be considered as hired when he was introduced to the employer at the end of the employment office procedure. But the most accredited interpretation of this system offered a different view. The conclusion of the placement procedure gave rise to a right to enter into a contract, the consequence being that, if the engagement was not taken up, because of the refusal of the employer to hire the worker identified by the employment office, the employee was entitled to compensation for damages.

Needless to say, that this system of hiring procedures mandatorily channelled through a public employment service, is rare in comparative terms. Even in the context of this legal framework, the consensual nature of the employment relationship could not be denied. This is because some categories, for example, workers with a share in the business, people working for their family business or employed in companies with less than 3 employees, could be hired directly and these categories increased progressively over time. More importantly, the system itself was largely and increasingly ignored in practice. The labour contract was often stipulated by conclusive conduct, while certification followed in cases when hiring had to be authorised by the local employment office.

Even more meaningfully, a nucleus of free will has always been recognised by the Italian jurisprudence with reference to the system of compulsory employment quotas. This mechanism was introduced in 1968 (Act N 482) and never repealed or significantly changed. It is based on a placement system for certain categories of socially or physically disadvantaged, *e.g.* orphans, widows of various categories, including victims of terrorist attacks, or handicapped persons. These categories are deemed to deserve special protection in order to fully implement the right to work enshrined in the Constitution (art. 4). The Italian labour courts have always recognised (see recently the Court of Cassation 8 february 1986, N. 816-817) that the existence of an obligation to stipulate an employment contract (employers, with more than 35 workers, are bound to hire a quota, 15 %, of employees from the above mentioned categories) cannot imply the remedy of specific performance (*i.e.* enforcement: art. 2932 Civil Code) of this duty. Admittedly, statutory law does not adequately specify the fundamental elements of the contract (*e.g.* pay, working time and the like) and leaves these effectively in the hands of the contracting parties.

2.3 LIMITATIONS ON MANAGERIAL PREROGATIVES

As for the content of the contract, it must be stressed that the limits imposed by legislation or collective bargaining, although very rigid indeed, have not created a set of rules which prevent employers from exercising quite extensive managerial prerogatives. It may be useful to consider personnel classification matters, regulated by industry-wide agreements which traditionally differentiate the order of workers in terms of wages and other employment conditions, on the grounds of their skills and by evaluating the work they do (job evaluation). Once hired, employees have the right (art. 13, Act N.300 of 1970) to be classified at the level which corresponds to the job assigned to them, with appropriate treatment as regards pay and other employment conditions. Afterwards, the employer may change the job assignment with two limitations: (a) no reduction of pay and (b) job equivalence (i.e., the new job must have a content similar to the original one, requiring skills corresponding to those acquired by the worker).

The same art. 13 of the Statute of Workers' Rights (Act N. 300/1970) states that any agreement, collective or individual which provides that an employer can unilaterally change the job position beyond the above mentioned limitations is null and void. This way of restricting the content of the employment contract may be considered an example, typical in that historical phase, of static guaranteeism, i.e. of the inviolability of protective provisions and the inalienability of rights deriving from them. More generally, (art. 2113 of the Civil Code) invalidity also affects waivers and transactions concerning the worker's rights which have been laid down not only in imperative norms of the law but also by collective agreements. Needless to say, this rule is also based on the assumption that the weakness of the employees' position which prevents them from exercising their own rights fully and that severe limitations must, therefore, be placed on their negotiating power.

Recent case law has weakened these principles. For instance, according to recent rulings of the highest courts[9] employees may be downgraded on a consensual basis (i.e. deviating from art. 13, Act N. 300/1970) when and if this arrangement proves to be more favourable to them, e.g., if this were the only way of keeping them in employment.[10]

---

9   See, e.g., Court of Cassation 7 september 1993, N. 9386.

10 E. Manganiello, *Dequalificazione consensuale e interessi prevalenti*, in *Rivista Giuridica del Lavoro*, N.2, II, 1994, at p. 380.

Another judgement[11] stated that decisions affecting promotion are the unilateral prerogative of the employer and not the subject of bilateral relations between the parties to an employment contract. It has been re-affirmed that the power to award a rating is exclusively the right of the employer. This prerogative cannot be compromised by the claims of an employee since it is intrinsic to an employer's right to organise a job rating system in the way he considers most convenient and effective.

2.4 JURIDIFICATION OF EMPLOYMENT LAW

These trends cannot conceal the increasing process of juridification that has affected the Italian system of individual employment law unlike collective labour relations, which to a large extent, are not regulated by legislation, and has progressively restricted the individual autonomy of contracting parties.[12] The post-War history of Italian labour law was dominated by a strong trade union pressure towards equalitarianism. This meant not simply an effort to reduce differences in terms of working conditions between blue and white-collar workers, or between small companies and major corporations, but also a demand for equal fixed-sum pay increases for all. Contractual freedom was largely restricted by union victories at the bargaining table, such as the abolition of lower groups of grades and the consequent advancement of workers to higher grades, simply on the basis of seniority, and the adoption of a single classification system overriding the distinction between blue and white-collars.

Nevertheless, in the historical period under consideration the role of the contract of subordinate employment was assured, although actual contractual freedom was highly limited. This is demonstrated, for example, by the regulation of overtime. While supplementary work/extra hours (*i.e.* activity performed within the maximum statutory limit of 48 hours a week) may be made compulsory by collective bargaining, legal overtime (*i.e.* exceeding the 48 hours a week or 8 hours per day limit) always implies individual consent, even if made "compulsory" by a collective agreement.[13] A similar

---

11   Court of Cassation 16 June 1989, N.2907.

12   G. Giugni, *Giuridificazione e deregolazione nel diritto del lavoro italiano*, in Id., *Lavoro Leggi Contratti*, Bologna, 1989, at p. 437.

13   B. Veneziani, *The transformations of the labour force and the organisations of firms*, in Id. (ed.), *Labour flexibility, the law and collective bargaining in EC countries*, Roma, 1992, at p. 51.

conclusion may be drawn from the fact that clauses in an individual contract of employment which are more favourable than those in collective agreement are deemed to be valid. In other words, the parties have always been allowed to derogate *in melius* from both the collective agreements and the law. This general rule was not extended to instances of absolute inviolability openly stated by statutory law itself.

The hegemony of the legal model based on a subordinate employment relationship and codified in art. 2094 (Civil Code) is characteristic of this period of legal/collective interventionism, although it has not disappeared altogether in the present phase of flexibility (see para. 3 *infra*). It is not by chance that some employment relationships were classified as "special" in comparison with the general model and because of the particular type of subordination involved (see apprenticeship: art. 1, Act N. 55/1 955; domestic work: art. 21, Act N. 339/1958; homeworking/outwork: art. 1, Act N. 877/1 973).

The above-mentioned supremacy can also be clearly observed in the priority granted to both part-timers (art. 5; Act. N. 863/1984) and workers on a fixed-term contract (art. 23, Act N. 58/1 987) when new employees are hired on a full-time open-ended basis by the same employer. Far from being legally obsolete, the vitality of the legal model codified in art. 2094 is revealed[14] when one looks at the rules for renewing fixed-term contracts. These are renewable only once, for a second term not longer than the first one (art. 2, Act N. 230/1962). The sanction for violating this rule is the conversion of a fixed-term contract into one of continuous employment from its very beginning. Conversion is also provided for if working activity continues beyond the limit of the 6 months (or less, if laid down differently in collective agreements) during the probation period (art. 2096 of the Civil Code), or if the deadline established by the training/work contract (a maximum is 1 or 2 year, depending on circumstances: Act N. 863/1 984 and subsequent amendments) is exceeded. An almost identical regime is laid down for the apprenticeship contract (art. 19, Act N. 25/1955).

The rule of conversion underlines the consent which is inherent to the employment relationship, although it sweeps away the actual contractual arrangement in favour of the dominant model of an open-ended subordinate employment relationship. At the same time, this rule replaces the will of contracting parties, making the general model of the subordinate employment contract prevalent every time statutory law is violated. Interestingly, the sanction consists of substitution of a freely negotiated contractual

---

14   L. Montuschi, *loc.cit.* footnote 3 *supra*, at p. 42.

arrangement with a sort of legal order based on a fiction (conversion means that the contract is deemed to have been concluded from its very beginning on an open-ended basis). A special sanction which contradicts the more general consequence provided by art. 2126 of the Civil Code is the case of annulment of a labour contract, *i.e.* that the legal and contractual effects of an employment contract remain in force only for the time during which the employment relationship actually lasted and the work was performed.

2.5 ATYPICAL WORKING PRACTICES

It is by no means surprising therefore, that in this period, some forms of atypical working practices have been marginalised. In Italy as elsewhere, the typical model of the employment contract (fulltime & open-ended) has led to the marginalisation of employment arrangements which are very popular in some industries. Meaningful examples are self-employment in the building/construction industry and seasonal work in work in agriculture.[15]

Equally useful in understanding the evolution of Italian labour law in the post-War period is the stringent regulation of contracting/subcontracting, *i.e.* allocating work out on contract. The general principle is that the contract can not be for labour only, *i.e.* simply "using" employees hired by the second contractor. This kind of arrangement is considered to be labour-only subcontracting and is, consequently, forbidden by Act N. 1369/1960. Contracting and subcontracting are not prohibited in themselves. Labour-only subcontracting (*i.e.* the mere performance of work) is outlawed to the extent that it involves the supply of personnel to an entrepreneur-user by intermediaries who cannot considered to be real employers, since they lack the typical characteristics of employers such as means of production, managerial structures, financial means etc.

The assumption is that the position of the formal employer and that of the real entrepreneur are artificially separated in order to bypass labour law protection. As a consequence of this illegal practice, the legislation states that subcontracted workers are considered to be employed by the actual employer-user to all intents and purposes. Once again, the sanction is based on the conversion of a contractual arrangement into a series of regulations imposed by statutory law, since the "false contractor" is replaced by the real entrepreneur. Legislation goes beyond the mere existence of an employment contract and gives priority to the actual work done. An employment

---

15   B. Hepple, *Labour Law and the New Labour Force*, in A. Gladstone et al. (eds), *Labour Relations in a Changing Environment*, Berlin/New York, 1992, at p. 288.

relationship is established with the genuine employer on the basis of statutory law only and previous contractual arrangements are swept away.[16]

2.5.1 The Concept of Subordination

The model contract provided by art. 2094 is based on the basic concept of subordination. As we said earlier, this norm of the Civil Code focuses more on the definition of the subordinate employee than on the employment contract. The key-feature, which also distinguishes it from self-employment (see para. 4 *infra*), is the concept of subordinate status. Work is assumed to be performed in a subordinate status when the employee makes the commitment "to collaborate in the undertaking (...) in the employment and under the direction of the employer". In other words, the employee must be subject to the authority of somebody (who that person is depends on the actual organisation of management).

It has frequently proved to be difficult to identify subordinate status. To make this identification easier, the legal concept has been linked with socioeconomic criteria (*e.g.* the economic weakness of the employee) and based on the existence of elements like fixed periodical pay, fixed working hours, incidence of risk, and the exercise of disciplinary powers. More recently, case law has stated that the definition of a subordinate relationship cannot be decided on the grounds of absolute and abstract criteria, but simply by approximation, on a case by case basis.

The traditional approach left limited room for contractual arrangements on an individual basis. Under the classical conception, the change of status (from unemployment to employment) did not involve real contractual activity. Acceptance of a contract meant agreeing to be subordinate to an employer under conditions imposed by the State or negotiated elsewhere, *i.e.* by collective bargaining. But this stereotyped model of subordination has been severely challenged by many factors. Some, particularly technology, have considerably changed the dependent status of the employee who finds himself more autonomous in performing his job, although he remains subordinate to the organisation of the undertaking as a whole.[17] More than that, new types of work giving rise to new kinds of employment relationships

---

16   O. Mazzotta , *Autonomia individuale e sistema del diritto del lavoro*, Id., Diritto del lavoro e diritto civile, Torino, 1994, at p. 134.

17   B. Veneziani, *New Technologies and the Contract of Employment*, in The *International Journal of Comparative Labour Law and Industrial Relations,* vol. 2, 1986, N.6, at p. 131.

have emerged.[18] Once that happened, a new season, historically speaking, had begun: an era of flexibility which implied a sort of rebirth for the employment contract - a painful rebirth from the ashes of legislative and collective interventionism.

3. The Present. Flexibility and Job Creation Policies in a Changing Labour Market

The general rule of numerical recruitment which was largely ineffective and frequently ignored in practice was formally repealed by art. 25 of Act N. 223/1991. This made direct recruitment the general rule. Aside from this fundamental innovation, the Act has left the standard job placement system unchanged. Public authorities still have a monopoly on placement services and private mediation is in principle sanctioned both administratively and penally. But, in practice, private employment agencies are to some extent tolerated for skilled production work and work requiring high white-collar qualifications. And, in these cases, public employment offices simply ratify the selection made by the employers.[19] This demonstrates that the modernisation of legal mechanisms in the regulation of labour market in Italy is always behind the actual evolution of employment patterns.

3.1 THE SYSTEM OF PUBLIC PLACEMENT

The system of public placement still lays down rules which limit employers' freedom to conclude employment contracts. Act N. 223/1991 lays down that all companies with over 10 employees must hire at least 12 % of 'disadvantaged' workers (*e.g.* those registered as unemployed for more than 2 years). This quota may be increased to 20% in the depressed areas of southern Italy and is in addition to the 15% quota for handicapped employees established by Act N. 482/1968. An attempt at further modernisation was made with Act N. 56/1987 which introduced the Regional Employment Bureaux (*Agenzie Regionali per l'Impiego*), technical, project-oriented institutions whose task it is to improve the match between demand and supply on the labour market. The *Agenzie* are supposed to support initiatives

---

18   F. Santoni, *Rapporti speciali di lavoro*, Torino, 1993.

19   L. De Luca, M. Bruni, *Unemployment and labour market flexibility: Italy*, Geneva, 1993, at p. 114.

to promote employment opportunities and also to improve co-ordination of central government and regional measures. However, their action is effective only in a few areas in northern Italy.

The relaxation of limits imposed by the public placement system on the freedom to conclude a contract of employment was due mainly to the profound changes in the labour market which occurred in the historical phase under consideration (from the late 1970s up to the present time): the changing gender and age composition of the workforce; the shift from production to the service sector; the growth of a variety of atypical (or marginal) work relationships with the increased importance of temporary and casual employment. These are amongst the most important factors that, in the last 20 years or so, have modified the pattern of work in Italy, from full time employment in the "core" of the labour market towards more flexible arrangements in the area of peripheral jobs. In this respect, much attention has to be paid to the underground and informal economy, a second labour market which operates alongside the official one. As a matter of fact, the development of informal employment was also due to the enactment of stringent regulations on recruitment, dismissals and personnel administration as a whole. The dynamism and volume of submerged non-criminal activity remains quite substantial.

3.2 FLEXIBILITY AND DISCRETION OF THE EMPLOYER

The need for more flexibility has not led to the employer being given total discretion in staffing decisions. In the Italian context, the adoption of a laissez-faire or market liberalisation logic would have been impracticable.[20] But, certainly, personal consensus and, at least to some extent, a sort of individual bargaining now typifies the legal regulation of part-time work as laid down by Act N. 863/1984. Within the limits set by collective agreements, individual autonomy may determine the working hours (including their distribution on a daily or weekly basis) which should be specified in writing by the individual contract of employment. In the contract, the parties may also agree to establish flexible arrangements (so-called "elastic clauses") in the distribution of working hours although the number of working hours has to be agreed upon from the outset. Furthermore, a flexible distribution between a minimum and a maximum total is allowed on a yearly basis. This does not involve any

---

20   T. Treu, *Employment Protection and Labor Relations in Italy*, in C.F. Buechtemann (ed.), *Employment Security and Labour Market Behavior*, Ithaca., 1993, at p. 392.

obligation for the employee to be available simply on request of the company. On-call labour in a precontractual situation where a potential job is promised, is outlawed in Italy.[21]

3.2.1 Statutory Regulation of Part-Time Work

Statutory regulation of part-time work is, perhaps, the most important example of the new perception of contractual freedom in the current period of legal flexibility in Italy.[22] Collective bargaining is supposed to establish the proportion of full and part-timers in an enterprise, in order to avoid part-time becoming a systematic way of substituting full-time employment with less onerous contracts. The increased recognition of individual autonomy has paved the way for further arrangements. Job-sharing agreements may be considered as a variation on part-time work. The stipulation of two employment contracts for two job performances implies an arrangement not simply with the employer but also between the workers. Some experiments are taking place in order to reconcile work with family life[23] and the social parties have made agreements encouraging the practice of weekend working.

Unlike the general model of full-time work, in the part-time employment contract the tasks to be performed (and, as said earlier, the working hours) must be stipulated in writing. A copy of this contract has to be sent to the labour inspectorate. This means that a part-time employee may not perform tasks other than those specified in the employment contract. The written agreement is required *ad substantiam* , *i.e.* in the absence of this requisite the contract must be deemed null and void. The consequence, in this case, is not conversion into a full-time relationship (see para. 2 *supra*) which would obviously penalise the employee himself. The part-timer will only receive remuneration proportional to the work performed. The absence of any statutory provision laying down the conversion rule implies the application of the general principles of the Civil Code.

---

21   P. Alleva, *Quali prospettive per il mercato del lavoro?*, in Notiziario Giuridico, 1994, N.6, at p. 16.

22   M. Pedrazzoli, *Flexibility in Working Time*, in Associazione Italiana di Diritto Comparato, Italian National Reports to the XIIIth International Congress of Comparative Law, Montreal 1990, Milano, 1990, at p. 304.

23   M. Biagi, *Working Life and Family Life: Policies for their Harmonisation. The Italian case,* in Comparative Labour Law Bulletin, N. 30 (forthcoming).

Although part-time work differs from the general model of the employment contract only in the reduction of working hours (like full-time work it is based on an exchange of work and pay and it is the same in terms of subordination and power to decide job performance), the written form is necessary to enable the labour inspectorate to control abuse. Even stricter formalities are laid down for the transformation of a full-time into a part-time contract. Again, with the aim of protecting the employee's free will, the written agreement must be filed with the local labour office which must release confirmation after hearing the interested employee. Recently, the government has put forward proposals to lift further legal restraints, especially the ban on overtime.

The written form requirement for atypical employment contracts (such as fixed-term and part-time) demonstrates that they are seen as exceptions and deviations in comparison with the (more favourable) general model and that consequently employees need special protection. For this reason, national industry-wide collective agreements normally require the employer to provide employees with a written statement specifying essential information (*e.g.* the exact place of work, the job position according to the classification scale agreed collectively, the remuneration, the length of trial clause, *etc.*). This information is provided to let the employee know his/her rights under the contract of employment. Furthermore, Act N.300/1970 places the employer under the obligation to specify in writing the disciplinary rules. From this perspective, the Italian system seems to meet the requirements of the EEC Directive of 14 October 1991 on employee rights to information about conditions applicable to their contract or employment relationship. More generally, this Directive confirms that both the development of new forms of work and the increasing diversity of types of employment do require greater transparency and improved protection against possible infringement of employees' rights.[24]

3.3 THE THREEFOLD MEANING OF FLEXIBILITY

In Italy, the meaning of flexibility is at least threefold, *i.e.* contractual, functional and numerical.[25] It may be achieved, first of all, by new

---

24   J. Clark, M. Hall, *The Cinderella Directive? Employee Rights to Information about Conditions Applicable to their Contract of Employment Relationship*, in Industrial Law Journal, Vol. 21, No 2, june 1992, at p. 107.

25   S. Negrelli, *Economic flexibility and society in Italy*, in The International Journal of Human Resource Management, Vol. 3, N. 2, September, 1992, at p. 194.

contractual arrangements which deviate from the general model in terms of duration of the relationship (fixed-term and temporary work), the number of linkages established (interim work), special regulation of working hours (part-time and job sharing). But flexibility also deals with different utilisation of workers already employed, *e.g.* widening the range of tasks each employee may be required to perform (job enlargement, job rotation). Finally, flexibility may be conceived in numerical terms (adjusting the size of the workforce to the fluctuating needs of the enterprise). A connection may be established between contractual and numerical flexibility in the sense that the periphery of the workforce, unlike the core, by definition does not enjoy security of employment. For the purpose of this paper, the concept of a flexible firm in Italy, with special attention to the segmentation of the workforce into a core and a periphery is of special importance.

Although the increased flexibility of employment relationships is caused, or at least intensified mainly by economic developments, the effects of changes towards greater flexibility in employment law should not be underestimated.[26] Certainly in Italy, the law has not allowed employers the freedom to stipulate any form of work contract they choose. Nevertheless, legislative innovations introduced in this period, also in order to foster job creation, have been quite remarkable. They all provide greater scope for individual autonomy in making contractual arrangements.

3.3.1 Fixed-Term Contracts

Fixed-term contracts are still considered as exceptions to open-ended relationships. Act N. 230/1962 proclaims that "the contract of employment is to be considered as being of unspecified duration" except in cases identified by legislation. The Italian courts were originally rather restrictive in interpreting the legal limitations provided by statutory law. However, both subsequent legislation and collective bargaining have significantly increased the scope for using fixed-term contracts. In addition to reasons originally laid down - seasonal work; replacement of a permanent employee temporarily absent due to illness; maternity leave; extraordinary, occasional work; *etc.* - Act N. 56/1987 lays down that it is up to collective agreements to identify further circumstances where this kind of contract may be stipulated. According to recent Government proposals, this system should be liberalised and legislation should no longer set down any maximum duration or define situation in which fixed-term contracts may be used.

---

26   P. Davies , M. Freedland, *Labour Legislation and Public Policy,* Oxford, 1993, at p. 575.

While the courts no longer consider fixed-term contracts unfavourably, these have not yet acquired the same status as open-ended relationships. Undoubtedly fixed-term work has a social solidarity value, since it has played an important role in job creation policies in Italy since the early 1980s. It is in this context that work-training contracts must be considered. First introduced in 1984, they afford young workers aged 15-31 the possibility of combining work experience and training activities. Employers have been given financial incentives in the form of social security contributions relief that cut labour costs of young trainees by some 30%. The law provides for a maximum 2 years term for this contract (12 months in case of a lower-level skill) and, according to very recent amendments, an "entry-level" salary for the trainees, though collective bargaining may establish some forms of "reduced" pay. The success of this new employment arrangement in the 1980s was probably due to a favourable economic climate: this seems to be confirmed by the drop in new participants in the economic slowdown of the early 1980s. Only about half of the work-training relationships became permanent contracts. Admittedly, high turnover is relatively common among young people, but it is very likely that some enterprises have hired trainees as cheap labour.

3.3.2 The Training-Work Contract

The regulation of the training-work contract is probably the best example of a legislative trend based on the need to do away with the inflexible protective standards typical of the previous period (see para. 2 *supra*). It is not simply a question of less protection for the individual employee. Since the trainee is employed under a fixed-term contract, s/he may be dismissed only for a "just cause", *i.e.* in case of serious misconduct. The training-work contract is perhaps the symbol of typological diversification of employment contracts, since the relationship is no longer based on the classical trade off (work performance vs remuneration). The duty of the employer to provide training represents a fundamental innovation, bringing labour law more into touch with the real needs of an ever-changing labour market. After the training-work contract has expired, the employee, on the one hand, has additional opportunities to enter the labour market with higher skills, while the employer, on the other, is in a better position to evaluate the prospective permanent employee (not simply based on the trial period). All in all, for both contractual parties, this involves a greater scope for more effective individual negotiations.

In Italy, the training-work contract is not the only form of employment arrangement which promotes job creation. Other relationships fulfil the same function in various ways. Frequently, atypical employees do not have to be included in the calculations that determine the threshold for the application of laws and collective agreements. This means that employers and employees stipulate contracts which are nonexistent as far as the identification of the number of workers is concerned. But these 'virtual' employment relationships probably represent a distortion of the job-creation perspective of labour market oriented legislation.

Apprenticeship also still plays a relevant role, particularly in artisan firms where collective bargaining has introduced a huge differentiation in pay between apprentices and skilled workers performing the same job. Furthermore, the relaxation of working regulations in job-promoting policies is normally coupled with substantial State assistance towards social security contributions. This has been the case in the past with apprenticeship contracts and it is still the case today as regards the regulation of the reinstatement or re-employment contract (the *contratto di reinserimento*) for workers who have been made redundant and are registered on the "mobility list". It is not worth analysing this new contractual arrangement in greater detail because it does not differ significantly from the general model of art. 2094 of Civil Code.[27]

3.3.3 "Works of Social Interest"

The fulfilment of a job creation function has led legislation to open new frontiers which deviate from the classical Civil Code perspective. It is in this light that the emergence - in statutory terms - of employment relationships which are openly defined as different from the model of subordinate employment contract codified in art. 2094 can be understood. A number of Acts (the last one being N. 451/1994) have stated that public bodies (*e.g.* municipal authorities) can promote "works of social interest", such as environment conservation projects, assistance for the handicapped and old citizens, etc., using long-term unemployed people registered in the "mobility list" (*i.e.* made redundant) and those receiving payments from the Wage Guarantee Fund. Legislation says that "using young people in the projects ... does not lead to the establishment of an employment relationship" (art. 15, Act. N. 451/1994).

The way in which "works of social interest" are performed is clearly subordinate, but the economic and social function of this contract is quite different. There is no exchange of work and pay. Job performance is a condition for getting unemployment benefit plus a modest additional pay in

---

27   L. Zoppoli, *Il contratto di reinserimento nella legge 23 luglio 1991, n. 223*, in Rivista giuridica del lavoro, N. 1 , parte 1, 1993, at p. 84.

the case of actual work.[28] In terms of legal protection, only a few basic principles, such as an insurance system against accidents at work, plus health and safety regulations, apply to this kind of work arrangement. This contractual arrangement is also based on a degree of cooperation amongst at least three different parties - the public body, the social security system, the worker - and, as such, is very different from the classical employer-employee relationship.[29] This proves that, under the present system, only legislation, and not individual parties, has the power to deviate completely from the general model codified in art. 2094.[30]

3.4 EXTRA-LEGAL FACTORS

Aside from the job promotional function of some new employment patterns discussed above, contractual freedom depends largely on extra-legal factors, such as labour market conditions and the professional qualification of the worker. Both an experienced manager and a talented cook may conduct a real negotiation with the prospective employer. Additionally, the logic of enterprise promotion may imply a sort of risk transfer in the individual employment relationship, thus paving the way for deals on an individual basis.

A good example of this is profit-related pay. Partial payment of employees by a share of company profits may increase productivity and improve quality, boost employee motivation and introduce greater flexibility to adjust labour costs. A variety of performance indicators have been adopted so far, linking pay to company performance indicators including gross operating profit and sales, quality and waste reduction. Examples of items which are frequently negotiated individually are fringe-benefits, ranging from the free use of a company car to the provision of housing, etc. This kind of arrangement is provided by collective agreements but some room for individual deals is left, albeit to varying degrees, depending on how advanced participative management style in the particular context is.

---

28   P. Ichino, *Subordinazione e autonomia nel diritto del lavoro*, Milano, 1989, at p. 248.

29   L. Zoppoli, *La corrispettività nel contratto di lavoro*, Napoli, 1991.

30   L. Montuschi, *loc. cit.* footnote 3 *supra,* at p. 33.

3.5 PUBLIC SECTOR EMPLOYMENT

There are two further trends that are worth mentioning to offer a more comprehensive overview of the current phase. The first is the reform of public sector employment. The main innovation introduced by a Government Legislative Decree (N. 29/1993), implementing Act N. 421/1992, is that the employment relationships of public employees have been privatised. They are now regulated by the Civil Code through individual and collective employment contracts, as is the case for private employees. In the past, public employees had a separate employment status which only a few categories such as diplomats, magistrates, prefects, directors-general of public administration departments, the armed forces, the police and university professors have retained. Without going too much into detail, it may be emphasised that traditional powers of employers in the private sector (disciplinary sanctions, dismissals and transfers) now have extended to the public sector. This radical reform, which is following the signature of the first "private" collective agreements will presumably create more space for the individual employment contract, since part-time work, together with merit-pay, flexitime, etc. can now be included.

3.6 CHOICE OF CONTRACTUAL *NOMEN JURIS*

The second trend which must be emphasised is the impressive effort made by the labour courts to stress the role of parties' intention in choosing the contractual *nomen juris*. This means that current jurisprudence is much more open than in the past to the will of the employer and the employee in negotiating their own deal. In order to ensure the applicability of labour law, their room of manouvering is still limited to the area of the subordinate employment contract as defined by art. 2094. But there is no doubt that case law is more sensitive and eager to determine what the parties actually intended to stipulate, *i.e.*, the substantial content of the contract, rather than simply looking at the surface and considering the formality of written agreements. This promising attitude[31] of the courts will make it easier in the future to experiment with new conceptions of working activity regulation.

---

31   M. Bartesaghi, *Il lavoro subordinato nel dilemma del nomen juris e della prestazione ambigua,* in Rivista giuridica del lavoro, 11, N. 3, 1993, p. 532 et seq.

4. The Future. Managing Human Resources Via Social Dialogue: the Ethics of Participation

In Italy and elsewhere a process of individualisation in employment relations has taken place and it is still underway. This has not implied any dismantling of statutory protection in the area of the employment contract[32] by means of a deregulatory process based on the abolition of those legislative controls which limit managerial discretion.[33] Governmental intervention to achieve more flexibility in employment has not removed statutory control of workers' rights. The freedom of individual employers and employees to reach their own agreement on terms which suit them has been widened without repealing fundamental pieces of legislation such as the Statute of Workers' Rights (Act N. 300/1970). Individualisation in employment relations by no means implies the untimely death of labour law or the loss of its autonomy: it means the rediscovery of a genuine contractual perspective, both in collective and individual terms.

This is due also to the continuing important role of the trade unions, both at macro and micro-economic level. Although most union members are still concentrated in the public sector and in the traditional manufacturing industries, collective bargaining, industry-wide as well as in the workplace is still vital in many sectors. The individualisation process has undoubtedly increased the potential for conflict between the trade unions and the rank-and-file[34] particularly in the area of "concession" bargaining. Since collective agreements do not have a universally binding effect in Italy - at least in strict legal terms - non-unionised employees frequently, and successfully, claim that their employment contracts are not affected by provisions which deviate from legislation or previous collective agreements. This has led to unions increasingly holding secret ballots to ratify collective

---

32   Lord Wedderburn, *Labour Law: From Here to Autonomy?*, in Industrial Law Journal, Vol. 16, N. 1, 1987, at p. 15.

33   B. Napier, *Deregulation, Flexibility and Individual Labour Law in the United Kingdom*, in The International Journal of Comparative Labour Law and Industrial Relations, vol. 4, N. 4, 1988/89, at p. 206.

34   S. Liebman, *Individuale e collettivo nel rapporto di lavoro*, Milano, 1993 and F. Scarpelli, *Lavoratore subordinato e autotutela collettiva*, Milano, 1993.

agreements,[35] a solution which, whatever else it might achieve, has not solved the problem of the real representative power of the trade unions.

Union influence is still particularly important in major Italian corporations.[36] In Italy, as elsewhere, there is a general trend towards the decentralisation of production units with employees being scattered in smaller establishments where they are less accessible to trade union activity. As a consequence, small entrepreneurs have been the main beneficiaries of this trend towards flexible individualisation. This is not due to any lessening of protective legislation: on the contrary, Act N. 108/1990 has even extended protection against unjustified dismissals to firms employing fewer than 15 workers. The reason lies in the communication systems which exist in small working units which favours better understanding between the employer and the employees.[37]

4.1 THE TREND TOWARDS INDIVIDUALISATION

This trend toward individualisation also includes elements like individual appraisal, individual goal setting, individual pay systems and direct communication with individuals. These employer-led initiatives undoubtedly stem from the increasingly widespread application of human resource management techniques[38] which are not necessarily seen as an attempt to marginalise trade unions and collective bargaining. Improving direct communication with employees is not itself incompatible with a simultaneous

---

35   P. Lambertucci, *La disponibilità collettiva dei diritti individuali*, in *Diritto delle Relazioni Industriali*, N. 2, 1993, p. 189 *et seq.*

36   M. Terry, *Workplace unions and workplace industrial relations: the Italian experience*, in *Industrial Relations Journal*, vol. 24, N.2, June 1993, p. 138 *et seq.*

37   J-M. Servais, *Labour Law in Small and Medium-Sized Enterprises: An Ongoing Challenge*, in The International Journal of Comparative Labour Law and Industrial relations, Vol. 10, N.2, Summer 1994, p. 119 *et seq.;* G. von Potobsky, *Small and medium-sized enterprises and labour law*, in International Labour Review, Vol. 131, N. 6, 1992, p. 601 *et seq.;* M. Biagi, *Small and Medium-Sized Businesses, Industrial Relations and Managerial Culture: The Italian Case and Comparative Remarks*, in R. Blanpain, M. Biagi, *Industrial Relations in Small and Medium-Sized Enterprises,* Bulletin of Comparative Labour Relations, N. 26, 1993, at p. 30.

38   J. Storey , N. Bacon, *Individualism and collectivism: into the 1990s*, in The International Journal of Human Resource Management, vol. 4, N.3, September 1993, p. 665 *et seq.*

collective approach, preserving collective bargaining as the preferred system for introducing flexible arrangements. "Bargained flexibility", which is widely accepted by Italian industrial relations scholars and practitioners, requires the continuing participation of collective actors. Personalisation of employment contracts will very likely increase in the foreseeable future, but this will not involve any shift from the collective bargaining process as far as decisions on the terms of contract are concerned. In other words, it is totally unrealistic to think that individualised employment contracts in Italy will spread only as a corollary of decreasing recognition of (the role of) the unions: a process of modernisation in human resource management in this country will be possible only if promoted jointly by the social partners.

4.2 SELF EMPLOYMENT ARRANGEMENTS

The alternative to the above-mentioned perspective is the strengthening of another trend which is simultaneously emerging in current working practices, *i.e.* the shift from subordinate employment to self-employment arrangements. According to art. 2222 of the Civil Code, self-employment is defined as performance of work under an independent service contract (*locatio operis vs locatio operarum*). This contract involves the performance of a task or a service without the ties of subordinate status and this is what differentiates it from the employment relationship codified in art. 2094.

Needless to say, self-employment is not governed by protective labour legislation: its legal regulation is based simply on rules covering contracts of exchange and on the assumption of parity between contracting parties. More recently, amendments to the code of civil procedure (Act. N. 533/1973, art. 409, n. 3) have extended the jurisdiction of the local labour magistrate (*pretore del lavoro*) to disputes affecting quasi-subordinate relationships (*rapporti di parasubordinazione*), *e.g.* contractual arrangements identifiable as quasi-subordinate by the continuous, coordinated and mainly personal nature of the working activity performed. These quasi subordinate employees (*lavoratori parasubordinati*) are covered by social security and welfare benefits very similar to those enjoyed by subordinate employees.

The level of self-employment is very high in Italy: it accounts for as much as 30% of the workforce. Frequently, it is considered to be an alternative to wage employment, a decisive flexibility enhancing instrument built on personal collaboration rather than on hierarchical subordination. In independent work (*lavoro autonomo*) the employee is responsible for the successful completion of a predetermined piece of work. This kind of freelance relationship is highly attractive to employers who are increasingly tempted to resort to self-employment as preferred model, particularly in the service sector. The advantages are clear in terms of labour cost adjustment: savings of social contributions and total flexibility (functional as well as numerical). Frequently, dual jobholding (moonlighting), a practice still frequent even during downturns in the economy, is based on self-employment which also arises from the significant increase in the practice of contracting out work formerly done by permanent employees.

The courts have shown a degree of high sensitivity towards the ambiguous co-existence of genuine and non genuine self-employment arrangements (*e.g.* bogus consultants or undefined collaborators). For a long time "pony express" work has been a matter of discussion. The final conclusion has been that it is actually subordinate employment, since subordination derives from the way the work is organised, even if the workers do not obey formal orders. In order to avoid this kind of problem, it seems preferable[39] to operate on the assumption that the worker is covered by labour legislation, with the burden of proof upon the person who alleges that the worker is independent. Or, to put it in other terms, to provide protection for all forms of "personal work", replacing the concept of "subordinate" with that of "dependent" employment which would include the area of quasi-subordination.[40]

4.3 THE INCREASE IN THE VARIETY OF ATYPICAL EMPLOYMENT RELATIONSHIPS

The future development of labour law in Italy will very likely see an increase in the variety of atypical employment relationships. The trilateral "social pact" signed on 23rd July 1993 provides for the asocial legitimation (not yet legalisation) of temporary agency work based on a series of regulations drafted by the social partners.[41] This liberalisation interestingly combines administrative/government controls, collective bargaining and individual/contractual flexibility. Amongst the most meaningful principles stated in the 1993 framework agreement are: temporary work agencies would require authorisation from the Ministry of Labour; temporary agency work placements would be on the basis of a written contract, lasting not more than

---

39   B. Hepple, *Restructuring Employment Rights,* in Industrial Law Journal, vol. 15, 1985, at p. 75.

40   P. Ichino, *op. cit.* footnote 28 *supra*, p. 264 *et seq.*

41   M. Tiraboschi, *"Agenzie" di servize e cooperative di produzione e lavoro,* in: il Lavoro nella Giurisprudenza, N.6, 1994, p. 559 *et seq.*

6 months, renewable only once; temporary workers would be entitled to the same remuneration as similar permanent workers in the user company; temporary workers could be used to replace absent employees where a fixed-term contract is not feasible, but in no case to substitute workers on strike, to carry out simple tasks, or by companies which have carried out collective dismissals in the previous 12 months. Finally, agencies would have to guarantee all temporary workers a monthly fixed bonus/wage, to be determined by collective agreements, in order to cover periods when they are not employed by a user company. The last principle, which is highly controversial, represents a compromise revealing that present outlawing of temporary work provided by Act 1369/1960 may be removed only via social dialogue, *i.e.* on the grounds of a mix of collective and individual flexible intervention.

Not less meaningful in terms of deviation from the general model is telework which represents a clear shift in the centre of gravity of the employment contract.[42] Telework, which is developing as a new form of homework, is not yet widespread in Italy but it is noteworthy as an example of the greater autonomy of choice given by the courts to the parties in classifying employment relationships.[43] This trend will hopefully be strengthened in the future as the result of pressure from the growing popularity of atypical forms of employment.

Flexibility is not to be confused with precariousness and cannot be achieved simply by expanding the area of atypical or insecure work: if the present trend continues, it could lead to counterproductive side effects. In the short run an increase in these kinds of marginal workers has led to an enthusiastic belief, a sort of collective illusion, that this could be the solution to the need to enhance the competitiveness of Italian companies (as well as in other countries).[44] But, in the long run, the social costs associated with an enlarged flexible/secondary workforce might exceed any short term competitive advantage gained. An economic system requires a highly skilled

---

42   A. Adlercreutz, *Sweden,* in Blanpain R. (ed.), *International Encyclopaedia for Labour Law and Industrial Relations,* vol. 9, 1982, at p. 28.

43   M. Tiraboschi, *Autonomia e subordinazione nelle tecniche di interpretazione dei precedenti giudiziari,* in Rivista giuridica del lavoro, N. 2, 11, 1994, p. 353 *et seq.*

44   R.U. Miller, *The Impact of Contingent Employment on Workers' Rights: A Comparative Analysis,* in R. Blanpain R., J. Rojot, H. Wheeler, *Employee Rights and Industrial Justice,* Bulletin of Comparative Labour Relations, N. 28, 1994, at p. 47.

and educated workforce and, as the experience of training-work contract in Italy has shown (see para. 3 *supra*), employers are not going to invest time and money to train workers hired on a precarious basis. This is not to say that a considerable portion of these workers do not want to be employed under atypical conditions, but the challenge that this trend represents must be considered carefully.[45]

4.4 THE REAL RISKS FOR LABOUR LAW IN THE FUTURE

The real risks for labour law in the foreseeable future are not so much individualisation or flexibilisation of the employment contract, but labour costs and the consequent increase of social dumping on a world-wide scale, with companies (including Italian companies) relocating abroad, in Central Europe as well as in the Far East. In order to avoid this risk, the two sides of industry should pursue jointly a common goal to exploit the only competitive advantage left to industrialised countries in times of complete internationalisation of economy and markets and to develop a better educated human capital by investing massively in training people at work. This seems to be the only alternative.

The question is not so much one of more versus less regulation. The real issue is what kind of social protection is compatible with this need. The answer is not simple. But some points seem to be clear. The first is that it is time to radically rethink the very idea of the employment contract. The future trend will speed up the change from hierarchical to functional subordination, giving rise to contractual arrangements based more on the values of collaboration and democratisation.[46] Through the employment contract, the employee now claims to have a say in controlling his own performance and frequently feels that s/he is not simply doing a particular job but acting for the company as a whole. S/he expects to be somehow involved in participative management.[47] The time for disciplinary measures and authoritative orders has passed and appropriate ways of motivating a

---

45 J.P. Hiatt, L. Rhinehart, *The Growing Contingent Workforce: A Challenge for the Future*, in The Labour Lawyer , Vol. 10, N. 2, Spring 1994, at p. 147.

46 B. Hepple, *op. cit.* footnote 15 *supra*, at p. 294.

47 M. Biagi, *Managing Industrial Relations as a Competitive Advantage: From Formalism to Training in Managerial Initiative*, in R. Blanpain, M. Biagi, *Participative Management and Industrial Relations in a Worldwide Perspective*, Bulletin of Comparative Labour Relations, N. 27, 1993, p. 15 *et seq.*

new, more demanding workforce, on a personal as well as collective basis, must be found.

In more technical legal terms, this means that before contractual arrangements on an individual basis can be developed, new and different kinds of external regulatory sources must be found.[48] In the current situation, there are too many legal regulations that cannot be deviated from by private, individual or collective agreement. The employee is no longer unable to express and promote his own interests and the present system, based on inviolable norms, is, therefore, rather obsolete and is frequently bypassed by clandestine individual agreements. In future legislation, the number of provisions which may be deviated from *in pejus* at least by collective bargaining, should be increased. Even more interesting would be to assign to the social partners the task of identifying via collective bargaining the extent to which employment relationships should be governed by labour laws.

Secondly, in the future, labour law will deal much more with employment in general than with single jobs. The need of social protection will shift from regulation of individual aspects in the working relationship (*e.g.* hiring and firing procedures) towards the promotion and development of human capital in employment. The "internal marketing" approach, which derives from human resource management techniques and which considers employees as customers, must be carefully discussed. Beyond the rhetoric,[49] this perspective represents an appropriate response to both managerial programmes and the individual expectations of many skilled employees. Also, collective bargaining conducted in some major corporations (including Fiat, Olivetti, Zanussi, etc.) is now paying increasing attention to total quality projects.

Human resource management is essentially based on making the best use of the skills of employees. It places the management of human capital at the centre of business planning. A variety of tools is currently being developed in Italy as elsewhere. These include teamworking, quality circles, lean production and just-in-time manufacturing, customer care training, performance-related pay, profit-sharing, share-options, etc. The focus is, undoubtedly, on the individual rather than the collective body of the workforce. If the goal is to improve performance by developing employee

---

48   M. D' Antona, *loc. cit.* footnote 2 *supra,* at p. 484.

49   C. Hales, *'Internal marketing' as an approach to human resource management: a new perspective or a metaphor too far?,* in Human Resource Management Journal, vol. 5, N. 1, Autumn 1994, at p. 62.

commitment with a view to the final objective of avoiding the reallocation of investment abroad, this, in turn, entails a more participative relationship with the trade unions and long term investments in training. In other words, genuine attempts to develop a social partnership at the micro as well as the macro level, become essential.

The impact of human resource management techniques on employment regulations is now under consideration.[50] The question is not one of preserving the ambiguous cultural identity of Italian labour law.[51] It is, rather, time to admit that the social differentiation is now based on professional know-how. The only way to get access to social promotion is through continuous education.[52] If labour law in the past was aimed primarily at protecting values such as job security, a new law of human resources is emerging which promotes employment opportunities, preferably through vocational and continuous training. An improvement of the training system in order to ameliorate the long-term accumulation of human capital within the enterprise is widely debated in Italy right now.

It would be a dangerous illusion to continue to see the employment relationship as one essentially involving the buying and the selling of a commodity called labour. Contemporary employment is a relationship between human beings, but there is a risk of potential dehumanisation due to the hierarchical organisation of business. Basic human rights in this context must continue to be protected.[53] To override the unavoidable conflicts that arise between those who decide and the others who simply implement these decisions, it is indispensable that some ethical values, such as cooperative participation, are shared by both parties. This approach could realistically reconcile opposing views of the employment relationship, which is seen by employers essentially as the contractual basis for employee's enforceable

---

50   L. Gaeta, *Qualità totale e teoria della subordinazione*, in Diritto delle Relazioni Industriali, N. 1, 1994, p. 3 *et seq.*

51   O. Mazzotta, *loc. cit.* footnote 16 *supra,* at p. 135.

52   G. Giugni, *Una lezione sul diritto del lavoro*, in *Giornale di diritto del lavoro e relazioni industriali*, N. 62, 1994, at p. 210.

53   H.N. Wheeler, *Employee Rights as Human Rights*, in R. Blanpain, J. Rojot , H.N. Wheeler, *Rights and Industrial Justice*, in Bulletin of Comparative Labour Relations, N. 28, 1994, at p. 13.

obligations, while the latter sees it as a cooperative undertaking in which profits should be equitably distributed.[54]

The transition from a contractual to an ethical approach will be long and difficult. The ethics and the culture of participation will be developed gradually once the two sides of industry realise the need for a partnership to face the challenge coming from newly industrialised and the developing countries, which offer foreign investors incomparable conditions in terms of labour costs. Social clauses in international trade agreements may represent a defense for the workforces of advanced industrialised nations,[55] but an alliance of employers and employees, based on converging business and ethical considerations, is the only way to give direction to an area of law whose object is the protection and the promotion of the interests of people at work.

---

54   J. Rojot (1994), *Ethics and Employee Rights at the Workplace, Ibid.,* at Blanpain,p. 6.

55   M. Biagi, *L'Accords Nordamericano di cooperazione sul lavoro,* in *Il Lavoro nella Giurisprudenza,* luglio 1994, N. 7, p. 677 *et seq.*

Bibliography

- Adlercreutz A. (1982), *'Sweden'*, in Blanpain R. (ed.), *International Encyclopaedia for Labour Law and Industrial Relations*, vol. 9.
- Alleva P. (1994), *Quali prospettive per il mercato del lavoro?*, in Notiziario Giuridico, N.6, p. 15 et seq.
- Anderman S.D. (1992), *Labour Law. Management Decisions and Workers' Rights*, London.
- Carabelli U. (1992), Italy, in Veneziani B. (ed.), *Law, Collective Bargaining and Labour Flexibility in E.C. Countries*, Rome, p. 345 et seq.
- Bartesaghi M. (1993), *Il lavoro subordinato nel dilemma del nomen juris e della prestazione ambigua,* in Revista giuridica del lavoro, 11, N. 3, p. 532 et seq.
- Biagi M. (1993), *Small and Medium-Sized Businesses, Industrial Relations and Managerial Culture: The Italian Case and Comparative Remarks*, in Blanpain R., *Industrial Relations in Small and Medium-Sized Enterprises,* Bulletin of Comparative Labour Relations, N. 26, p. 13 et seq.
- Biagi M. (1993), *Managing Industrial Relations as a Competitive Advantage: From Formalism to Training in Managerial Initiative*, in Blanpain R., Biagi M., *Participative Management and Industrial Relations in a Worldwide Perspective*, Bulletin of Comparative Labour Relations, N. 27, p. 15 et seq.
- Biagi M. (1994), *L'Accordo Nordamericano di cooperazione sul lavoro*, in Il Lavoro nella Giurisprudenza, luglio, N. 7, p. 677 et seq.
- Biagi M. (1995), *Working Life and Family Life: Policies for their Harmonisation. The Italian case,* in Comparative Labour Law Bulletin, N.30 (forthcoming).
- Castelvetri L. (1994), *Il diritto del lavoro delle origini*, Milano.
- Clark J., Hall M. (1992), *The Cinderella Directive? Employee Rights to Information about Conditions Applicable to their Contract of Employment Relationship*, in Industrial Law Journal, Vol. 21, No 2, june, p.106 et seq.
- D' Antona M. (1991), *L'autonomia individuale e le fonti del diritto del lavoro*, in Giomale di Diritto del Lavoro e Relazioni Industriali, N. 51, p. 455 et seq.
- Davies P., Freedland M. (1993), *Labour Legislation and Public Policy,* Oxford.
- De Luca L., Bruni M. (1993), *Unemployment and labour market flexibility: Italy*, Geneva.

- Gaeta L. (1994), *Qualità totale e teoria della subordinazione*, in Diritto delle Relazioni Industriali, N. 1, p. 3 et seq.
- Giugni G. (1989), *Diritto del lavoro (voce per un' Enciclopedia)*, in Id., Lavoro Legge *Contratti*, Bologna.
- Giugni G. (1989), *Giuridificazione e deregolazione nel diritto del lavoro italiano*, in Id., Lavoro Leggi Contratti, Bologna.
- Giugni G. (1994), *Una lezione sul diritto del lavoro*, in Giomale di diritto del lavoro e relazioni industriali, N. 62, p. 209 et seq.
- Hales C. (1994), *'Internal marketing' as an approach to human resource management: a new perspective or a metaphor too far?*, in Human Resource Management Journal, vol. 5, N. 1, Autumn, p. 50 et seq.
- Hepple B. (1986), *Restructuring Employment Rights,* in Industrial Law Journal, vol. 15, p. 69 et seq.
- Hepple B. (1992), *Labour Law and the New Labour Force*, in Gladstone A. et al. (eds), *Labour Relations in a Changing Environment*, Berlin/New York.
- Hiatt J.P., Rhinehart L. (1994), *The Growing Contingent Workforce: A Challenge for the Future*, in The Labour Lawyer , Vol. 10, N. 2, Spring, p. 143 ss.
- Ichino P.(1989), *Subordinazione e autonomia nel diritto del lavoro*, Milano.
- Lambertucci P. (1993), *La disponibilità collettiva dei diritti individuali*, in Diritto delle *Relazioni Industriali*, N. 2, p. 189 et seq.
- Liebman S. (1993), *Individuale e collettivo nel rapporto di lavoro*, Milano.
- Manganiello E. (1994), *Dequalificazione consensuale e interessi prevalenti*, in Rivista Giuridica del Lavoro, N.2, 11, p. 380 et seq.
- Mazzotta O. (1994), *Autonomia individuale e sistema del diritto del lavoro*, in ld., Diritto del lavoro e diritto civile, Torino.
- Miller R.U. (1994), *The Impact of Contingent Employment on Workers' Rights: A Comparative Analysis*, in Blanpain R., Rojot J., Wheeler H., *Employee Rights and Industrial Justice*, Bulletin of Comparative Labour Relations, N. 28, p. 47 ss.
- Montuschi L. (1993), *Il contratto di lavoro fra pregiudizio ed orgoglio giuslavoristico*, in Lavoro e Diritto, N. 1, p. 21 et seq.
- Napier B. (1988/89), *Deregulation, Flexibility and Individual Labour Law in the United Kingdom*, in The International Journal of Comparative Labour Law and Industrial Relations, vol. 4, N. 4, p. 206 et seq.
- Negrelli S. (1992), *Economic flexibility and society in Italy*, in The International Journal of Human Resource Management, Vol. 3, N. 2, September, p. 191 et seq.

74 Marco Biagi

- Pedrazzoli M. (1990), *Flexibility in Working Time*, in Associazione
  Italiana di Diritto Comparato, *Italian National Reports to the Xlllth
  International Congress of Comparative Law, Montreal 1990*, Milano, p.
  283 et seq.
- von Potobsky G. (1992), *Small and medium-sized enterprises and labour
  law*, in International Labour Review, Vol. 131, N. 6, p. 601 et seq.
- Rojot J. (1994), *Ethics and Employee Rights at the Workplace*, in
  Blanpain R., Rojot J., Wheeler H.N., *Employee Rights and Industrial
  Justice*, Bulletin of Comparative Labour Relations, N. 28, p. 3 et seq.
- Santoni F. (1993), *Rapporti speciali di lavoro*, Torino.
- Scarpelli F. (1993), *Lavoratore subordinato e autotutela collettiva*,
  Milano.
- Servais J-M. (1994), *Labour Law in Small and Medium-Sized Enterprises:
  An Ongoing Challenge*, in The International Journal of Comparative
  Labour Law and Industrial relations, Vol. 10, N.2, Summer, p. 119 et
  seq.
- Storey J., Bacon N. (1993), *Individualism and collectivism: into the
  1990s*, in The International Journal of Human Resource Management,
  vol. 4, N.3, Sept., p. 665 et seq.
- Streeck W. (1988), *Status e contratto nella teoria delle relazioni
  industriali*, in Giornale di Diritto del Lavoro e Relazioni industriali, p.
  673 et seq.
- Terry M. (1993), *Workplace unions and workplace industrial relations:
  the Italian experience*, in Industrial Relations Journal, vol. 24, N.2, June,
  p. 138 et seq.
- Tiraboschi M. (1994), *"Agenzie" di servize e cooperative di produzione e
  lavoro*, in il Lavoro nella Giurisprudenza, N.6, p. 559 et seq.
- Tiraboschi M. (1994), *Autonomia e subordinazione nelle tecniche di
  interpretazione dei precedenti giudiziari*, in Revista giuridica del lavoro,
  N. 2, 11, p. 353 et seq.
- Treu T. (1993), *Employment Protection and Labor Relations in Italy*, in
  Buechtemann C.F. (ed.), *Employment Security and Labour Market
  Behavior*, Ithaca., p. 391 et seq.
- Veneziani B. (1986), *Labour Law Research in Italy*, in Edlung S. (ed.),
  Labour Law Research in Twelve Countries, Stockolm.
- Veneziani B. (1986), *The Evolution of the Contract of Employment*, in
  Hepple B. (ed.), *The Making of Labour Law in Europe. A Comparative
  Study of Nine Countries up to 1945*, London/New York, p. 31 et seq.
- Veneziani B. (1986), *New Technologies and the Contract of Employment*,
  in The International Journal of Comparative Labour Law and Industrial
  Relations, vol. 2, N.6, p. 117 et seq.

- Veneziani B. (1992), *The transformations of the labour force and the organisations of firms*, in Id. (ed.), *Labour flexibility, the law and collective bargaining in EC countries*, Roma.
- Vranken M. (1989), *Autonomy and individual labour law: a comparative analysis*, in the International Journal of Comparative Labour Law and Industrial Relations, Vol. 5, p. 1 00 et seq.
- Wedderburn Lord (1987), *Labour Law: From Here to Autonomy?*, in Industrial Law Journal, Vol. 16, N. 1, p. 1 et seq.
- Wheeler H.N. (1994), *Employee Rights as Human Rights*, in Blanpain R., Rojot J., Wheeler H.N., *Rights and Industrial Justice*, in Bulletin of Comparative Labour Relations, N. 28, p. 12 et seq.
- Zoppoli L. (1991), *La corrispettività nel contratto di lavoro*, Napoli.
- Zoppoli L. (1993), *Il contratto di reinserimento nella legge 23 luglio 1991, n. 223*, in Rivista giuridica del lavoro , N. 1 , parte 1, p. 69 et seq.

PAST, PRESENT AND FUTURE ROLE OF THE EMPLOYMENT CONTRACT IN LABOUR RELATIONS IN SWEDEN

Reinhold FAHLBECK

1. Structure of collective bargaining and of collective agreement regulation in Sweden[1]

The Swedish labour market is highly organised. The overall rate of unionisation is around or above 80 % of the working population.[2] Union membership is fairly evenly distributed among the three main sectors of the labour market: private, local government and national (state) government. Unionism is divided into three main federations, one for blue-collar employees, one for white-collar employees and one for professionals. Today this division is largely an anachronistic remnant of a more class-oriented society and there are tendencies towards unification. In the blue-collar sector, workers belong to industry-wide unions federated into the Swedish Confederation of Trade Unions (known as LO after the abbreviation of its Swedish name). LO accounts for approximately 50% of all employees in Sweden. White-collar employees are unionised to a great extent as well. Industry-wide industrial unions, mainly belonging to the Central Organisation of Salaried Employees (TCO), organise the bulk of them. Among professionals the unionisation rate is somewhat lower in the private sector than in public service where it often reaches the 90 % level. The majority of unionised professionals belong to national craft unions amalgamated into a central federation (SACO).

---

1 This paragraph (as well as the next) relies heavily on the corresponding text in my contribution to a recently published major introductory book on Swedish law designed for foreign readers: *Swedish Law. A Survey* (Juristförlaget, 1995).

2 A July 1994 OECD report puts the overall unionisation rate in Sweden at 80 - 90 % of the working population and states that the rate is still rising. That corresponds to official statistics in Sweden; see *e.g.* Government White Paper, *Ny anställningsskyddslag*, SOU 1993:32 (ISBN 91-38-13332-6), chapter 5.

L. Betten (ed.), The Employment Contract in Transforming Labour Relations, 77-103.
© *1995 Kluwer Law International. Printed in the Netherlands.*

Employers in the private sector are also highly organised. Most private sector employees work for employers who either belong to an industry-wide organisation of employers or sign a collective agreement of their own. True, a good portion of small companies are not covered by collective agreements but the standards of the collective agreement in the particular sector of the economy often serve as a model nevertheless (see para. 2 *infra*).[3] The Swedish Employers Federation (SAF) completely dominates. Its some thirty-five member organisations represent virtually every facet of private industry.

In the public sector, agencies represent the national (state) government and the local governments for the purpose of collective bargaining and employment matters generally.

The size of the company is not much of a factor in terms of unionisation rates. Nor is sex, age, geographical location or branch of industry. The unionisation rate among part-time employees may be lower than the average but not very much. Swedish unions consider it their mission to organise all employees. Union membership is not on the decline in Sweden. On the contrary, it continues to rise despite the already extremely high unionisation rate. Sweden is a very corporative society and the union movement is but one of the many organised groupings.

On the employer side the picture is much the same. The SAF has adopted a policy of trying to disentangle itself from the corporative structure of which it has become part. It has taken quite a few steps in that direction. However, in a partial reversal of that policy the SAF early in 1995 agreed to serve on a tripartite committee on labour and employment law reform together with the government and the union movement.[4]

Collective bargaining in Sweden is very centralised. Traditionally bargaining in the private sector has taken place at three levels, *national* between SAF and the employee federations, *industry-wide* between industry-wide organisations on both sides and *local* between the company and the local union.

Legally binding agreements are concluded at all levels of bargaining. Due to limitations in their by-laws, the national federations are not authorised to enter into legally binding *collective* agreements but many agreements entered

---

3   Well over ninety per cent of employers in Sweden employ less than 20 people. However, the total number of people employed by them is only around thirty per cent of all employees. Many of these employers are not covered by a collective agreement, perhaps as many as fifty per cent. *Ibid*, at p. 159 *et seq.*

4   See Government Committee Directive 1995:30. See also at footnotes 22 and 36 *infra*.

into by them assume that quality when ratified by member organisations. Traditionally, the industry-wide level has been the focus of bargaining. Some agreements cover vast sections of the economy. For instance, one single agreement for blue-collar employees covers the bulk of Swedish engineering industry, core of Swedish economy, and, though renegotiated at intervals, the agreement dates back to 1905.

The traditional three-tier classification of employees has no legal standing in Sweden. With very few exceptions Swedish labour legislation makes no distinction between employees in terms of this classification. To some extent legislation has been used to overcome existing differences in collective agreements between employees of these different categories. However, the classification still plays an enormous role in the actual functioning of the labour market. Trade union structure is fashioned to it. Collective agreements reflect it, which means that more often than not there are separate agreements at places of work.[5]

There is a trend for employees to co-operate across the traditional borderlines and in some sectors collective regulation now covers all employees, but this trend is still very much in its infancy.[6] Employers have started referring to all employees as "participators" ("cooperators"), regardless of educational background.[7]

Comprehensive, industry-wide collective agreements exist in every sector of the Swedish economy. Standards apply to workplaces regardless of size *et cetera*. By far the great majority of employees are covered. That includes management representatives, from production line foremen and supervisors to managers close to the top of the hierarchical pyramid. This is so both in the private and in the public sector. Such all-encompassing coverage obviously reduces the need for individual employment contract regulation.

---

5   Indeed there often are four, the fourth being that covering foremen. The foremen's union belongs to the white collar federation but it often signs a collective agreement of its own nevertheless.

6   In the public sector, the distinction has been abolished, there being only "employees". However, old traditions die hard so the union structure still basically reflects the historical classification.

7   The word "collaborators" would better fit the Swedish word used (*medearbetare, Mitarbeiter* in German) but because of its treacherous undertone the word had perhaps better be avoided.

The industry-wide agreements leave some matters to local bargaining but only precious little for individual bargaining.

Few nations with a market economy and privately owned industry have centralised bargaining as Sweden. Strong forces today advocate less centralisation. To some extent that has already materialised. The process may continue but given the very centralised nature of Swedish society at large it does not seem likely that the process will bring about a truly profound change. Led by the private sector employer organisation SAF, there is also a move towards a system that allows for more individual bargaining. The union movement is adamantly opposed to a dismantling of the industry-wide bargaining structure and so far it has basically been successful. The union movement has accepted some decentralisation and deregulation. These trends have changed the rule-making structure but so far not to any truly significant degree.

Flexibilisation of work and of the work force is a fact in the Swedish labour market, private as well as public. This will be discussed further in paragrpah 4 *infra*.

2. Coverage and characteristics of Swedish labour and employment law

Under Swedish law, agreements to perform work fall into two major categories: employment work agreements and (independent) contract work agreements. Labour law is concerned with employment work. The distinction between the two is of great importance. Whereas the employment relationship is covered by a vast body of law, the opposite is true with regard to contract work. Furthermore, labour law on the whole aims at protecting one party to the contract, *i.e.* the employee (often referred to as the weaker party). As a consequence employment law is binding upon employers in the sense that provisions in employment contracts contrary to regulation in statutes or collective agreements are void.

Despite the importance of this distinction between the two categories of work agreements, Swedish statutory law offers no definition of either.[8] Rather, it is the task of the courts to establish the line of demarcation in the various legal areas where the need arises. An important body of law has emerged. The lodestar to distinguish between the two is the degree of

---

8   See generally T. Sigeman, *The Concept of Employee: Some Comparisons between British and Swedish Law*, in A. Neal, & A. Victorin, editors, *Law and the Weaker Party* (London 1992), volume V.

dependency of the party performing work on the opposite party, employees by and large being heavily dependent whereas contract workers are much less dependent (eg self-employed professionals, such as attorneys or dentists, or independent contractors and craftsmen). Typically, the contract is for employment work when the party performing work becomes part of an organisational structure established by the other party. The vast majority of the working population are employees and the employment work category has slowly but steadfastly gained ground on contract work. Those holding management positions, high or low, are also employed.

The very distinction between an employee and a contract worker might be seen as important when discussing the role of individual employment contracts. (After all, the vast majority who perform paid work are employees). For reasons to be explained below that is not the case.

Swedish employment law covers virtually all employees. Precious few categories are excluded. For instance, employees representing management are covered with only very limited exceptions, *e.g.* a rule in the 1982 Employment Protection Act which excludes top management people from coverage by that statute. This comprehensive coverage clearly reduces the need for individual contractual regulation.

Public employment accounts for no less than some forty per cent of the entire work force in Sweden, local government employment accounting for three fourths of public employment. Public servants are all employees, there no longer being any exemptions for "public servants" or the like.[9] Previously, public employment law was considered to belong to the public law category. That has all changed in the past three decades. With only marginal exceptions, even public employment is now considered to belong to the private realm and public employees are covered by existing employment legislation in almost exactly the same way as private sector employees. In other words, the distinction between public and private employment has largely been abolished.

Legal rights and obligations under employment law are part of private law (civil law). The same is true with regard to (collective) labour law. Swedish law does not make much of a distinction between the two. On the contrary, they are closely intertwined. Again, there are (virtually) no distinctions between public and private sector employment here either.

---

9   Judges are also employees though protected by constitutional safeguards.

2.1 DISMANTLING OF EMPLOYERS' PREROGATIVES

A characteristic feature of Swedish employment law is a set of *employer prerogatives* established in the late 19th century. Traditionally, these prerogatives were phrased in the following way: Employers are entitled
- to hire and fire at will and to employ workers whether unionised or not;
- to direct and distribute the work.

These prerogatives were far-reaching indeed. However, they had been accepted by the union movement (LO) in an epochal "compromise" between labour and management in 1906. These managerial prerogatives were upheld by the Labour Court as "generally prevailing principles of law" in the formative years of that court following its establishment in 1928.

The 20th century has seen a gradual and partial dismantling of these unilateral rights through legislation. Traditionally, the labour market parties opposed legislative intervention, the notion of "the freedom of the labour market parties" being cherished. However, starting in the early 1970's, Sweden witnessed massive legislative activity in labour relations. Some rather far-reaching limitations of employer prerogatives were introduced, most notably the substitution of the "fire-at-will" doctrine by a *just cause* requirement. Legislation on equal opportunity between women and men at places of work has further limited employer prerogatives. Within its field of application, that legislation also introduces a general standard of objectivity. These two bodies of law might have the potential to serve as a harbinger for the introduction by case law of a generally prevailing standard of objectivity with regard to all employer decisions.[10] The "Cinderella Directive" on employer obligations to inform employees about employment conditions has a similar potential for such a development.[11] However, at this present time Swedish employment law is far from imposing a general norm of objectivity

---

10   The Danish labour law professor Ruth Nielsen is a leading scholar on EC employment
     law. As is well known professor Nielsen has often stated that under EC individual
     employment law there is indeed already a generally applicable objectivity norm. See
     e.g. Nielsen, *Employers' Prerogatives* (forthcoming). This being so, professor Nielsen
     maintains, a concomitant objectivity norm has been introduced into individual
     employment law of each member State. However, in my opinion, the thesis of
     professor Nielsen is overstated but there certainly is a strong trend in this direction.

11   Directive 91/533/EC on employee rights of information.

but the trend is unmistakable. In the absence of substantive rules on matters covered by the prerogatives, employers still enjoy their traditional authority.

The employer prerogatives limit the role of employment contracts since much of the terrain for individual employment regulation is already occupied by unilateral employer authority. The implications of this state of affairs have been immense and are still of paramount importance.

2.2 THE ROLE OF EMPLOYMENT LEGISLATION

Employment legislation covers many aspects of working life. Still, the employment relationship is only partly covered by legislation. There simply is no such thing as a comprehensive employment law code.[12] Government proposals in 1910 and 1911 to introduce such legislation failed. The last attempt was made in the mid 1930's. It also failed. This time the reason was opposition from the blue-collar sector of the labour market to provisions in the proposals distinguishing between blue-collar and white-collar employees. In the past two decades, many have advocated that the numerous scattered statutes concerning the individual employment relationship be codified. A codification would be in perfect harmony with Swedish legislative traditions and add yet another code to the fifteen-odd codes already existing. Nothing has come out of these proposals. In recent years, the 1982 Employment Protection Act has begun to emerge as a centrepiece of employment law. First enacted in 1974, this piece of legislation was one of the many scattered employment law statutes, albeit arguably the most important. As indicated by its name, the Act deals with protection for employees against dismissal by the employer. Originally, it was strictly confined to issues concerning the termination of employment contracts. Lately, the scope of the Act has widened considerably as a result of Sweden joining the EU. Several EC directives have been transposed into the 1982 Act.[13] Its central role has

---

12   The situation in the Nordic countries differs considerably in this respect. Denmark, like Sweden, has no comprehensive legislation. However, that may soon change since preparations are under way in Denmark to introduce such a statute. Finland has the most comprehensive regulation, the 1970 Statute on Employment Contracts. In Norway the Work Environment Act has a central position, yet is far from comprehensive in employment matters.

13   Directive 75/129/EEC, as amended by Directive 92/56/EEC, on collective dismissals; Directive 77/187/EEC on transfers of undertakings, Directive 91/533/EC on employee rights of information ("Cinderella directive").

been greatly enhanced by these developments but the act is still far from being a codification of individual employment law generally.

> *To give just two examples of the non-existence of statutory law regarding the employment contract, reference can be made to the fact that there are simply no statutory rules on procedures to conclude a private sector employment contract. Nor are there any such rules regarding formal requirements here, e.g. if the agreement must be put in writing to be valid. The decisive factor is whether or not the parties have agreed to enter into an employment relationship.*
>
> *This can be done by signing a written contract or by oral agreement, explicit or implicit. General contract law applies. To some extent the courts have fashioned rules specifically relating to the employment relationship. Obviously, a comprehensive employment code would at least address issues such as these.*
>
> *The EC "Cinderella" directive[14], now transposed into section 6a of the Employment Protection Act, has not brought about any change in this respect.*
>
> *The information required under that directive must be in writing but the information need not necessarily be part of the employment contract, separately provided information being perfectly permissible.*

Constitutional law has played an important role in creating an independent and impartial public service. Today, constitutional law plays only a very marginal role. The independence, impartiality and irremovability of the judiciary enjoys constitutional protection. Apart from that, constitutional law does not deal with employment law in substance. Equality between women and men is guaranteed by the Constitution as is protection against ethical discrimination but, in both respects, the Constitution refers to statutory law for substantive regulation.

So far, existing legislation on the employment relationship does not promote regulation by individual employment contracts much. First, statutes cover most employees. Only truly top management employees and civil servants are exempted. Second, statutory regulation in most instances is rather general and provides for minima only, leaving detailed matters to be regulated by the labour market parties, primarily by means of collective agreements. Third, labour legislation is binding upon individual employers and employees in most instances and to the extent that it can be set aside,

---

14   *Ibid.*

that authority is primarily vested in the labour market parties, again by means of collective agreements.

2.3 COLLECTIVISATION

This state of affairs reflects another characteristic feature of modem Swedish employment regulation, namely that of collectivisation. Up until the 1970's, the employer had the right to unilaterally decide a number of matters now subject to statutory regulation (*e.g.* the 1974/1982 Employment Protection Act) or union participation by means of negotiations (the 1976 Joint Regulation Act[15]). In either case, established unions[16] have far-reaching rights to enter into agreements of vital importance for the individual employee. Statutes fail to a large extent to provide employees with such "rights" that cannot disposed of by the established union(s) together with the employer. The 1976 Act does not provide individual employees with any "rights" within the domain of joint regulation at all nor does it substitute employer managerial prerogatives to direct and distribute work with any specific, detailed rules regarding the direction and distribution of work.

Instead, the Act invites established unions to participate at their own discretion in the dynamic process of directing and distributing work. In most instances where employer managerial prerogatives have been curtailed, previous unilateral discretion on the part of the employer has been replaced by a regime of bilateral discretion at the hands of the employer and the established union(s). The collective interest of the employee community prevails over the interest of the individual employee.

---

15   The 1976 Act is the focal piece of Swedish (collective) labour legislation and governs virtually the entire area of industrial relations. When introduced it was hailed as an epochal turning-point in the running of private enterprises but experience has proven such expectations to be wrong. The Act does introduce a scheme for negotiations regarding all matters of importance at workplaces, private and public, but final decision-making powers remain firmly in the hands of management. The designation of the Act is a misnomer and the Act should rather have been entitled *e.g.* "Act on Collective Labour Relations and Union Consultation".

16   The expression "established unions" refers to unions (and their local bodies) that are parties to a collective agreement covering the place of work. By and large consultation rights under the 1976 Joint Regulation Act are confined to these unions.

2.3.1   *The Paramount Importance of the Collective Agreement*

Collective agreements are of paramount importance. Given the high unionisation rate and the fact that most employees work for employers who are parties to collective agreements or members of organisations that have signed such agreements on their behalf, it follows that the overwhelming majority of Swedish employees is covered by collective agreements. As was pointed out above (para. 1), agreements also cover most employees in managerial positions. Collective agreement regulation is more or less exclusive in some areas concerning the individual employment relationship, *e.g.* most conspicuously regarding pay where no legislation at all exists in Sweden (not even on minimum wages).

Legally speaking, the collective agreement will or will not have a mandatory normative effect on individual employment contracts. It all depends on the collective agreement. The reason is that the relevant statutory regulation provides that "employers and employees bound by a collective agreement are not legally entitled to enter into contracts that are in contravention of that agreement" (S. 27, 1976 Joint Regulation Act). The statutory rule leaves it to the parties to the collective agreement to decide the extent to which individual employers may contract with their employees. As a matter of actual practice, collective agreements often provide for binding minima but allow for improvements by workplace collective agreements or individual contracts.

Non-unionised employees are in a different position. So are employees working for employers not bound by any collective agreement. Here freedom of contract prevails. There is no mechanism under Swedish law to extend collective agreements[17] or - in other words - to arrive at an *erga omnes* effect.[18] However, under prevailing labour market practices and well established case law collective agreements have an impact on the working conditions of non-unionised employees as well.[19]

---

17   Finnish, Icelandic and Norwegian law provide for such extension. The Finnish rules are particularly comprehensive.

18   See generally R. Fahlbeck, *Collective Agreements - A Crossroad Between Private Law and Public Law* (Acta Societatis Juridicae Lundensis No. 95, 1987, ISBN 91-544-1931-X). For an abridged version see Comparative Labor Law Journal, volume 8 (1987).

19   This principle also applies to employees who are members of a union other than the one that is covered by a collective agreement at the workplace. Such unions are very rare in Sweden but prominent examples exist. The syndicalist union movement is one. It is tiny in terms of membership but it is vocal and activist. Break-away unions are also

It is generally accepted that collective agreements carry an obligation for the employer to apply standards that are no less favourable that those spelled out in the agreement to non-unionised employees as well. In that way employers will not benefit from employing non-unionised manpower. Difficult issues revolving around the application of this principle are not uncommon. This author is of the opinion that these are often resolved in ways that result in "outsiders" being discriminated against.

Many places of work are not covered by a collective agreement.[20] Here individual employment contracts are of prime importance. True, the collective agreement in the sector of the economy concerned often serves as a model for individual agreements nevertheless. The traditional attitude among unions and the social democratic party, since long the dominant political force in Sweden, is, nevertheless, that this is a problem. The attention of the newly appointed tripartite government committee on labour and employment law reform is drawn to this circumstance. The committee has not been expressly told to submit proposals in this respect but it certainly is free to do so. The instructions to the committee also point at the recently adopted EC directive on work councils (94/45 EC) and the issue of transposing an EC directive by means of collective agreements, an issue that Sweden has not faced before.[21] The implications of these statements in the instructions might well be that the committee will propose some kind of mechanism for the extension of collective agreements.[22]

---

very rare in Sweden. Every now and then they spring up and - primarily because of their rarity - they attract much publicity.

20   Cf footnote 3 *supra*.

21   The relationship between collective agreements and individual employment contracts is much the same in Denmark as in Sweden. Also, Denmark has no mechanism for extending collective agreements. The Danish experience demonstrates the difficulty, or impossibility, of using "traditional" collective agreements for transposing an EC directive. See Commission v. Denmark, case 143/83,ECR 1985 p 427. The European Court here found Danish transposition of a directive (75/117, equal pay for men and women) by means of "traditional" collective agreements not acceptable.

22   *Op. cit.* footnote 4 *supra* at pp. 6 and 7.

2.4 THE ROLE OF THE LABOUR COURT

Case law provides much legal regulation. The Labour Court has a central position in
Swedish industrial relations.[23] The court was created primarily to be instrumental in promoting industrial peace but it seems justified to say that its most prominent contribution has been in the area of individual employment law rather than in collective labour law. The reason is that the court has been called upon to rule on the scope of employer prerogatives. In doing so, the court originally accepted the *de facto* state of affairs in this respect in the days of its inception in 1928 and also, by so doing, profoundly influenced the balance of power between the labour market parties and the rule making structure.

2.5 OTHER INFLUENCES

Generally prevailing employment contract principles based on actual contract regulation prevailing in large sectors of the labour market are by and large non-existent. The managerial prerogatives provide the only truly important exceptions. However, the Labour Court has also developed a doctrine of "good labour market practice" as a standard for adjudication. It would be difficult to define this standard other than in very general terms *i.e.* in terms that are as general as the phrasing of the standard itself. Labour market parties are supposed to behave like "good guys" rather than "bad guys" and not in contravention of *bonos mores*. Litigants evoke this standard rather often but the Labour Court has been very judicious in actually applying it. There is, however, one instance of great importance where the principle has been routinely applied. Personnel management by the employer is to be exercised in ways that are not contrary to "good labour market practice". Restrictions on employers are not severe. The court has refrained from becoming involved in detailed matters concerning personnel management. It has taken a rather cavalier position reminding employees that "strong words and unfriendly treatment occur in all spheres of life". Application in areas other than personnel management has, so far, been on an *ad hoc* basis.

Regulation of a quasi-contractual kind does not exist in Sweden with regard to the employment relationship. It is true that employers often adopt work rules and rules of conduct. These rules have the potential of assuming a

---

23   See generally R. Fahlbeck, *The Role of Neutrals in the Resolution of Shop Floor Disputes*. Comparative Labor Law Journal, volume 9 (1987).

contractual or quasi-contractual character. Employer organisations have strongly advised member companies against allowing that to happen. The rationale is that such a development might undermine employer prerogatives and turn some of them into a mutually binding contractual relationship effectively barring the employer from unilaterally changing or repealing the rules, should he/she so desire. Swedish employers have been successful in not allowing such unilaterally established rules to turn into contractual ones.

In sum: Labour regulation in Sweden shows an intricate and close interplay between employer prerogatives, legislation, collective agreements, case law and union participation in day-to-day decision making at workplaces. Individual employment contracts are of minor importance as regulatory instruments.

3. Development and Role of the Contract of Employment

The employment contract first emerged towards the end of the Middle Ages. Around 1350 Sweden got its first statute-book of nationwide applicability. The rules in that statute-book laid down that the relationship between masters and servants was based on a contract, freely entered into by both parties, including the employee/servant. Statutory regulation of the relationship between master and servant was to last for some 500 years. Naturally it developed over time but the contractual basis for the relationship remained unaltered. Contracts for hiring were for a limited period only, mostly for one year, so contracts had to be renewed periodically. This accentuated the contractual nature of the relationship. However, apart from the bare fact of hiring and becoming hired there was not much else the parties could contract about. State government regulation took care of everything else, including remuneration.

The relationship between the parties was strictly hierarchical and based on the subordination of employees/servants. Servants were at the disposal of masters and their duties were far-reaching. In matters such as *when, where* and *how* to perform work the master decided. Servants owed their masters *fidelity* and *loyalty* and were subject to discipline (short of dismissal, except for just cause *i.e.* truly serious misbehaviour).

This regulatory structure collapsed in the middle of the 19th century. The liberal state philosophy that replaced it favoured free bargaining between buyers and sellers regarding employment contracts. Under the motto "From status to contract" the "free" employment contract came into existence. In reality, freedom of contract did not mean much to most sellers/employees since the buyer/employer side came to dominate completely in the newly created markets for human labour. Buyers/employers dictated conditions. This market situation gave rise to a *de facto* state of affairs whereby employers made all the decisions at industrial places of work. The law was largely silent, referring only to the actual contents of contracts. At the turn of the century the social situation in Sweden was tense, as in most other European countries, with a vast proletariat forming a revolutionary potential. Organisations came into existence on both sides of the labour market. As was pointed out in paragraph 2, the then infant national federations LO and SAF reached a compromise. The compromise was, of course, not concerned with the employment contract as a legal instrument. The employer prerogatives that it expressly confirmed, mirrored the actual relation between employers and employees at the time. In turn, these prerogatives meant that there was not much need for individual contractual regulation since the employer prerogatives covered virtually the entire employment relationship. Indeed, the position of employers under the 1906 compromise was much stronger than that of masters under the previous regulation. Only the basis was the same: a contract for work.

From another point of view also, the 1906 compromise meant that individual contracts were to play an insignificant role. It established the union federation LO (and its member organisations) as legitimate representatives of workers. The compromise was in itself a collective regulation between the organisations on both sides and consequently the compromise implicitly pointed at collective regulation.[24]

For much of this century, the individual contract of hiring has contained virtually no individual specifications at all. In the blue-collar sector, employment conditions were said to be collective and blue-collar workers were commonly referred to as "collectively employed worker" (*kollektivanstallda*) The term is still sometimes used but has become increasingly misleading in so far as it is used to distinguish between blue-collar and white-collar employees.

Traditionally, the employment contract of blue-collar employees had only one individual element, *i.e.* the date of commencement of employment. Everything else was regulated elsewhere, primarily through the applicable collective agreement. A simple reference to that agreement was enough. The

---

24   As stated in para. 2, employment law reform throughout the 20th century can be seen as
      a gradual dismantling of the 1906 compromise. With regard to (collective) labour law
      the situation is completely different. The 1906 compromise here was a great victory for
      organised labour. The employer concession in 1906 was to recognise and accept
      employee unionism and a pledge not to interfere with employee right of association.

normative effect of collective agreements (S. 26, 1976 Joint Regulation Act) assured contractual bonds between the parties with regard to the rules spelled out in the collective agreement. During the span of the employment relationship individual bargaining could, and often did, occur at intervals regarding personal pay increases. Employment contracts of white-collar employees had at least two individual elements, *i.e.* the date of commencement of employment and the initial pay. Unlike blue-collar collective agreements those for white-collar people did not contain rules on initial pay (other than perhaps some minima). Much the same was true for most professionals as well. People in sensitive positions privy to trade secrets may have had to sign a secrecy clause and still others a clause not to compete upon termination of the employment relationship but such clauses were - and still are - rather standardised. For example, a 1969 master agreement on restrictive covenants in employment contracts covers most of the private sector, so by and large there is no need to specifically tailor such a clause. A reference to this master agreement will suffice. Only truly high echelon employees bargained directly with employers and had much of employment conditions embodied in an individual contract of hiring.

3.1 THE LIMITED ROLE OF THE INDIVIDUAL CONTRACT OF EMPLOYMENT

By and large, this state of affairs is still valid for the overwhelming majority of the working population. The substance of the employment contract is simply derived from other sources. In addition, unless otherwise agreed between the parties, the employment contract is for an unlimited period of time, permanent employment.[25] Paraphrasing the slogan "from status to contract" the situation can be described as a move "from status to contract and back!"

One example to illustrate the limited role of individual employment contracts! The example chosen is simple and concerned with day-to-day operations at workplaces, transfers and alterations in work tasks, i.e. job

---

25   The 1982 Employment Protection Act allows for fixed-term employment only in specific, restricted situations. These restrictions are one of the most sensitive issues in Swedish employment law. For a discussion of the, somewhat divergent, rules on fixed-time employment in the original 1974 Employment Protection Act and its 1982 successor see R. Fahlbeck, *Employment Protection Legislation and Labour Union Interests: A Union Battle for Survival?* Stanford Journal of International Law, volume XX (1985). See further on fixed-term employment para. 4 *infra.*

classifications. In some legal systems, job classifications play an important role. An employee is hired to perform a job with a specific job classification. That may mean that he/she cannot be transferred to some other position if that position falls under some other job classification. Nor can, if such is the case, work task alterations be ordered. Such transfers/alterations would mean a change of the employment contract, so the employer would not be in a position to effect the transfer/alteration unilaterally. The employment contract would have to be renegotiated.

Under Swedish law the point of departure here is freedom of contract. If the contract means that the employee has been hired to perform a specific job spelled out in the employment contract, then that settles the issue. Traditional contract interpretation will be used to resolve disputes regarding work tasks. Many employment contracts are of this kind.

However, the overwhelming majority of employees, both in the private and in the public sector, work under contracts that are differently structured. It is a principle of long standing under Swedish law that collective agreements are based on the principle that employees are obliged to perform all tasks that meet two standards: the tasks must be part of the core work performed at the place of work and the employee must be qualified to perform these tasks. Stated differently, the principle is that employees are obliged to perform all tasks that are covered by the applicable collective agreement. Most collective agreements are of the industry-wide type and cover all work tasks at the specific place of work so this way of describing the work tasks an employee can be ordered to perform is in fact just another way of phrasing the same principle. The basis for the doctrine is contractual but the contract here is not the individual contract of hiring but the collective agreement. Unless the parties to the individual employment agree to something else, the principle of the applicable collective agreement will apply. Swedish employers have been very careful not to allow employment contracts to limit the managerial freedom that the overriding principle gives them. Indeed, the overriding principle mirrors the actual state of affairs in private industry at the time when collective agreement regulation came into existence. As can easily be surmised, this principle is a manifestation of the managerial prerogatives discussed above (para. 2). In one of its very first rulings the Labour Court accepted this contractual principle.[26] Initially

---

26   Nicknamed the "29:29-principles" after Labour Court ruling 1929 number 29 where they were laid down.

limited to the blue-collar sector, the principle now extends to virtually the entire labour market.

Obviously the principle discussed here does not leave much room for a prominent role for employment contracts. It is an exponent of the very collectivist nature of Swedish employment law. Recent years have seen some important changes. They are a consequence of the just cause requirement for termination of employment contracts by the employer laid down in the Employment Protection Act.

Now, if important changes in the work situation of an employee take place, the employee might find himself/herself in a position that is, from the employee point of view, an entirely new job. That may or may not be the case strictly legally speaking. If it is, then the employment contract has to be renegotiated, in accordance with generally prevailing principles of contract law. There is nothing new here: the novelty is concerned with the situation where the alterations are within the boundaries of the employment contract. Neither employee consent nor renegotiation is required. But the Labour Court has laid down the rule that if the alterations are such that, from an objectively justified point of view, the employee is justified in thinking that he/she has got a new job, then the employer is authorised to undertake such alterations only for just cause.   Furthermore, aggrieved employees can challenge the employer's decision before a court and the court can issue an order of specific performance, reinstating the employee. Failure to obey such an order does not *per se* amount to the Swedish equivalent of contempt of court[27] but the employer is in breach of contract and thus liable to pay damages to the employee.

This principle represents one of the rare situations where the Labour Court has created new law. The court reasoned that the logic of the Employment Protection Act would be best served with a principle of this kind. The absence of such a principle would undermine the effectiveness of

---

27   The equivalent, called *vite*, is a private law sanction in the form of a sum of money to be paid to society in case of non-compliance. Unlike the situation in most other fields of the law, *vite* in labour and employment cases can only rarely be commuted into a prison sentence. *Vite* is virtually never prescribed in employment cases and no prison sentence has ever been imposed for failure to pay the stipulated *vite*.

the act and constitute an important loophole.[28] A body of case law has come
into existence.

The discussion in the previous paragraphs serve to illustrate the traditionally
insignificant role of individual employment contracts under Swedish law.

4. The Employment Contract in a Changing Work Environment

In 1982, the labour market parties in the private sector signed yet another
epoch-making master agreement.[29] The agreement has wide ramifications
for the private sector but it has also set much of the tone for the entire labour
market. Entitled "The Development Agreement" it is a Song of Songs in
praise of cooperation, mutual understanding and accommodation as well as
of business efficiency. It vibrates with the dynamism of change but also with
the optimism of change. Consequently, it stresses the need for business
flexibility and the concomitant continuous process of adaptation, both for
companies and for employees. It underlines the necessity of continuous
learning and skill formation but at the same time acknowledges the
legitimacy of employee expectations to experience a rewarding and fulfilling
professional life. The agreement is miles away from looking at employees as
an anonymous mass with uniform and limited horizons. On the contrary,
here the employee is treated as an individual with legitimate expectations of
his/her own.

---

28   Nicknamed "the sauna bath principle" it was established by Labour Court ruling 1978
     number 89. In that case the legality of an employer order to, in fact, demote an
     employee who had been found in the sauna rather than at his work site - an extremely
     costly pulp processing machine - was at issue. In line with Swedish traditions to
     compromise, the court found for the employer on issues of principle but for the
     employee in the case at hand. An irrelevant but sunny and encouraging addendum!
     Today "the sauna bath employee" of yore is an attorney of law. Portraying him in a
     recent article the leading Swedish labour law monthly quotes him as saying that the case
     that turned him into a celebrity of sorts made him change career. The reason? His faith
     in the legal system was greatly strengthened by the ruling of the court! Lag & Avtal,
     May issue 1995:5.

29   Four master agreements stand out, i.e. the 1906 compromise between SAF and LO, the
     1938 agreement between SAF and LO on procedures for negotiations, settling disputes
     and for avoiding industrial warfare, the 1946 agreement between SAF and LO on work
     councils and the 1982 agreement between SAF and all union federations in the private
     sector on efficiency and participation.

It is obvious that the 1982 agreement represents an individualistic approach to the employment relationship. But the agreement is not concerned with legal niceties concerning the balance between different forms for legal regulation, *i.e.* collective agreements versus individual employment agreements.

The fifteen-odd years that have passed since the "Development Agreement" was signed have certainly proved the visions of the agreement right. It has been a period of stunning technological advance. The information technology and concomitant telecommunication systems have revolutionised our ways of perceiving human interaction. The work environment has changed dramatically. The era of standardised mass fabrication in huge factories is being replaced by smaller and leaner production facilities where the contribution of each individual becomes much more quantifiable and visible. The importance of each individual's professional knowledge has increased considerably. Manufacturing has increasingly become computerised, turning many blue-collar workers into highly specialised technicians. The number of employees in manufacturing industries has gone down dramatically. The service sector is becoming the dominant sector of the economy. Work processes and employee qualifications here are much more individualised than in traditional manufacturing. Workplaces in this sector are smaller. The distance between employee and customer is shorter and they often meet. The participation of women has increased by some twenty per cent. In 1991, women began outnumbering men in the Swedish workforce for the first time.

The manpower structure of workplaces has changed too. A core of employees are employed on a full time basis and are considered permanent employees in the sense that they are not likely to be dismissed. Surrounding them are layers of others. Part-time employees and employees on fixed-term agreements form one. Since they are employees, their ties to the workplace are often quite strong and, in many cases, of long duration. Many turn into core employees. Yet another layer is composed of contract workers, employed by independent contractors doing business with the company where the contract worker actually performs his/her work. Specialisation has become more and more common. Fewer companies produce "everything" that goes into their products. This has led to an increase in sub-contracting but also to closer contacts between the purchasing firm and the sub-contracting firm as a result of ever more exacting technical requirements.

Temporary hiring of manpower has become legal in Sweden and such manpower represents yet another layer.

4.1 FORMS OF ATYPICAL WORK

The various forms atypical work just mentioned have proliferated. By now it is in fact anachronistic to refer to them as atypical. They are so common that they are atypical only in a historical sense. In addition, a whole array of other kinds of arrangements entailing flexibility exist, in particular flexible working time and various forms for time off.[30]

Unions take part in all facets of the flexibilisation process. They also organise "atypical employees" and unionisation rates are not considerably lower than the average rate. To the extent possible standards in collective agreement apply to "atypical employees" in just the same way as to "typical employees". Where not possible collective agreements often establish standards specifically designed for "atypical employees".

To what extent have all these developments influenced regulation by means of individual employment contracts? That will be discussed in the following subparagraphs.

4.1.1 Part-Time Employment
Part-time employment is one form of atypical employment. As a prevalent practice it is a recent phenomenon, dating back no longer than to the 1960's.[31] It has grown very rapidly and is now quite common. By definition, "part-time employment" means work where working hours do not exceed 34 hours per week. In 1992, approximately 25 per cent of all employees were part-timers. Two prime reasons are routinely cited, the growth of public sector employment and the massive entrance by women on the labour market. Public sector employment has grown very considerably in the past few decades and now accounts for nearly forty per cent of the work force. Part-time employment is over-represented here and accounts for well over fifty per cent of all part-timers. Women have favoured part-time work

---

30   See, generally, R. Eklund, *New Fortuns and Aspects of Atypical Employment Relationships. Swedish report to the XIth World Congress of Labour Law and Social Security*; A. Numhauser-Henning, *Hiring Procedures in Sweden* (Acta Sociatatis Juridicae Lundensis No. 82, 1986, ISBN 91-544-1801-1); A. Numhauser-Henning, *Fixed-Term Contracts of Employment and Temporary Work, Swedish report to the ILO* (stencil, Lund, 1988) and A. Numhauser-Henning, *Flexibility in Working Time from the Swedish Horizon. Swedish National Report to the XIIIth International Congress of Comparative Law*, Montreal 1990 (Acta Instituti Upsaliensis Iurisprudentiae Comparativae XVI, S. Strömholm & C. Hemström, editors, Uppsala 1990.

31   For a recent survey of part-time work see *op. cit.* footnote 2 *supra*, chapter 18 and Appendix.

because of traditional gender roles that leave most of the house work to them. They make up the bulk of part-timers, accounting for some 85 to 90 per cent of them. Among men part-time work is most common at the beginning and towards the end of their professional life. With women age is much less of a factor. The trend among part-timers is to increase their working time and many switch to full time work. Previous rapid increases in the number of part-timers abated towards the end of the 1980's and the absolute number has receded somewhat in recent years.

To some extent, part-time employment has promoted individual employment contract regulation. One individual element is added to the employment contract, i.e. the number of working hours. Swedish law does not contain any mandatory rules on standard numbers of working hours for part-time work although collective agreements often recommend a specific number of hours. An individual agreement is needed for every employee. Both statutes and collective agreements contain rules in other respects, however, so the additional element of individualisation is basically confined to the agreement on the number of working hours. This means that the tremendous increase in part-time employment has not led to any significantly increased role for individual employment contract regulation.

4.1.2 Fixed-Term Employment

The same is true with regard to fixed-term employment.[32] Paralleling the evolution and structure of part-time employment in may respects, fixed-term employment as a common phenomenon is relatively recent, did increase rapidly but is no longer doing so, is much more common in the public sector and among women (though to a considerable lesser degree). In the past five to ten years around ten per cent of all employees have been employed on a fixed basis at any given time.[33] The percentage has decreased slightly.

---

32   Cf generally *op. cit.* footnote 2 *supra*, chapter 12 and Appendix.

33   Given statutory maxima on the length of fixed-term employment contracts these should rarely exceed six months. However, many employees find themselves moving from one fixed-term employment to another in a seemingly endless succession. The reason is that one form for fixed-term employment is that of deputising for an absent employee. In particular at workplaces where many women of fertile age are employed, *e.g.* hospitals, there will be numerous vacancies at any given time. The expression "deputy mess" (or even "deputy hell") has been coined. Such practices are legal since the vacancies are genuine and the employer is acting *bona fide*.

Young people, aged 16 to 24, are much overrepresented and account for around half of all employees with fixed-term contracts.[34]

The various forms for fixed-term employment have undoubtedly much contributed to flexibilisation of working life. Have they also enhanced the role of individual employment contract regulation? The answer in Sweden is: not much. The reason is that statutes and collective agreements contain detailed rules on fixed-term employment, leaving precious little room for individual bargains. Again in parallel with part-time work, fixed-time work adds one element to the contract of hiring since the law requires that the parties agree on fixed-time employment. In the absence of an agreement to that effect the employment contract will considered to be for an unlimited period of time, permanent employment. The parties will also have to agree on the length of the contract. The Employment Protection Act as well as many collective agreements contain detailed rules on lawful maximum lengths but there is nothing that forbids shorter fixed-term contracts so the individual parties here enjoy freedom of contract.

4.1.3 Distance Work
Distance work has become a reality for some. Few work full time away from the premises of their employer but an increasing, yet still small, number of employees do so occasionally. One study showed that the majority of distance workers were white collar employees in higher positions, virtually all men and in most cases at the initiative of the employee. Most commonly employees work at home on computers linked to the employer's data system. Personal contract element are necessary but collective agreement regulation also exists.

4.1.4 Hiring Out
Hiring out of employees is yet another form for flexibilisation. The 1993 Act on Private Employment Exchange and Hiring Out of Employees applies.[35] The statute is an archetypal exponent of deregulation. It marks an end to a

---

34   It should be pointed out that in this context probationary employment is not counted as fixed-term employment.

35   See generally R. Fahlbeck, *Employment Exchange and Hiring Out of Employees in Sweden.* Tidsskrift for Rettsvitenskap 1995. For an earlier treatment of the subject see *Temporary Work in Modern Society. A Comparative Study.* Editors: W. Albeda, R. Blanpain & G.M. Veldkamp (Kluwer 1978). My text there on Sweden gives a fuller account of previous law and practice that the 1995 article, which of course is primarily concerned with new situation created by the 1993 Act.

regulatory structure that had existed for nearly sixty years. It is also an archetypal exponent of the present international surge towards decentralisation. A rigid and strongly centralised system is replaced by a flexible system where the local market place is the stage.

What arguments were forwarded to justify the revocation of the rules banning private employment exchange and hiring out of employees? When the rules came into existence in the 1930's and early 1940's, they were prompted by abuse and unsatisfactory conditions, sometimes even downright exploitation of job seekers. Three distinctive yet closely connected phenomena make for a situation so different from those prevailing then that fears of yore are no longer relevant or at leat not very worrisome. Those are the existence of (1) a free, comprehensive, high quality public employment exchange, (2) strong labour unions covering virtually the whole labour market and (3) extensive labour and social legislation protecting employees.

Employment exchange is not of interest here but hiring out of employees is. Also referred to as temporary work or hiring out of manpower it is a contractual relationship between an employer, the "hiring out firm" (temporary work firm, manpower firm), and a third party, the user, where under the employer puts one of more of its employees at the disposal of the third party for the purpose of performing work that is part of the activity of the third party. Such a worker is the employee of the hiring out firm but is wholly or partly under the authority of the user firm and is to perform work ordered by the user, possibly of a continually changing nature (depending on and within the limits of the worker's employment contract with the employer and the contract between the employer and the third party user). The hiring out firm must charge the user a fee of some kind. (If no fee is charged the arrangement will usually be referred to as "loan of workers". Incidentally, such an arrangement also represents a form for atypical work!)

The 1993 Act permits hiring out of manpower with virtually no restrictions. Since hiring out had previously been forbidden, manpower policies of Swedish employers did not include temporary work arrangements. Hiring out has undoubtedly expanded since becoming legal but it is still very much in its infancy and accounts for only a tiny portion of total employment in the country. No official statistics exist so far. Information provided by branch organisations indicate that as of January 1995 only some 0.001 to 0.002 per cent of all employed worked for hiring out firms. According to the same sources, estimates are that the corresponding figure for many Western countries is some 2 per cent of the working population. The figures reveal that temporary work has yet to grow considerably before becoming a factor of importance in the labour market. Nevertheless, it certainly represents yet another form for flexibility, constituting an atypical employment relationship of its own.

The 1993 Act contains virtually no substantive regulation of employment conditions. This seems to call for quite a few individual contract elements to govern the relationship between the temporary work firm and its employees. A list of such elements might include work tasks, working hours, workplaces that the employee accepts to be dispatched to, advance notice of assignments, availability for being contacted by the employer and remuneration. It would seem that the temporary work employment contract has to be rather personalised. Past experience both confirms and disconfirms this. Companies of the temporary hiring out type have existed for long in Sweden. Their legality was questionable and they were sometimes found to be in contravention of the existing ban on hiring out of workers. But they struggled on. Everyone agreed at the time that many were very well managed. Some even succeeded in securing collective agreements with the leading union in their breach of business. This gave them an aura of legality and was a confirmation of their seriousness. The fact that they signed collective agreements proves that even in a business as flexible and variable as that of temporary work, regulation by means of collective agreements is possible.

Now that temporary work firms have been legalised, there is every reason to believe that they will sign collective agreements with unions. Even so, one must assume that the scope for individual elements will be significant here. Collective agreements will probably cover all the issues mentioned above but that does not eliminate the need for individual acceptance of them. On the other hand, one must assume that temporary work firms will become as specialised as other firms in the service industry. That will be reflected in the collective agreements signed by them. Prospective employees will know by the services that the temporary work firm offers what job tasks they might be asked to perform and what other conditions they will be faced with. That will act to reduce the individual elements in the contracts of hire.

Apart from atypical work forms a vast array of other arrangements entailing flexibility exists. Working time flexibility, time off and early part-time retirement are the most important.

4.1.5 Flexible Working Time
Flexible working time has become a standard feature in recent years but is nevertheless of recent origin. Today, virtually the whole labour market is covered with a variety of flexible working time schemes. Around half the working population enjoys some kind of flexitime privilege, white-collar and professional employees to a considerable higher degree than blue-collar

employees. Flexitime can be calculated on a daily, weekly, monthly or yearly basis. Examples of all exist and sometimes they are combined.

They can provide for scheduling of working time or for the total number of hours worked per period or both. The degree of individual choice differs considerably between different collective agreements. For example summer working hours versus winter working hours are applied uniformly to all whereas most other flexitime arrangements allow for much individual choice. Proposals to introduce a lifetime flexisystem have attracted wide attention as have proposals to introduce sabbaticals as a regular benefit for but so far these proposals have not produced any concrete results. If realised, such arrangements would obviously give individuals a considerable amount of freedom of choice.

Employers have long sought to introduce business cycle variations in the total number of working hours. Until very recently their efforts have met with little success. The 1995 collective agreement for blue-collar workers in the engineering industry (see para. 1 *supra*) may have been a breakthrough. It allows for such agreements between the employer and individual employees. Under the agreement, those individuals that have accepted them would work longer or shorter hours than the rest of the workforce. Employee acceptance is strictly personal.

Virtually all arrangements concerning flexitime promote individual freedom of choice. In most instances employees are free to decide on their own without specific employer consent so employment contract regulation as such is scarcely promoted. The basis for flexitime schemes is invariably rules in collective agreements. The 1982 Working Time Act does not deal with flexitime.

Schemes for *time off* are numerous in Sweden. Most are of recent origin. Most are statutory. All allow for some individual choice, ranging from extensive freedom of choice, *e.g.* time off for studies, to rather limited freedom, *e.g.* the annual vacation.

Early retirement is an option offered by statue to employees who have reached 62 years of age. The option is strictly personal. In other words, the decision to take advantage of this option does not require an agreement with the employer.

5. Concluding remarks

This contribution consistently points at the relatively insignificant role in Sweden for regulation by means of individual employment contracts. As has been pointed out, the only group of employees that relies heavily on individual contract regulation is that of top management employees in the private sector but that group is very small, perhaps accounting for one per cent of the working population. The time has come to ponder the reasons for this state of affairs and to ask whether significant change is likely.

The insignificant role for individual contracts of employment undoubtedly represents a restriction on the freedom of contract of individuals. The restriction is partly response to the *de facto* failure from a social welfare point of view of the principle of freedom of contract in the 19th century. Unions and collective agreements came into existence to correct the imbalance that the market had produced.

More importantly, the restrictions are part and parcel of Swedish social fabric that antedates the 19th century and that manifests itself in a centralist, collectivist and corporative type of society where the lives of individuals have always to a large extent been shaped by the powers that be. Swedes are used to that and most Swedes would not consider the limitations here as restrictions. They are more looked upon as part of a social system that is to the benefit of all.

Countervailing forces exist and have always existed. Obviously the employer community advocates more individualistic social strategies.

At this very juncture employment and labour law is of central concern in Sweden. Everyone seems to agree that statutory regulation should be limited to the extent possible. In that sense there is an overall tendency towards decentralisation and deregulation. But consensus here does not necessarily mean other than that responsibility for employment regulations should be in the hands of existing national or industry-wide labour market organisations. It is quite another matter to advocate increased local union-management authority and even more so an increased role for individual employment contract regulation. By and large, advocates for the latter alterative find themselves facing strong opposition from unions and also from political parties to the left of the centre of the political spectrum.

To illustrate! In March 1995, the government appointed a committee and commissioned it with the task of promoting change in employment law. In its instructions to the committee the government reiterates a common view in Sweden, namely that "Conditions in the labour market should normally be regulated in collective agreements". Against that background the committee is expressly told to try to "find ways for how the labour market parties, by means of collective agreements, should themselves work out employment law rules to the maximum extent possible".[36]

Freedom of choice for individuals to tailor their professional life more to their own liking has increased stupendously in the last two decades as a result of the various forms for atypical and flexible work arrangements. That is one thing. Quite another matter is the techniques used to achieve this result. As was shown in paragraph 4, the techniques used have not resulted in a corresponding increase in employment contract regulation. Flexibilisation certainly has contributed to a more significant role for individual employment contracts. However, Swedish union want to be partners in the on-going process and they want to make contributions. One way of doing that is to be instrumental in formulating rules designed for flexible work organisations. Unions have done precisely that. Will the role of individual employment regulation increase at the expense of union-management regulation? Perhaps, but I would not bet on it.

True, it is perfectly conceivable that the role of collective agreements as regulatory instruments will diminish in the future. The prime reasons would be two. First, the trends towards decentralisation, deregulation and flexibilisation. Second, Sweden's recent joining of the EU means that EC labour law must be transposed in a way that meets EC requirements. In the present context the important aspect is that EC regulation must be made *erga omnes*. Swedish collective agreements are not (yet) suited for that (see para. 2 *supra*). Also, EC employment law seems to accord the individual employee a more prominent role than does Swedish employment law, which is more collectivistic (see para. 2 *supra*). But these different trends do not all work in the same direction. The first reason does work in the direction of promoting regulation by means of individual employment contracts. On the other hand, implementation of EC directives cannot be achieved by employment contracts. EC employment law certainly centres on the individual but it is also formal and rather legalistic. Add to all this the resilient nature of industrial relations systems and the conclusion probably is that nothing much will happen to enhance individual employment contract regulation. Freedom of choice will in all likelihood continue to increase to the benefit of all employees but that will probably continue to take place within frameworks established by statutes and collective agreements rather than by strictly individual contracts. Continuity in change? "Plus ça change, plus ça reste le même"? That I would bet on!

---

36   *Op. cit.* footnote 4 *supra* at pp 4 and 6.

THE ROLE OF THE EMPLOYMENT CONTRACT IN JAPAN

Ryuichi YAMAKAWA

1. Overview of the Law of Employment Contracts and Other Contracts of Services

In Japan, the Civil Code provides for a certain regulation of the employment contract. According to article 623 of the Civil Code, the employment contract is defined as a contract through which an employee promises to render personal services and an employer promises to pay for such services. However, there are two other types of contracts relating to the provision of services: the service contract and the delegation contract. The purpose of the service contract is to guarantee completion of a given project, while the purpose of the employment contract is only to render the service itself. On the other hand, the delegation contract is a contract through which a person entrusts a certain task to another. Under this contract, a trustee has considerable discretion in performing the entrusted task, while under the employment contract an employee is subject to an employer's direction and supervision.

The regulation of the employment contract provided in the Civil Code is quite limited and not sufficient for the protection of workers. It is, rather, the Labour Standards Act and other labour and employment laws, including the body of case law, which provide such protection. Although the Labour Standards Act applies to "workers", the scope of this concept should be determined with an emphasis on substance rather than formality. Thus, even though a contract formally falls under the category of a service contract, it may still be regulated by the Labour Standards Act if, for example, the contractor actually works under the direction of the client in the same manner as an employee. In this sense, a contract covered by the Labour Standards Act is called a "labour contract."

L. Betten (ed.), The Employment Contract in Transforming Labour Relations, 105-128.

1.2 THE LABOUR MARKET AS THE BACKGROUND FOR JAPANESE EMPLOYMENT CONTRACT LAW

As explained below, the labour market in Japan has substantially influenced the law regarding employment contracts. One of the most important features of the Japanese labour market is the practice of "lifetime" employment. However, it is necessary to note at the outset that people outside Japan have sometimes misunderstood this concept. First, the employment contract in Japan does not last for one's "lifetime". Most Japanese companies have a mandatory retirement system, providing for retirement usually at the age of 60.[1] This is why in recent years this practice is often called a "long-term" employment practice.

Furthermore, this employment practice is found mainly in large companies. Smaller companies have much weaker job security. In recent years, however, even employees of large companies cannot expect to stay until they reach retirement age. A recent survey reveals that, at the age of 55, only about 50 % of employees have remained in the company where they were first hired.[2] Many middle-aged employees go to work for subsidiaries or other related companies, even though they often continue to be employees of the companies that originally hired them (shukko).[3]

In recent years, "farming-out" has become one of the important means of securing employment. Even in large companies, not all employees enjoy long-term employment. There is a considerable number of part-timers or other "atypical" workers who work under a fixed term contract. Such atypical workers are likely to be made redundant at times of labour cutbacks.

Finally, the lifetime employment practice does not mean that the employer promises their employees not to dismiss them until their retirement age. The employer has a right to dismiss employees, although case law limits the exercise of this right through the doctrine of unfair dismissal. In fact, as a specialist on the labour market points out, employers begin to discharge employees when they suffer a deficit for two years running.[4] Still,

---

1   See Japan Institute of Labour, *Japanese Working Life Profile* 77 (1994).

2   The Ministry of Labour, *White Paper on Labour 1994*, at p. 43.

3   See generally, Kazuo Sugeno, Shukko (Transfers to Related Firms): *An Aspect of the Changing Labour Market in Japan*, Japan Labour Bulletin Vol. 28, no. 4 (1989).

4   Kazuo Koike, *Shigoto no Keizaigaku* (*Economics on Employment*) at pp. 102-103 (1991).

employers certainly believe that they must try hard to avoid dismissal. In this sense, the lifetime employment practice is more of a philosophy than a stringent rule.

2.   The Development and Role of the Employment Contract in Japan

As stated above, the Japanese Civil Code has several provisions regulating the employment contract. Enacted in 1890, the Civil Code is one of the first modern statutes in the area of private law. Some of its provisions regarding employment contracts protect employees. For example, article 625 (1) provides that the employer shall not transfer his/her employment status to a third person without the consent of the employee, since such a transfer may affect the employee's interest in terms of for whom he/she is supposed to work for. However, such protection is far from sufficient. Among others, article 627 (1) provides that when parties to an employment contract do not set a fixed term for employment, either party may cancel the contract at two week's notice. In other words, subject only to a two week's notice, the employer has the freedom to discharge his/her employees at will. In addition, the Civil Code has no provision regarding working hours, the method of the payment of wages or workers' safety, not to mention the provision for equal employment opportunities.

2.1 THE LABOUR STANDARDS ACT AND OTHER STATUTES

When Japan began its industrialisation process, labour problems such as long working hours and night work came to be widely recognised. Thus, in order to supplement the insufficiency of protective provisions for workers under the Civil Code, the Factory Act was enacted in 1911. This Act prohibited child labour under the age of 12. It also prohibited employers from having minors under the age of 15 and women do night work between 10 p.m. and 4 a.m., and limited work hours to 12 hours a day or less. Although the Factory Act was later amended to include more protective provisions, and other statutes for labour protection were enacted before World War II, this statutory protection was quite limited in both scope and contents. Thus, after World War II, Japan enacted the Labour Standards Act. Article 27 (2) of the Constitution of Japan, which states that "standards for wages, working hours, rest periods and other working conditions shall be determined by law" provided a basis for enacting the Labour Standards Act, which remains one of the most basic labour protective statutes.

The Labour Standards Act has one section entitled "labour contracts" containing several articles that regulate the employment contract. These regulations include a limitation on the period of probationary employment (up to one year), the employers' duty to disclose terms and conditions of employment before hiring, a requirement of 30 days notice in the case of discharge and so forth. Regulations regarding working hours, the method of the payment of wages, and work rules are provided in other sections. For most of these regulations, the Labour Standards Act provides a system of criminal sanction against employers who violate it, in addition to the provision that entitles workers to take private action for violation of the minimum standards that it establishes.

There is a number of other statutes regulating the employment contract. These statutes include the Minimum Wages Act, the Industrial Safety and Health Act, and the Worker Dispatching Act. In recent years, the number of statutes regulating employment contracts or individual employment relations has increased. Some have a new style of regulation such as the good-faith effort provisions, as in the case of the Equal Employment Act of 1985 and the Part-Time Worker's Act of 1993. This new style of regulations will be discussed later.

Japanese courts have developed a number of rules on employment contracts in its body of case law, especially in the areas where the Labour Standards Act provides no regulation. In fact, the courts have played a very important role in the regulation of employment contracts. One of the most famous examples is a limitation on the dismissal of employees (see para. 3.2 *infra*). This is an area in which neither the Civil Code nor the Labour Standards Act provides sufficient protection of workers.[5] Furthermore, as described below, most of these case laws have taken into account the employment practices of Japanese companies.

3.   The Role of the Individual Employment Contract

In Japan, an employer and an employee rarely conclude a written employment contract, especially when the employee is hired for regular employment, *i.e.*, full-time and without a fixed term. The Labour Standards Act does not require employers to put an employment contract in writing. Work rules usually provide for the terms and conditions of employment and

---

5   Article 3 of the Labour Standards Act prohibits the employer from discriminating against the employee because of the employee's nationality, creed, and social status. Thus, a discriminatory discharge is prohibited.

they are very important because of this. As shown below, case law has held that the content of work rules, if reasonable, may be incorporated into an employment contract.[6] This case law is important because it means that the provisions of work rules, rather than the worker's individual consent, can constitute the basis for each employee's contractual obligations. Furthermore, it is not easy for individual employees to incorporate their own requests into their employment contract. As a result, the role of an individual employment contract has been relatively unimportant.

3.1 THE ROLE OF STATUTORY REGULATION

As stated above, the Labour Standards Act has several provisions regulating employment contracts. Under article 13 of the Act, an employment contract that stipulates working conditions which do not meet the standards of the Act shall be invalid with respect to such parts, and such parts shall be governed by the statutory minimum standards. This means that the Labour Standards Act has a preemptive effect over an individual's consent, if the conditions consented to are inconsistent with the standards of the Act. Thus, coupled with the criminal sanctions against violations, the Labour Standards Act imposes strong and strict regulations on employment contract.

The scope of regulations under the Labour Standards Act is, however, still quite limited, especially as regards employment contracts. Enacted in 1947, the Labour Standards Act did not foresee problems that have arisen in the course of Japan's post-war economic development. Confronted by such unforeseen problems, Japanese courts have developed a body of case law to compensate for the deficiencies in the Labour Standards Act and the Civil Code. Although in recent years, Japan has enacted a number of statutes relating to the employment relationship, case law still plays a very important role.

3.2 THE ROLE OF THE DOCTRINE OF UNFAIR DISMISSAL

Although neither the Civil Code nor the Labour Standards Act has a general provision delimiting reasons for the dismissal of employees, the courts have established a case law principle that employers cannot discharge employees without showing a sufficient just cause. The Supreme Court states, "even when an employer exercises his right of dismissal, it will be void as an abuse of the right if it is not based on objectively reasonable grounds and cannot

---

6   See *infra* footnote 18 and accompanying text.

receive social approval as a proper act".[7] Thus, even if an employee has made a mistake, the court examines every factor in his/her favour in order to determine whether the dismissal is so excessively harsh as to constitute an abuse of the right of dismissal.

The doctrine of unfair dismissal applies to a dismissal in the case of a reduction in the labour force when an employer's business goes into decline. Case law has shown that there are four requirements for an employer to be able to discharge employees in such a situation: (1) a business necessity for reducing the number of employees, such as serious financial difficulties; (2) attempts by the employer to avoid dismissal by implementing other means including a reduction in working hours, transfer of employees and the solicitation of voluntary retirement; (3) a fair standard by which the employees to be discharged are selected; and (4) adherence to a procedure that the employer has followed before carrying out dismissal, *i.e.*, consultation with unions or workers about the need for and method of implementing redundancies.[8]

The doctrine of unfair dismissal is so deeply rooted that regular workers in Japan enjoy a considerable degree of employment security. This doctrine has, as its background, the lifetime employment practice connected with the seniority-based wage determination system. In Japan, it is very difficult for regular workers, once discharged, to find a new place of employment in which they can enjoy at least equal terms and conditions of work, since, in many Japanese companies, wages and related conditions are largely determined by the years of service (the recent change is shown below). In this sense, case law reflects the reality of the labour market and of employment practices.

3.3 FLEXIBILITY: TRANSFER AND OVERTIME WORK

In contrast to the limitation on dismissals, employers in Japan have wide discretion with respect to personnel deployment and overtime.

3.3.1 Transfers and Farming-outs

As regards transfers, case law has established that an employer has a right to transfer an employee to a new workplace or position within a company unless the employment contract, work rules, or collective bargaining

---

7   Nihon Shokuen Seizou, 29 Minshu 456 (Sup. Ct. Apr. 25, 1977).

8   See, generally, Kazuo Sugeno, *Japanese Labor Law 100* (Leo Kanowitz ed. 1992).

agreement specifies, explicitly or implicitly, the employee's job or place of work.[9] In fact, most work rules contain a provision to the effect that the employer has a right to transfer where there is a business necessity to do so. Moreover, the Supreme Court has ruled that an employee is obliged to accept the transfer order to a distant workplace even if the employee must leave his family behind because of a spouse's work or children's education.[10] (There is an exception to this rule which is based on the abuse of right doctrine: when the employee must care for a sick family member, the transfer order may be deemed an abuse of the employer's right, and, therefore, void.[11] Transfers within a company take place quite often, and have various functions such as career development through rotational assignment, utilisation of an employee's ability through re-allocation, and the adjustment of the workforce in case of a downturn in business.

Employers have a right to order their employees to work for another firm on certain conditions. This employment practice, called *"Shukko"* or farming-out, is unique in that the employee retains the employment relationship with the original employer while working under the direction of another.[12] Usually such an employee is supposed to return to the original employer, and the original employer retains a right to discharge him/her. Thus, according to the interpretation of the Ministry of Labour, the employee during the *Shukko* period has a dual employment relationship both with the original employer and the new employer.[13] Like transfers within a company, farming-out plays a number of roles. Sometimes it is carried out as a means of controlling subsidiaries or related companies. Employers also utilise farming-out for employee career development. Farming-out is, furthermore, one of the most important methods for adjustment of the work force in the times of recession.

Courts have taken a slightly more restrictive position on the employer's right to order farming-out than in the case of transfers within a company, since the employee, once farmed out, must work under the direction of an employer with whom he/she did not originally conclude an employment

---

9   *Idem*, at p. 369.

10   Toa Paint, 1198 Hanrei Jiho 149 (Sup. Ct. Jul. 14, 1986).

11   *E.g.*, Nihon Denki, 19 Rominshu 1111 (1968).

12   See Sugeno, *supra* footnote 3.

13   Circular (Kihatsu) No. 333, Jun. 6, 1981.

contract.[14] However, when farming-out is an established practice in the
company and the employer has made a sufficient effort to minimise the
detrimental effect on the employee's working conditions (*e.g.* wages and
severance pay), the farming-out order is often held to be binding on the
employee.[15]

3.3.2 Overtime Work

Article 32 of the Labour Standards Act restricts working hours to 8 hours a
day and 40 hours a week. According to article 36, however, if an employer
has entered into a written agreement (a so-called "article 36 agreement") with
either a trade union organised by a majority of workers at the workplace or,
if such a union does not exist, with a person representing a majority of the
workers, and has filed this agreement with the Labour Standards Inspection
Office, the employer may extend working hours in accordance with the
provisions of the agreement. An "article 36 agreement" merely exempts
employers from liability for violations of article 32. The circumstances under
which an employer may, from the viewpoint of contract law, order
employees to work overtime, has been a matter of debate for some time.

In 1991, the Supreme Court held that an employer may issue such an
order when 1) the employer has concluded and filed with the competent
Labour Standards Inspection Office an article 36 agreement and 2) the work
rules have a provision that entitles the employer to order overtime work for
"reasonable" reasons.[16] As stated below, provisions in work rules may, if
reasonable, be integrated into the content of employment contracts. The
Court has stated that an overtime provision in the work rules is "reasonable"
even if the reasons for overtime stated in the provision include rather abstract
ones such as "when it is necessary to attain production goals", and "when the
extension of working time is required by the special nature of the work".
Since work rules in Japanese companies very often contain such a provision,
employers have wide latitude in ordering overtime work under the Supreme
Court decision.[17]

---

14   See generally, Sugeno, *supra* footnote 8, at p. 378.

15   *Idem.*

16   Hitachi Seisakujo Musashi Kojo, 45 Minshu 1270 (Sup. Ct. Nov. 28, 1991).

17   See generally Kazuo Sugeno, *The Supreme Court's Hitachi Decision on the Duty to
     Work Overtime,* Japan Labor Bulletin vol. 31, no. 5 (1992).

3.3.3   Relationship with Employment Security

Flexibility regarding transfer and overtime is correlated to restrictions on the employers' right to dismiss employees.[18] While employers are not free to discharge employees even in the case of a downturn in business, they may transfer (or farm-out) redundant employees to divisions or related companies where they can be absorbed. Also, when employers have a work overload, they can order their employees to work overtime without hiring new regular workers (it should be noted that employers sometimes hire part-time or dispatched workers). This means that they do not need to discharge the employees whom they would have hired when an additional workforce was necessary. In other words, transfers and overtime are a means of workforce adjustment in place of discharge. Management flexibility is, in a sense, the price that is paid for employment security.

3.3.4 Collectivism: Work Rules as a Source of Contractual Duties

The Labour Standards Act requires enterprises where ten or more workers are regularly employed to provide work rules and file them with the Labour Standards Inspection Office. Work rules should contain provisions regarding 1) working hours, rest periods, rest days, leave, and matters related to shift changes as well as 2) the method for determination, computation, and payment of wages, the dates for payments and closing accounts for wages, and matters concerning pay raises. Also to be included are matters regarding retirement allowances, bonuses, safety and health, training, workers' compensation, disciplinary action and so on, if employers want to establish schemes for these matters. In fact, most work rules contain all these provisions and function as the law or norm of the workplace.

Theoretically, it has long been debated whether work rules are contracts or legal norms, *i.e.* norms with the force of law. The background to this debate is the fact that work rules made unilaterally by employers bind employees like contracts or statutes. The Supreme Court has held that provisions in work rules are, if reasonable, incorporated into the individual employment contract.[19] The essence of this reasoning is that it is customary for work rules to regulate employment relations. This is, in a sense, contract theory. According to this theory, provisions in work rules are regarded as provisions in an employment contract and are called the "comprehensive" or

---

18   See generally Kazuo Sugeno, *Management Flexibility in an Era of Changes: The Court's Balancing of Employer and Employee Interests*, Japan Labor Bulletin vol. 30, no. 6 (1991).

19   Denden Kosha Obihiro Kyoku, 470 Rodo Hanrei 6 (Sup. Ct. Mar. 13 986).

"fixed form" contract.[20]

Moreover, the Supreme Court held that, when employers make a "reasonable change" in work rules, the changed rules have a binding effect on individual employees even if they do not consent to the change.[21] The "reasonableness" of the change of work rules is determined by 1) the necessity for the change, 2) the degree of disadvantage suffered by employees as a result of the change, 3) the improvement of working conditions implemented in relation to the change and 4) the effort made to obtain the consent of employees, especially where a vast majority of the employees have already consented to the proposed change.

Under the contract theory, changes in work rules unilaterally made by an employer were not binding on employees if they did not agree with the proposed change. Thus, the holding of the Supreme Court that changes in work rules made by employers can bind even unconsenting employees seems to be inconsistent with the contract theory, which the Court apparently adopted. Although it is difficult to find a theoretical explanation for this judgement, some scholars point out that a practical reason behind it is the difficulty in dismissing employees in Japan.[22] The contract theory could lead to a conclusion that employers can dismiss employees when they do not agree to the proposed change, if such a change is based on business necessity. However, since the employer's right to dismiss is quite limited in Japan, it is very difficult to dismiss employees in these circumstances. On the other hand, it is natural that employers need to change as business necessity demands. Thus, to strike a balance between security in employment and the demand for flexibility in the employer's business activities, the Supreme Court has created an original case law principle that a reasonable change in work rules can be binding on employees.[23]

Another aspect of this case law is that it is collective in orientation. As a basis for its judgement, the Court emphasised the necessity for uniform treatment of working conditions under work rules.[24] In fact, the consent of a vast majority of employees plays an important role in determining the

---

20   See Sugeno, *supra* footnote 8, at p. 98.

21   Shuhoku Bus, 22 Minshu 3459 (Sup. Ct. (Grand Bench) Dec. 25, 1968).

22   Sugeno, *supra* footnote 8, at pp. 99-100.

23   See Sugeno, *supra* footnote 20.

24   Shuhoku Bus, 22 Minshu at 3464.

reasonableness of a change.[25] Thus, the Supreme Court has granted employers the power to make uniform changes in working conditions within the limits of reasonableness. Since a minority of employees are bound by the reasonable change in work rules even though they object to it, it is safe to say that this case law leans more to collectivism than individualism.

3.3.5 A Dual Labour Market: Atypical Employment

Japanese employment practices such as lifetime employment and seniority-based wage systems apply only to regular workers in large companies. Even in large companies, there is a number of non-regular or "atypical" workers who are not protected by the lifetime employment practice. Such atypical workers include part-timers, dispatched workers, and "contract workers", *i.e.* workers who work under a fixed term contract. These workers are easily dismissed in the course of a downturn in business[26] In this sense, employers can adjust their workforce by discharging atypical workers according to business circumstances, while retaining regular workers as long as possible.

Unlike some European countries where there are strict restrictions on the use of atypical employment, Japan has only a limited number of regulations in this area. Although recent legislation on part-time workers contains a few protective provisions[27] there is no requirement for their employment security or equal treatment. Also, while the employment of dispatched workers is permissible only for limited job categories that require high skills or experience,[28] Japanese labour law does not place limits on reasons for concluding fixed term employment contracts. Thus, atypical employment is largely free from regulation. As a result, employers enjoy considerable

---

25   Sugeno, *supra* footnote 8, at p. 100.

26   In the case of dispatched workers, the companies they were dispatched cancel the dispatching agreement.

27   For example, article 6 provides that the employer should make a good-faith effort to distribute part-time workers a document disclosing their working conditions.

28   These job categories are computer programming, machinery design and drafting, machinery operation for producing sounds and images for broadcast programs, production of broadcast programs, operation of office machinery, interpretation, translation and shorthand, secretarial work, filing, market research, management of financial affairs, the drafting of foreign exchange documents, the presentation and explanation of manufactured goods, tour conducting, cleaning of buildings, operation and maintenance of building equipment, and building receptionist and guide.

flexibility in the use of atypical workers. In this sense, atypical workers form a "peripheral" labour market where they cannot expect employment security, while regular workers belong to a "core" labour market where the lifetime employment practice and seniority system prevail.

In some cases, however, atypical workers can resort to protection against unjust dismissal. The Supreme Court has held that the doctrine of unfair dismissal applies to workers who work under fixed term contracts when their contracts have been repeatedly renewed and these are essentially similar to those of regular workers.[29] In such cases, the expectation of continued employment is worthy of protection, and employers cannot refuse to renew their employment contracts.

4. Changes in the Role of the Employment Contract

Notwithstanding the recent outcry about the "disintegration of the Japanese employment practices" amidst recession, long-term employment still remains a guiding principle for employers. Most of them are attempting to avoid dismissal of their employees through transfers and farming-out,[30] and intend to continue to do so in the future.[31] Recently the Ministry of Labour in Japan also reaffirmed its policy of supporting stable employment relationships.[32] This is because instability in employment inevitably affects workers' lives, morale and productivity. However, this does not mean that there will be no change in human resources management in the future. Many employers predict that their employment management will be in a dual-track style, in which the workforce consists of core employees who enjoy lifetime

---

29   Toshiba Yanagimachi Kojo, 28 Minshu 927 (Sup. Ct. Jul. 22, 1974).

30   The Ministry of Labour, *supra* footnote 2, at p. 41.

31   According to a recent survey conducted by the Nihon Keieisha Dantai Renmei (Japan Employers Association), 88.4 % of the respondents (354 large companies) answered that they will basically support the long-term employment system. *Nihon Keieisha Dantai Renmei, Shin Nihon Teki Keiei System Tou Kenkyu Project Ni Kansuru Anketo Chosa Houkoku (The Report of Questionnaire Survey Relating to the Research Project on the New Japanese-Style Management)* 12 (1994).

32   Ministry of Labour, *White Paper on Labour 1993*, at p. 72.

employment and peripheral employees who do not.[33] Even now, there is a peripheral labour market consisting of atypical workers such as part-timers and contracted workers. It is pointed out, however, that, in the future there will be an increase in the number of professional employees as well as of these workers. Professional employees have a high level of skill and a high degree of mobility in the labour market. They may opt for a fixed term contract if this means that they can earn a high salary. The lifetime employment practice may be modified in this respect.

There are other factors that may affect the lifetime employment practice. One of the most important factors is the change in the seniority-based wage system, which has provided workers with considerable incentive to remain in the same company. The seniority system functioned very well when Japan's population was young and its economy still developing as it enabled employers to continue to increase the number of managerial positions as well as wages. However, in the context of Japan's ageing society, coupled with the limitations on economic growth in the context of international competition, employers have difficulty maintaining the seniority-based wage determination system. Thus, many companies feel that they can no longer maintain such schemes.[34] In fact, they are now beginning to change their wage systems into one based on merit. The annual pay system is a typical examples of these changes.[35] Workers may now find that they have less incentive to remain in the same company and an increase in the mobility on the part of workers may, in turn, influence the lifetime employment practice.

4.1 THE INCREASING IMPORTANCE OF INDIVIDUAL EMPLOYMENT CONTRACTS

As stated above, the role of employment contracts is quite limited in Japan. Many scholars point out, however, that individual employment contracts will

---

33 See *Nihon Keieisha Dantai Renmei, Shin Nihon Teki Keiei System Tou Kenkyu Project Chukan Houkoku (The Intermediate Report of the Research Project on the New Japanese-Style Management)* 15-17 (1994).

34 According to the survey mentioned in note 31, 82.7 % of the respondents answered that the wage increase based on seniority should be reconsidered. Nihon Keieisha Dantai Renmei, *supra* footnote 31, at p. 49.

35 See Naoyuki Kameyama, *Management Restructuring and Multi-faced Manpower Procurement*, Japan Labor Bulletin vol. 31, no. 7 (1992).

become more important in the future.[36] One of the most significant reasons is the diversification of working style. Already working style has been diversified through the increase in part-timers, dispatched workers and contracted workers. In the future, the trend towards diversification will be more pronounced. As opposed to traditional factory labour, which requires uniformity in working style, the service economy enables workers to adopt more flexible practices such as flexitime. The increase in the number of professional employees would also contribute to diversification. Furthermore, in an ageing society, there will be many more elderly workers in the labour market, and their style of working may be different from that of younger workers. The increase in the number of female workers may also lead to a changes. Lastly, as the harmonisation of working and family life becomes one of the most important issues for all workers, there will be many cases where employers must take into consideration each worker's family circumstances. This tendency towards diversification will inevitably increase the importance of individual employment contracts.

At the same time, there will be a parallel increase in the number of disputes about individual employment contracts. This is especially true where employees are not unionised, since in this case it is difficult for employees to use collective bargaining or joint consultation to prevent employers' from abusively exercising rights. From a different viewpoint, it will become very important to clarify the content of each worker's contract, as it may not be easy to presume. At present, the Ministry of Labour is considering an amendment to the Labour Standards Act, focusing on the regulation of employment contracts. (In Japan, although legislative power belongs to the Diet, the executive branch often prepares legislation.) A study group established by the Ministry of Labour has published a report which examines points to be discussed for legislation.[37] Although the report has made several suggestions such as the clarification of all working conditions in the form of written documents, the form the legislation will take is not clear at this time. Also, the report does not appear to propose any drastic alterations to the current case law on employment contracts.

---

36 See, *e.g.*, Kazuo Sugeno & Yasuo Suwa, *The Future of Labour Law in the Structurally Changing Labour Market*, 418 Nihon Rodo Kenkyu Zasshi (Monthly Journal of Japan Institute of Labour) 2 (1994).

37 *Kongo No Rodo Keiyaku Hosei No Arikata Ni Tsuite (On the Future of Labour Contract Law)* (Ministry of Labour ed. 1993).

4.2 POSSIBLE CHANGES IN THE STYLE OF STATUTORY REGULATION

The change in the role of the employment contract may result in the change in the style of statutory regulation. Traditionally, the Labour Standards Act has one of the strongest systems for regulating employment relations. First, the standards of working conditions provided by the Labour Standards Act has a preemptive effect: any part of an employment contract that does not meet the statutory standards is void, and such parts are to be governed by the standards. An individual worker's consent is irrelevant, if the agreed standard is below the statutory standards. Secondly, the Labour Standards Act provides for criminal sanctions against employers for violations of its provisions. These sanctions include imprisonment and fines. Thirdly, the Labour Standards Act has established a system of administrative supervision by the Labour Standards Inspection Offices at the local level, and these offices are ultimately controlled by the ministry for Labour. The Labour Standards Inspectors are authorised to inspect workplaces, to order the production of documents, and, in the event of criminal investigation, to exercise the duties of police officers. Many other labour protective statutes, *e.g.*, the Minimum Wage Act and the Industrial Health and Safety Act have followed this style of regulation.

Although such a strict enforcement mechanism is necessary for enterprises engaging in traditional factory operations or construction, "soft" or more flexible methods of enforcement may be suitable in the future, at least for certain sectors such as the services. Where the style of working is likely to be more flexible and diversified, it will be necessary to take into account an individual worker's circumstances. Uniform regulations that disregard an individual's consent without exceptions may be too rigid and lack flexibility. Also, since the interpretation of criminal statutes do not allow flexibility, the system of criminal sanctions may not be suitable for regulating diversified employment relationships. Civil statutes may be suitable for coping with various types of disputes arising from such employment relationships. To be sure, the enforcement of labour statutes must be effective, and workers' rights must not be lightly abrogated. For this purpose, however, we should consider enhancing dispute resolution systems for individual workers, a topic to which we will turn later.

As a matter of fact, some Japanese labour statutes already have less strict regulations than the Labour Standards Act. For example, the Equal Employment Opportunity Law of 1985 has no criminal sanction. Although the unequal treatment of female workers with respect to dismissal, mandatory retirement, training and fringe benefits is illegal and void, there is no penal provision for these violations. Furthermore, the Equal Employment Opportunity Law has a so-called "good faith effort" provisions regarding recruiting, hiring, assignment, and promotion. Although employers are required to make good-faith efforts to attain equality for female workers regarding these matters, judicial remedies for violations of these provisions are not available under the Equal Employment Opportunity Act itself. Some recently enacted statutes such as the Part-time Labour Act have also adopted such good faith effort provisions.

Under some statutes, an individual worker's consent functions as a requirement for exemption from regulation. For example, although the Labour Standards Act ordinarily disregards individual consent, article 64-3, item 5, exempts employers from the prohibition of night work for female workers on the basis of individual consent. This applies only to taxi drivers and is subject to the approval of the Labour Standards Inspection Office. In the future, it may be, likely that such exemptions based on an individual consent will become more diffuse, as the role of individual employment contracts becomes increasingly significant.

4.3 POSSIBLE CHANGES IN EMPLOYMENT CONTRACT LAW

Case law on employment contracts may also evolve as the trend towards diversification and individualism becomes stronger. As stated before, the Supreme Court has allowed employers considerable discretion in ordering transfers and overtime.[38] This case law applies mainly to regular workers, who have generally been men. As a result, it is often difficult for them to harmonise family life and working life. However, as the population ages and more women enter the work force, the proportion of elderly and female workers will increase, and these may prefer family life to working life. The lifestyle of male workers may also change, as is already beginning to happen.[39] Such changes in attitude toward lifestyles might ultimately affect the discretion of employers regarding transfer and overtime. It should be noted, however, that the employers' discretion in these aspects is, as stated before, closely related to the lifetime employment practice. If the lifetime employment practice is to be maintained, the employers discretion may survive at least to a certain degree, unless other alternatives are available for maintaining a balance between security in employment and business

---

38   See *supra* footnotes 9-17 and accompanying text.

39   The Ministry of Labour, *White Paper on Labour 1991*, at p. 53.

necessity.

On the other hand, when the employer's discretion is restricted through individual agreements or other instruments, the doctrine of unfair dismissal may undergo some modification. As a matter of fact, recent lower court decisions already indicate this trend. In cases where foreign employers had hired executives for specific jobs, the courts held that employers may dismiss these without considering possibilities for transfer or demotion if they failed to perform their jobs.[40] In such a case, the employment contract specifies the employee's job, and the employer cannot transfer him/her to other positions. If this type of hiring for a specific job or position increases and has the effect of limiting the employer's discretion, the doctrine of unfair dismissal may be limited accordingly.

5.   The Employment Contract and Collective Bargaining Agreement

As is the case in many other industrialised countries, the unionisation rate in Japan has been declining in recent years. As opposed to 46.2 % in 1950, 24.4 percent of workers were unionised in 1992.[41] Scholars have long debated the causes for this decline.[42] It is often pointed out that change in the industrial structure is one of the major reasons: with the development of a tertiary industry in the Japanese economy, the proportion of white collar workers has been increasing, and this has resulted in a decrease in the proportion of factory workers, who are more conducive to organisation. Also in relation to this economic change, the number of part-time workers has also increased and these are not so interested in union membership either. Moreover, workers' standard of living has improved greatly in the last two or three decades. Although unions in Japan stress the attainment of sufficient wages to live a comfortable life, such goals are not as attractive to workers as in the past. Of course unions are trying hard to find new strategies to attract workers including the promotion of reduction in working hours. The results of these effort, however, remain to be seen. On the other hand, some scholars have pointed out the need to introduce an employee representation

---

40   *E.g.*, Ford Jidosha, 35 Rominshu 140 (Tokyo High Ct. Mar. 30, 1984).

41   The Japan Institute of Labour, *Japanese Working Life Profile* 48 (1994).

42   See generally Tsuyoshi Tsuru, *Why Has Union Density Declined in Japan?* Japan Labor Bulletin vol. 33, no. 11 (1994).

system such as Works Councils.[43] They contend that unorganised workers need a permanent employee representation system to voice their concerns and protect their interests in the workplace. Other scholars have cast doubts about on this concept, questioning the relationship between an employee representation system and trade union law, though many agree with the need to protect of the interests of unorganised workers.[44]

5.1   THE ROLE OF THE COLLECTIVE BARGAINING AGREEMENT

Article 16 of the Trade Union Law provides that "any portion of an individual labour contract contravening the standards of work ... provided in the collective agreement shall be void. In such a case, the invalidated part of the individual labour contract shall be governed by the provisions of the standards." This is called the "normative effect" *(normative Kraft)* of a collective bargaining agreement. Since Japanese theory on the collective bargaining agreement has been considerably influenced by the German labour law theory, this terminology has its origin in German law. In addition, the Trade Union Act contains provisions for the extension of the effect of a collective bargaining agreement within the workplace as well as within a given local region. As to extension within the workplace, article 17 of the Law provides that the normative effect of a collective bargaining agreement shall be extended in a particular workplace to the same kind of workers as are covered by the agreement when three-fourths or more of the workers of the same kind employed in the workplace are bound by the agreement. Article 18 provides for the extension of a collective bargaining agreement in a local region.

Another effect is called a "contract obligation effect" *(obligatorische Wirkung),* a notion that also originated in German theory. This means that a collective bargaining agreement as a contract creates an obligor-obligee relationship between an employer and a union.

5.1.1 *The Principle that the Most Favourable Provision Should Apply*
Although Japanese legal theory on the collective bargaining agreement has been influenced by German law, there are a few important differences

---

43   *E.g.*, Satoshi Nishitani, *Legislative Problems Concerning the Employee Representative System in Japan*, 356 Nihon Rodo Kyokai Zasshi (Monthly Journal of Japan Institute of Labour) 2 (1989).

44   *E.g.*, Katsutoshi Kezuka, *A Proposal to Reform the Employee Representation System at the Workplace*, 79 Nihon Rodo Ho Gakkai Shi (Journal of Labour Law) 129 (1992).

between them. For example, German legal theory has established and incorporated into statutory law the principle that the most favourable provision should apply *(Begünstigungsprinzip)*. Under this principle, while a collective bargaining agreement provides for minimum working conditions, workers are free to conclude a more favourable agreement. In Japan, however, it has not been determined whether working conditions provided by collective agreements are minimum standards or exclude more favourable provisions in individual employment contracts. Although case law is not clear on this issue, many scholars take the position that this principle does not generally apply in Japan.[45] They contend this is because, Japanese collective bargaining agreements are usually concluded on an enterprise or company-basis, and the parties to the agreements often regard the conditions contained in them as uniform rather than minimum standards. This rule is not without exception, however. A collective bargaining agreement may contain a provision that is meant to allow treatment to vary according to individual workers' circumstances. As diversification in working style develops, the inclusion of this kind of provision is likely to increase.

5.1.2 Changes in the Role of Collective Agreements

There are two changes in the role of the collective agreement. First, the decline in the unionisation rate results in a decline in the role of the collective bargaining agreement as a tool for determining the content of an employment contract. In other words, unions are gradually losing their influence in the determination of terms and conditions of employment. This is especially true with respect to certain types of workers such as part-timers whom unions often fail to organise.

The second change lies in the function of the collective bargaining agreement in unionised workplaces. In order to cope with recessions, employers often attempt to bargain with unions in order to obtain their cooperation (concession bargaining). When they conclude collective bargaining agreements that lowers wages or other terms and conditions of work, a question arises whether such a collective agreement can effectively change the content of individual employment contracts. Although the Supreme Court has not ruled on this issue, a number of lower courts have answered in the affirmative.[46] Scholars who support such decisions contend that the collective bargaining agreement is the outcome of the give and take

---

45   *E.g.* Sugeno, *supra* footnote 8 at p. 514.

46   *E.g.* Nihon Truck, 36 Rominshu 691 (Nagoya High Ct. Nov. 27, 1985).

process of bargaining, and that a concession in one respect may be connected with a gain in another.[47] However, courts have, in dicta, added one exception to this position: if the collective agreement provision at issue is "unreasonable," it may not affect the individual employment contract.[48] This is, in a sense, a backstop measure to protect individual workers' interests, although the definition of "unreasonableness" is unclear at present.

5.2 "MAJORITY AGREEMENT": A DEVICE FOR DEREGULATION

In Japan, the collective bargaining agreement cannot violate mandatory provisions in labour statutes. Unlike some European labour laws, the Labour Standards Act and other similar statutes do not allow parties to collective bargaining agreements to provide exceptions to the statutory standards. However, the Labour Standards Act has a somewhat similar device through a "majority agreement. " Under article 36 of the Labour Standards Act, for example, an employer may extend working hours beyond the statutory maximum or have workers work on rest days, when the employer has entered into a written agreement with either a trade union organised by a majority of workers at the workplace or, if such a union does not exist, with a person representing a majority of workers, and has filed such an agreement with the Labour Standards Inspection Office. Thus, exceptions to the prohibition on working more than 8 hours a day are granted on the condition that the representative of the majority of workers in the workplace concludes a written agreement to allow such an exception. Since such a representative is not necessarily a trade union, this agreement is called a "majority agreement," as distinct from a collective bargaining agreement.

The majority agreement generally lacks the normative effect of a collective bargaining agreement. Thus, even when a majority agreement has a provision to the effect that employees are obliged to work more than eight hours a day, it is not binding unless the majority agreement is concluded by a trade union and regarded as a collective bargaining agreement under the Trade Union Act. In this sense, a majority agreement functions only as a means of exemption from statutory regulations, e.g., the mandatory effect and criminal sanction of the Labour Standards Act. One exception to this principle is the implementation of planned annual leave (annual leave provided through majority agreements). A lower court decision held that a

---

47   E.g. Sugeno, *supra* footnote 8, at pp. 514-515.

48   Nihon Truck, 36 Rominshu 695.

majority agreement providing planned annual leave has a binding effect on employees and that they may not take leave on the days that are not specified in the majority agreement.[49]

Although the Labour Standards Act allowed for this deregulation through majority agreements at the time of its enactment in 1947, a recent amendment extended this to a number of provisions, mainly in the area of flexible working hours. Deregulation through majority agreements is, in a sense, one of the devices for promoting flexibility in a changing economy while protecting workers' interests by way of the majority's consent. In order to protect workers' interest, however, it is essential to secure fairness in the election of the person who represents the majority. Since the Labour Standards Act does not have provisions for election process, it should be pointed out that employers sometimes exert undue influences in this respect.[50]

6. Agenda for the Future

Japan's labour and employment law is now in the process of considerable change as is its economy. The direction of this change, however, is not certain at all. The following are some points to be discussed in considering the future prospects of Japanese law on employment contracts.

6.1 CAN THE CASE LAW ON SECURITY AND FLEXIBILITY SURVIVE?

Despite the absence of statutory provisions restricting dismissal, case law has established security in employment through the doctrine of abusive dismissal. As a means of striking a balance between employment security and the necessity for workforce adjustment, case law has allowed employers considerable flexibility in ordering transfers and overtime. This body of case law is based on the two major employment practices of Japanese companies: the lifetime employment and the seniority-based wage systems. Although the recent recession appears to have introduced a tendency for employers to abandon these practices, the Ministry of Labour and the majority of large

---

49   Mitsubishi Jukogyo, 43 Rominshu 477 (Nagasaki Dist. Ct. Mar. 26, 1992).

50   The Ministry of Labour, *Roshi Kyotei Ni Okeru Kahansu Daihyo Sha Ni Kansuru Chosa Kenkyu Kai Hokoku (The Report of the Study Group on the Majority Representation in the Labour-Management Agreement)* (1989).

companies still intend to preserve security in employment.

However, the diversification of working styles as well as employment management may affect this case law when the individual employment contract specifies the employee's job or place of work. Changes in the seniority-based wage systems may also have an affect. It is possible that labour mobility will increase as the realisation that long term employment does not provide wage increases gives workers more incentive to change jobs. In the long run, it may not be very difficult for discharged employees to find new jobs that are as favourable as their previous jobs. This might affect the doctrine of unfair dismissal, and, in turn, the employers' discretion to order transfers and overtime.

6.2 FROM COLLECTIVISM TO INDIVIDUALISM?

Traditionally, employment contracts in Japan have not dealt with workers' individual circumstances. Rather, work rules uniformly provide the terms and conditions of employment. Case law on work rules has enabled employers to unilaterally establish and change employees' terms and conditions of employment on condition that these changes are reasonable. This makes it possible for employers to deal with employment relations on a collective basis irrespective of the objections of a small minority of employees.

However, as the workplace becomes more diversified, it is likely that the conflict of interests among employees will become stronger. What is reasonable for some employees may be unreasonable for others. For example, if an employer intends to change its seniority-based wage system and make it more merit-based, such a change will lead to loss of earnings by older workers, while benefiting younger workers. In a case like this, it is difficult to determine "reasonableness" and new criteria for work rules will be necessary. At present, however, it is not at all clear what is the better paradigm. Apart from the case law on work rules, the employment contract itself may become more individualistic. As described above, the working style is likely to be more diversified in the future. In this respect, too, it may become difficult to continue to treat employment contracts on a collective basis.

6.3 DEREGULATION FROM STRICT REGULATION?

As regards the statutory regulation of employment contracts, statutes without criminal sanctions or those with good-faith effort provisions are already increasing. Although, in some areas, strong enforcement is still necessary, regulations without criminal sanctions will be a trend for the future. This "soft" type of regulation is especially suitable for disputes about employment contracts, for which flexible resolution is better suited than criminal sanctions.

Next, when an individual agreement is important as a means of determining the terms and conditions of employment, deregulation through individual agreement, such as the exemption of the prohibition of night work for female taxi drivers, will be possible. This kind of deregulation may become more widespread in the future. If such individual deregulation is inappropriate, an alternative is deregulation through collective agreements or "majority agreements". In using this device, however, it is important to take into account the fact that the interests of different workers often conflict. Also important is fairness in the selection of the representative who concludes the majority agreement.

6.4 THE NECESSITY FOR A BACKSTOP: MORE EFFECTIVE SYSTEMS FOR RESOLVING INDIVIDUAL DISPUTES

As shown above, the role of the individual employment contract will increase in importance in the future. Consequently, there will be an increase in disputes over employment contracts. Apart from the necessity of providing suitable protection for employees with respect to the contents of a contract, it is necessary to emphasise the importance of providing for an effective system of dispute resolution. In Japan, the court is almost the only forum for the resolution of individual employment disputes. If an employee is protected by a trade union, the union can utilise the process of collective bargaining or resort to the adjustment procedure of the Labour Commission to resolve employment disputes. This is not often the case, however, given the current low unionisation rate. On the other hand, it is not easy for ordinary employees to file a suit to resolve their employment disputes, especially when the amount at stake is small compared to the time and money necessary for litigation. Thus, it is important to provide an effective system for resolving employment disputes.

Scholars have put forward several suggestions in this regard.[51] These include civil procedure reform to make the courts more accessible, the promotion of civil mediation administered by courts, and the reform of the

---

51   E.g., Akira Hamamura, *Rodo Keiyaku To Funso Shori Seido* (*Labour Contract and Dispute Resolution System*), 82 Nihon Rodo Ho Gakkai Shi (Journal of Labour Law) 131 (1993).

Labour Commissions, which have covered only collective disputes, to make it available for the resolution of employment disputes. Apart from providing forums, one alternative may be implementing assistance schemes for workers involved in disputes, such as counselling or instruction for workers in disputes as well as financial aid for litigation. Since discussion on this topic has just begun, it is necessary to consider the pluses and minuses of these alternatives.

THE CONTRACT OF EMPLOYMENT IN AUSTRALIAN LABOUR LAW

Breen CREIGHTON and Richard MITCHELL*

1. Master and Servant Law in Australia

All relevant rules of English common law and statute were assumed to have been transplanted to the Australian colonies at the time of European settlement.[1] *Inter alia*, this had the consequence that the emerging English law of employment, together with its underpinning in the law of master and servant, was imported wholesale into the various colonies. It also meant that early Australian unions were potentially subject to the same range of common law and statutory liabilities and disabilities as their British counterparts.

Starting with New South Wales and Van Dieman's Land (Tasmania) in 1823, each of the colonies acquired a measure of legislative competence. From an early stage, a significant focus of the legislative activity of the colonial assemblies was the regulation of the individual employment relationship.[2]

This can be attributed to a number of factors. Among the most significant were: (i) the perceived need to establish and maintain discipline amongst a workforce which consisted, to a significant degree, of emancipated convicts

---

* The authors thank Keith Redenbach for research assistance in the preparation of this paper.

1 The cut-off date for the automatic reception of English law in New South Wales, Tasmania, Victoria and Queensland was 25 July 1828 (see *Australian Courts Act* 1828 (UK), s. 24). The equivalent date for Western Australia was 1 July 1829, and for South Australia 28 December 1836.

2 For more detailed studies of this early provision see Merritt 1982; Quinlan 1986; Quinlan 1989; Quinlan & Gardner 1990. For an overview of the evolution of Australian labour law see Creighton & Stewart 1994: Chapter 2.

L. Betten (ed.), The Employment Contract in Transforming Labour Relations, 129-166.
© 1995 Kluwer Law International. Printed in the Netherlands.

or "ticket-of-leave men"[3]; and (ii) persistent labour shortages due to the lack of migrants or emancipists who were prepared to engage in wage labour rather than working on their own account. This was a particularly acute problem after the discovery of gold in the 1840s. Not only were agricultural workers, domestic servants etc liable to desert their employment in response to rumours of a fresh discovery, but the entire crews of ships were prone to similar behaviour as soon as they docked at a port within reasonable proximity to the goldfields.

To some extent the imported English Master and Servant Acts had the potential to deal with these kinds of problems.[4] They did, after all, create a range of offences relating to abandonment of work before the expiry of the term of a contract and other forms of employment-related misdemeanours. They were, nevertheless, considered to be inadequate to the needs of the emerging colonial economies in various respects. Consequently, all of the Australian legislatures adopted local variants upon contemporary British provision. All of these measures could be seen to be directed to the twin objectives of maintaining labour discipline and labour stability. They sought to do this by applying to a wider range of workers and creating a wider range of offences than their British progenitors. They also placed greater reliance upon imprisonment as a sanction; accorded very broad discretions to the local magistracy in terms of the administration of the legislation; and made special and detailed provision for the position of apprentices and indented immigrants.

Not only were these colonial measures more far-reaching than the British provision upon which they were modelled, they also remained operative long after the repeal of that legislation in 1875.[5] For example, New South Wales finally repealed its legislation only in 1980, while Western Australia retains residual provision even in 1995.[6] This measure is now entirely unused in practice, but it is important to appreciate that in some jurisdictions

---

3   These were convicts who were provided with a document (or "ticket") which entitled them to work and live freely within a given locality until such time as their original sentence expired, or they were given a formal pardon.

4   For more detailed consideration of this legislation see Simon 1954 and Orth 1991: Chapter 7.

5   The repeal was effected by the *Conspiracy and Protection of Property Act* of that year.

6   *Masters and Servants Act* 1892. This legislation is currently under review, and it seems reasonable to suppose that it will be repealed in the near future.

prosecution under master and servant legislation was commonplace right up to the start of World War II.[7]

The adoption of distinctive colonial master and servant legislation serves to emphasise that Australian labour law had begun to develop along a different trajectory than that of the United Kingdom even before the events of the 1890s precipitated the adoption of a highly distinctive system of conciliation and arbitration which has characterised Australian labour relations law for most of the 20th century. It is, however, important to keep these early developments in perspective. In the first place, the differences between the colonial and the British provision were differences of detail or of emphasis rather than of fundamental principle. Indeed, if the colonial provision *had* departed too radically from the metropolitan model, it is highly likely that it would have been disallowed by the imperial authorities.[8]

It is also important to appreciate that Australia in the late 19th and early 20th centuries was still very much a pre-industrial society. Master and servant legislation - along with statutory wage-fixing and the Poor Law - was an important factor in the maintenance of labour and social stability in pre-industrial Britain.[9] But industrial capitalism did not need that same kind of stability as. Rather, it wanted labour mobility and flexibility. Hence the emergence of the "prerogative contract" as a means of legitimating and regulating the relationship between individual units of labour and those to whom they sold their labour. Hence also the final abandonment of master and servant legislation three quarters of the way through the 19th century. The fact that these imperatives were still not dominant in 19th and early 20th century Australia does much to explain the longevity of master and servant legislation in this country.

1.1 THE EMERGENCE OF THE CONTRACT OF EMPLOYMENT

Authors such as Selznick (1969) and Fox (1974) have traced the emergence of the Anglo-American contract of employment to a fusion of principles of *laissez faire* contractualism, and principles and assumptions drawn from the law of master and servant. The latter in turn consisted of a mixture of the

---

7   See in particular the detailed study of the New South Wales legislation by Merritt 1982. See also *Ex parte McLean* (1930) 43 CLR 472.

8   For examples of situations where this did in fact happen see Quinlan 1986: 10; Quinlan 1989: 26-7; Quinlan & Gardner 1990: 73.

9   See further Simon 1954: 197-8; Wedderburn 1986: 141-2.

legislative principles embodied in the Master and Servant Acts dating back to the time of the Black Death in the 14th century and common law rules which treated the relationship between master and servant as analogous to that between the (male) head of a household and the members of his family. According to Selznick (1969: 130-36) and Fox (1974: 183-184) the purpose of this infusion of the principles of contract law with elements of the law of master and servant was to ensure that employers retained the element of domination or control which the efficient conduct of their enterprises demanded, whilst at the same time legitimating the treatment of labour as an article of commerce: "What resulted was a form of contract almost as far removed from the pure doctrinal form as the status relationship which had preceded it".[10]

This analysis is somewhat simplistic in certain respects: it is, for example, inherently unlikely that the judges who fashioned the emergent common law of employment consciously decided to "infuse" the principles of contractualism with the law of master and servant. It is much more probable that they developed and applied the law in the light of their perceptions of the principles which ought to apply as between what were commonly referred to as "masters" and "servants".[11] Nevertheless, the analysis is useful in that it serves to highlight the fact that the Anglo-American contract of employment cannot properly be seen as "the personal and voluntary exchange of freely-bargained promises between parties equally protected by the civil law".[12] First, because the parties were almost invariably in profoundly unequal bargaining positions, with the result that the "exchange" was neither "free" nor "voluntary". Secondly, because the legal principles which governed the relationship assumed, and were intended to legitimate, the domination of one party by the other. The parties could not, therefore, meaningfully be said to be "equally protected by the law".

As noted earlier, all relevant rules of English common law were assumed to have been imported into Australia at the time of European settlement. This would, of course, have included the principles relating to the contract of employment. Even after the cut-off date for the automatic reception of English law, the Australian courts continued to regard themselves as bound

---

10   Fox 1974: 184.

11   Indeed the usage has still not entirely disappeared - see for example the judgment of Clarke JA in *Connelly v Wells* (1994) 55 IR 73 at 94.

12   Wedderburn 1971: 77.

by the decisions of the English courts in common law matters.[13] It follows that the developmental process outlined above can safely be assumed to be directly applicable in the Australian context, and that the legal principles which governed the contractual relationship between Australian workers and their employers in 1900 would have been essentially the same as those which governed relations between British workers and their employers.

On the other hand it also seems clear that these common law principles were of less practical significance in the Australian context than in Britain. This is because most employment matters that came before the courts in this country did so by way of prosecutions under master and servant legislation, rather than common law litigation. Of course the underlying common law principles were still relevant, but the principal issue before the courts generally centred upon whether there had been a breach of the appropriate legislation, rather than upon the application of those underlying rules. Furthermore, as the 20th century progressed, the common law principles, and indeed the contract of employment itself, were increasingly marginalised in practical terms by the emergence of State and Federal systems of "compulsory" conciliation and arbitration.

1.2 THE EMERGENCE OF "COMPULSORY" CONCILIATION AND ARBITRATION

Australia enjoyed a prolonged period of economic growth between the 1850s and the late 1880s. This, together with the labour shortages noted earlier, enabled the emergent trade unions to secure terms and conditions of employment for their members which were equivalent to, if not in advance of, those which prevailed elsewhere in the world. For example building workers in Victoria secured the eight-hour day as early as 1856 - many years before their counterparts overseas. However by 1890 "boom" had turned to "bust", and employers decided to fight back. They elected to do so under the banner of "freedom of contract": that is, the assertion of their right to negotiate terms and conditions of employment directly with their employees without the intervention of any third party such as a trade union.

Starting with a dispute in the Victorian maritime industry in 1890, the employers inflicted a series of major defeats upon the union movement. In all instances, there was extensive recourse to both common law and statute

---

13   Decisions of the British courts are no longer binding in Australia (except where they pre-date the cut-off for the reception of English law), but they are nevertheless accorded great respect. For a helpful analysis of the present position see *Cook v Cook* (1986) 162 CLR 376 at 389-90 (per Mason, Wilson, Deane and Dawson JJ).

in support of the employer position. By 1894 the employers had largely attained their objectives. Trade union membership was decimated, collective bargaining had virtually disappeared, and the principle of freedom of contract had been resoundingly vindicated.[14] This had the inevitable consequence that in many instances employers were able unilaterally to impose terms and conditions of employment upon their employees on a take-it-or-leave-it basis. Their capacity to do so was considerably enhanced by a prolonged economic recession, with attendant high levels of unemployment.

The labour movement reacted to this situation in an interesting manner: they turned to the law. In particular, they embraced the notion that industrial disputes should be determined by means of compulsory conciliation and arbitration in situations where they could not be resolved through processes of collective bargaining - for example because of the employer's refusal to negotiate.[15] They also recognised that the colonial legislatures, dominated as they were by farming and commercial interests, were unlikely on their own initiative to pass legislation which was perceived to be favourable to organised labour. This recognition in turn played a significant role in the establishment of the Australian Labor Party in 1891, and its subsequent emergence as a major political force.

The processes by which support for the principle of compulsory conciliation and arbitration found practical expression is a complex and fascinating one.[16] It is, however, beyond the scope of this paper. For present purposes, it is sufficient to note that by the early part of the 20th century all Australian jurisdictions had adopted some form of statutory regulation of terms and conditions of employment. In some cases,[17] this consisted of a system of conciliation and arbitration whereby an independent court or tribunal attempted to secure resolution of disputes by conciliation. In default of agreement they could then proceed to impose an arbitrated

---

14   For brief accounts of these disputes see Turner 1976: 40-50; Hutson 1983: 43-6.

15   Support for this course was not, however, unanimous - see further Markey 1989.

16   See further Macintyre 1989; Mitchell 1989; Bennett 1994: 9-21.

17   Most notably Western Australia and New South Wales. See *Industrial Arbitration Act 1901* (NSW) and *Industrial Conciliation and Arbitration Act 1900* (WA). The New South Wales Act served as the model for the Commonwealth's *Conciliation and Arbitration Act* of 1904.

settlement by way of a legally enforceable award.[18] In such systems, disputes could be brought before the tribunal by unions or employers or employer organisations. Part of the reasoning behind this approach was the assumption that employers would come to recognise that it was pointless to refuse to negotiate with unions to which their employees belong, or could belong, because even if they did so, the union(s) concerned could simply bring them before the appropriate court or tribunal and obtain an arbitrated settlement. Of necessity, therefore, the operation of these systems implied a formal recognition of the role of trade unions.

Other States adopted a somewhat different approach in the form of wages boards. These consisted of equal numbers of representatives of employers and workers, plus an independent chair. In the event of disagreement between the two groups on the board, the chair could "arbitrate" by coming down in favour of either the employer or the worker position, but they could not impose a settlement of their own. Trade unions had no formal role in such systems, although in practice worker members of boards were very often union nominees. Most jurisdictions adopted at least some form of wages board provision at some stage, but by the late 1980s all had opted for conciliation and arbitration systems.[19]

Even more important than developments at the colony/State level was the fact that section 51(xxxv) of the Constitution of Australia, which became operative on 1 January 1901, gave the newly-established federal Parliament power "to make laws for the peace, order, and good government of the Commonwealth with respect to...conciliation and arbitration for the prevention and settlement of industrial disputes extending beyond the limits of any one State". This provision was used as the basis for the enactment of the *Conciliation and Arbitration Act* in 1904. This measure was subject to

---

18   In general terms, awards can be equated to collective agreements in European and North American labour law systems. It is important to appreciate, however, that awards of the Australian tribunals have the full force of an Act of Parliament. This means, for example, that a valid award of the federal tribunal would prevail over an inconsistent Act of a State Parliament (Constitution of Austrailia, section 109).

19   Victoria and Tasmania adhered most closely to the wages board model, and were the last to abandon it.

extensive amendment over the years, but was not finally repealed until 1988, when it was replaced by the essentially similar *Industrial Relations Act*.[20]

The Federal Act and its State counterparts have exerted a profound influence upon the evolution and practice of Australian labour law and labour relations over the last 90 years. Indeed, the basic terms and conditions of employment of some 80 per cent of the workforce are now regulated by awards of State or Federal industrial tribunals.[21]

2. The Role of the Contract of Employment in Australian Labour Law

Kahn-Freund (1954: 45) described the contract of employment as '"he cornerstone of the edifice" of the British system of labour regulation. Freedland (1976: 1) considers that "as a conceptual starting point" it "preserves a central position in a rapidly developing part of the law", whilst Wedderburn (1986: 106) sees it as "the fundamental institution" to which the British labour lawyer is "forced to return again and again". Australian commentators adopt a broadly similar view.[22] More recently, a number of commentators have suggested that such assessments need to be treated with a degree of caution.[23] It would certainly be misleading to suggest that the contract of employment is the "cornerstone" of either British or Australian labour law in the sense that it constitutes the principal source of the regulation of the terms and conditions of employment of the greater part of the workforce. But it *is* the cornerstone of the system in both countries in the

---

20   This Act has in turn been extensively amended on a number of occasions, most notably by the *Industrial Relations Reform Act* 1993. As will appear presently, the Government claimed that this highly controversial measure was intended to effect a fundamental shift away from regulation through conciliation and arbitration in favour of collective bargaining. Its critics claimed that it did not go nearly far enough in this direction.

21   The most recent Australian Bureau of Statistics (ABS: 1991) figures show that in May 1990 46.5 per cent of the workforce were covered by State awards, and 31.5 per cent by Federal. McCallum (1994a: 203-4) suggests that the figure for Federal coverage is now around 42 per cent, whilst that for the State systems has dropped to 44 per cent. He also suggests that these figures overstate the extent of non-award employment. On the other hand, data presented by Mitchell & Scherer (1993: 94) suggest that there has been a gradual decline in award coverage since the 1950s.

22   See for example Macken et al 1990: 25-8 and 63; Creighton et al 1993: 17-18; Creighton & Stewart 1994: 128; McCallum & Pittard 1994: 15-6.

23   See for example Wedderburn & Clark 1983: 145-6; Brooks 1988; Brooks 1993c.

sense that it provides the conceptual foundation for much of the rest of the system. Put differently, it is a construct whereby the relationship between the buyers and sellers of labour can be legitimated and regulated.

This can be illustrated at a number of levels. It serves as the trigger for both State and Federal systems of conciliation and arbitration.[24] The operation of protective and fiscal provisions relating to leave; unfair dismissal; severance pay; workers' compensation; superannuation; training; pay-roll tax; deduction of PAYE tax instalments and discrimination in employment depend to a greater or lesser extent upon the existence of contracts of employment - although it should be noted that such the application of legislation is quite frequently extended to non-employees by means of deeming provisions and extended definitions.[25]

Common law principles are often expressly or impliedly translated into legislation and awards. For example, awards have traditionally referred to the employer's right summary to dismiss employees for "malingering, inefficiency, neglect of duty or misconduct": a form of words which is normally interpreted by reference to the common law principles relating to summary dismissal for misconduct. Similarly, section 170DB of the *Industrial Relations Act* 1988 (Cth.) obliges employers to give certain minimum periods of notice (or pay wages in lieu thereof) except where "the employee is guilty of serious misconduct, that is, misconduct of a kind such that it would be unreasonable to require the employer to continue the employment during the notice period". It is probable that "misconduct" for

---

24   For example the "industrial disputes" which can be the subject of resolution through conciliation, arbitration or bargaining in accordance with the *Industrial Relations Act* 1988 (Cth.) must be "about matters pertaining to the relationship between employers and employers" (s.4(1)). In the past it appeared that this limitation was impelled by the wording of s.51(xxxv) of the Constitution. More recent decisions, such as *R v Coldham; Ex parte Australian Social Welfare Union* (1983) 153 CLR 297, suggest that this is not necessarily the case. However the Parliament has chosen to persist with the more restrictive form of words. This means, for example, that independent contractors may not be involved in arbitrable disputes for purposes of the Act. Although not subject to the same constitutional constraints (real or imagined) as the Commonwealth, the States have, by and large, also chosen to limit access to their systems to parties who stand in the relation of employer and employee - but see *Industrial Relations Act* 1991 (NSW), s.5(1) and Sched.1.

25   For some examples see Creighton et al 1993: 51-4.

these purposes would be interpreted by reference to the common law criteria, although there has not yet been any formal ruling on the matter.[26]

Although collective agreements are not a major source employment rights in Australia,[27] it is clear that at least part of their content may, in appropriate circumstances, be legally enforceable through the medium of the contracts of employment of the workers to whom they apply,[28] notwithstanding that the agreement may not be enforceable as between the collective parties.[29] Finally, the contract of employment does regulate at least part of the terms and conditions of employment of *all* employees. Self-evidently, it is of particular significance for the approximately 20 per cent of the workforce whose basic terms and conditions are not regulated by State or Federal awards. But it would also govern the terms and conditions of award-employees in relation to any matters not dealt with by the relevant award (or otherwise applicable legislation).

The most vexed issue which arises in this context is the precise nature of the relationship between contracts of employment and the awards whose operation they serve to trigger. Given that the existence of a contract of employment is crucial to the operation of both State and Federal systems, it might be supposed that this issue would have been resolved at an early stage in the development of the system. This is not, however, the case.

It is clear that the parties may by express stipulation incorporate the provisions of an award into a contract of employment.[30] It also seems reasonably clear that the parties may legitimately contract on terms which are more favourable than otherwise applicable award provision,[31] although the situation might be otherwise with "paid rates awards" which specify "actual entitlements, rather than minimum entitlements, in respect of wages and

---

26   Section 170DB was inserted in the 1988 Act by the *Industrial Relations Reform Act 1993*, which became operative in March 1994.

27   See further Creighton et al 1993: 858-61 and the discussion in Section 4.1 of this paper.

28   Creighton et al 1993: 111-18. See also *Re Homfray Carpets Pty Ltd* (1994) 36 AILR 326 and *Honeyman v Nhill Hospital* [1994] 1 VR 138.

29   See Creighton et al 1993: 873-82.

30   *True v Amalgamated Collieries (WA)* (1938) 59 CLR 417 and [1940] AC 537.

31   *Kilminster v Sun Newspapers* (1931) 46 CLR 284.

conditions of employment".[32]   But what of the situation where the parties have not made any express reference to the relevant award, or where they have expressly contracted in a manner which is inconsistent with such an award?

There have been indications in a number of cases over the years that the terms of applicable awards were incorporated in the contracts of employment of workers to whom they applied. For example in *True* Dixon J stated that:

"The right to payment of award wages is really a term imported by statute into the contract of employment, and imported independently of the intention of the parties".[33]

Other cases suggested, without actually determining, that awards were *not* incorporated in the contracts of employment of the workers to whom they applied.[34] However, it was not until 1988 that any Australian court expressed a decided view on the matter.

In *Gregory v Philip Morris*[35] a majority (Wilcox and Ryan JJ) of the Full Court of the Federal Court of Australia found that an award provision to effect that "termination of employment by an employer shall not be harsh unjust or unreasonable" was automatically incorporated in the contract of employment of an employee to whom the award applied, with the consequence that he could recover damages for breach of contract in respect of a dismissal which contravened this provision.

Wilcox and Ryan JJ considered that there were two bases upon which the award could be regarded as having been incorporated in the employee's

---

32   See *Industrial Relations Act* 1988, ss.4(1) and 170SA-170UE. Such awards are particularly common in the public sector. However they are by no means unusual in the private sector - see for example *AFMEU v Alcoa*, Aust. Ind. Rels. Comm., Unrep., 8 Dec. 1994.

33   (1938) 59 CLR 417 at 431. Support for the incorporation view can also be found in *R v Gough; Ex parte Meat and Allied Trades Federation* (1969) 122 CLR 237 at 245 (per Windeyer J) and *Mallinson v Scottish Australian Investment Co* (1920) 28 CLR 66 1 - but cf the approach to these cases adopted by Black CJ in *Byrne and Frew v Australian Airlines* (1994) 120 ALR 274 at 278-80. *Nunn v Chubb Australia* [1986] Tas R 183 also seems to lend support to the incorporation view, although it is not entirely clear from the reported judgment whether there was express or implied incorporation in that case.

34   See for example *Josephson v Walker* (1914) 18 CLR 691.

35   (1988) 80 ALR 455.

contract: (i) by force of statute, independently of the intention of the parties; or (ii) by reference to the implied agreement of the parties.[36] Neither approach is entirely unproblematic:[37] but of the two, the "importation by statute" option appears to be the more compelling.

In the period after 1988 the courts accepted this view more or less without question.[38] However in *Byrne and Frew v Australian Airlines*[39] a majority of the Full Court of the Federal Court determined that *Gregory* should not be followed. Four members of the Court considered that the incorporation by statute apporach could not be sustained as a matter of principle. However, they did not entirely rule out the possibility that award provision could be incorporated into a contract of employment in some circumstances. A majority were of the view that it could not be done in the present instance, and, indeed, Beaumont and Heerey JJ clearly thought that it was most unlikely that the *Shire of Hastings* test could ever be satisfied in such a case.[40]

This decision is not satisfactory in a number of respects, and at the time of writing it was on appeal to the High Court.[41] A decision on this appeal is not expected until later in 1995, but it is to be hoped that the Court will take the opportunity to provide some clear and internally consistent guidance as to the proper relationship between contracts of employment and awards. Pending such guidance, it must be assumed that awards do not automatically become part of the contracts of employment of the employees to whom they

---

36   The test which is used for this purpose in Australia is that laid down by the Judicial Committee of the Privy Council in *BP Refinery (Westernport) v Hastings Shire Council* (1977) 52 ALJR 20 at 26. To satisfy this test the term in question: (i) must be reasonable; (ii) must be "necessary to give business efficacy to the contract so that no term will be implied if the contract is effective without it"; (iii) must be so obvious that "it goes without saying"; (iv) must be capable of clear expression, and (v) must not contradict any express term of the contract.

37   See for example Naughton & Stewart 1988; Mitchell & Naughton 1989; Tolhurst 1992.

38   See for example the cases listed at Creighton et al 1993: 103-4.

39   (1994) 120 ALR 274.

40   (1994) 120 ALR 274 at 314-5.

41   For comment see Forsyth 1994; de Meyrick 1995; Brooks 1995.

apply, but that they may be incorporated on the basis of either express or implied agreement.[42]

3. The Contract of Employment as a Protective Device

It should be evident from the foregoing that the Anglo-Australian contract of employment was never intended to be a protective device in the sense of providing protection for employees against arbitrary behaviour by employers or potential employers.Reflecting the assumptions inherent in the relationship of "master and servant", it provided a means of legitimating the domination of the purchaser of labour over the vendor. This helps explain the central roles of *control* in identifying the existence of a contract of employment,[43] and of the duty of *obedience* in its performance.[44]

So long as the employer adheres to the terms of the contract, the common law is little concerned with the reasonableness of either its content, or the manner in which it is performed. For example, provided the employer gives the proper amount of notice to terminate the contract, the common law has not traditionally concerned itself with either the motive for, or manner of,

---

42 Express incorporation may be more common than is sometimes supposed. For example, it is not unusual for employees, when entering employment, to sign an undertaking to the effect that they "agree" or "understand" that their employment is "subject to the XYZ award of the Industrial Relations Commission". It is at least arguable that this has the effect of importing the terms of the relevant award into the contract of the employee concerned.

43 Traditionally, the employer's capacity to control the what, the how and the when of the job were regarded as the key determinant of the existence of a contract of employment - see *Yewens v Noakes* (1880) 6 QBD 530 at 532 (per Bramwell B) and *Performing Right Society Ltd v Mitchell & Booker Ltd* [1924] 1 KB 762 at 767 (per McCardie J). More recently, the Australian courts have tended to look to a range of factors in order to ascertain whether a given contract should or should not be regarded as a contract of employment. However control, or at least the residual right to exercise it, is still regarded as of the utmost significance - see *Stevens v Brodribb Sawmilling* (1986) 160 CLR 16.

44 This is conventionally described in terms of the employee's duty to obey those orders of the employer which can be said to be lawful *and* reasonable - see for example Creighton et al 1993: 181-6, and the sources cited therein. There are, however, some suggestions that in the Australian context the only issue which is relevant is whether the order is "lawful" - see for example McCarry 1984.

termination.[45] Furthermore, the employer can be relieved of even the obligation to provide notice where the employee is "guilty" of misconduct of such a character as to constitute repudiatory breach of the contract: most obviously by failure to obey the lawful reasonable orders of the employer. Even if the employer is erroneous in assuming that it is entitled to terminate the contract without notice, the common law has been extremely reluctant to countenance the notion that the employer should be ordered to reinstate the wrongfully dismissed employee.[46] Instead they must take their remedy in damages: damages, moreover, which will be assessed on the very restrictive basis laid down by the House of Lords in *Addis v Gramophone Company*.[47]

In principle, these same rules apply to the employee vis-a-vis the employer. The point is, however, that the consequences of termination are almost invariably much more serious for the former than for the latter. It seems to follow that employees have a much greater need of protection against arbitrary termination than do employers. In any case, the common law *does* provide a significant measure of protection for employers in the event of arbitrary termination by the employee. Quite apart from the protection which is inherent in the fact that the errant employee loses the benefit of accrued rights in her or his employment, the employer may be able to restrain competition by the ex-employee in certain circumstances, and has the right to refuse to provide a reference, thereby potentially damaging the employment prospects of the former employee. Employees lack equivalent protections, beyond the fact that post-employment restraints must

45   The situation may, of course, be otherwise if the contract contains express provision relating to either or both of these issues - see for example *McClelland v Northern Ireland General Health Services Board* [1957] 1 WLR 594 and *Stevenson v United road Transport Union* [1977] ICR 893.

46   The traditional view is that expressed by Fry LJ in *De Francesco v Barnum* (1890) 45 ChD 430 at 438. For discussion of more recent developments in this area see Macken et al 1990: Chapter 7; Creighton et al 1993: 264-88; Ewing 1993, and the sources cited therein.

47   [1909] AC 488. On more recent developments see Macken et al 1990: 292-306; Creighton et al 1993: 255-64; Ewing 1993: 423-9, and the sources cited therein. For a trenchant critique of *Addis* see Gray 1994.

not be "unreasonable",[48] and that references must not be wilfully false, defamatory or contain negligent mis-statement.[49]

The common law is also largely unconcerned with the fairness or otherwise of the substantive content of the contract. In essence, the parties are free to contract on whatsoever terms they choose, so long as they do not contract to do anything which is unlawful, or which is otherwise contrary to public policy.

Public policy is a notoriously difficult concept: "a very unruly horse" which is "never argued at all but when other points fail".[50] Nevertheless it is clear that if the parties do contract to do something which is inherently unlawful - for example to commit a crime, or to defraud the taxation authorities - then the entire contract may be struck down as illegal, or the offending provision may be severed from the rest of the contract.[51] There is a number of other manifestations of public policy which may be used to vitiate unfair or oppressive provisions of contracts of employment in certain circumstances. They are, however, of limited practical relevance.

The rule against servile incidents, for example, stipulates that an employee may not "attach to his (sic) contract of service any servile incidents - any elements of servitude as distinguished from service".[52] There are, however, very few reported instances of contractual provisions actually being struck down on this basis.[53]

Contractual provisions which provide for the imposition of fines or other forms of monetary penalty (such as forfeiture of wages) upon an employee as a sanction for breach of contract may run foul of the rule against penalties.[54] To avoid this, the employer must be able to show: (i) that the penalty constituted a genuine re-estimate of the damage to the employer in

---

48   See the discussion of the doctrine of restraint of trade, *post*.

49   On this latter see *Spring v Guardian Assurance Plc* [1994] ICR 596.

50   *Richardson v Mellish* (1824) 2 Bing 229 at 252; 130 ER 294 at 303 (per Borrough J).

51   See further Mogridge 1981, and the cases discussed therein.

52   *Davies v Davies* (1887) 36 ChD 359 at 393 (per Bowen LJ).

53   See however *Horwood v Millar's Timber and Trading Company* [1917] 1 KB 305. See further Macken et al 1990: 78-79.

54   See *Dunlop Pneumatic Tyre Co v New Garage & Motor Co* [1915] AC 79 at 86-88 (per Lord Dunedin).

consequence of the employee's behaviour; and (ii) that the amount of the penalty is either specified in, or can readily be ascertained from, the contract. Although it is relied upon from time to time, this rule cannot be regarded as a significant restriction upon the notional capacity of the parties to contract upon their own terms.[55]

A further potential constraint upon the content of contracts of employment is furnished by the doctrine of restraint of trade. As noted earlier, employers may seek to restrain the capacity of former employees to compete against them after the termination of the employment relationship and/or to protect the confidentiality of information obtained by former employees in the course of their employment. Historically, the common law courts viewed this kind of provision with considerable distrust: partly because "it is contrary to the public welfare that a man (sic) should unreasonably be prevented from earning his living in whichever lawful way he chooses" and partly because the public should not "unreasonably be deprived of the services of a man (sic) prepared to engage in employment".[56] Nevertheless, the courts have come to accept that post-employment restraints on competition or upon use of confidential information can be sustained provided they can be shown to be reasonable in the interests of the parties *and* of the public.[57]

Despite the common law's antipathy towards post-employment restraints, the courts have been most reluctant to apply the doctrine of restraint of trade to restraints which operate during the currency of employment.[58] This presumably reflects a perception that the parties having made their bargain, should stick with it. It is only where there are adverse implications for third parties, or the "public", that the courts should become involved.

Similar considerations appear to underpin the apparent inability of the courts to extend the equitable doctrine of unconscionability so as to mitigate the effects of inequality of bargaining power as between the parties to a contract of employment. That the doctrine is capable of such extension seems

---

55   For applications of the rule see *Arlesheim v Werner* [1958] SASR 136; *Ajax Insurance v Smith* (1960) 79 WN (NSW) 83; *Amos v Commissioner for Main Roads* (1983) 6 IR 293.

56   *Buckley v Tutty* (1971) 125 CLR 353 at 380.

57   See further Macken et al 1990: 80-3; Creighton et al 1993: 129-42.

58   See for example *Esso Petroleum Co Ltd v Harper's Garage (Southport) Ltd* [1968] AC 269 at 294 (per Lord Reid) and 328 (per Lord Pearce); *Buckenara v Hawthorn Football Club* [1988] VR 39 at 44 (per Crockett J); *Curro v Beyond Productions Pty Ltd* (1993) 30 NSWLR 337 - cf *Schroeder Music Publishing Co v Macauley* [1974] 1 WLR 1308.

clear: what is lacking is the will to do so. For example in *Commercial Bank of Australia v Amadio*[59] the High Court set aside a commercial contract which had been signed by an elderly couple who had only a limited command of English, and a very inadequate understanding of the commercial world. In the course of his judgment Mason J stated:

"[there is] an underlying general principle which may be invoked whenever one party by reason of some condition or circumstance is placed at a special disadvantage vis-a-vis another and unfair or unconscientious disadvantage is taken of the opportunity thereby created. I qualify the word "disadvantage" by the adjective "special" in order to disavow any suggestion that the principle applies whenever there is some difference in the bargaining power of the parties and in order to emphasise that the disabling condition or circumstance is one which seriously affects the ability of the innocent party to make a judgement as to his (sic) own best interests, when the other party knows or ought to know of the existence of that condition or circumstance and of its effect on the innocent party.'[60]

Clearly this principle is capable of application in a situation where a worker is driven by poverty and/or ignorance to accept grossly inequitable terms and conditions of employment. Equally clearly, the express disavowal of inequality of bargaining power as a vitiating factor is intended to guard against that very possibility.

A similar issue arises in relation to the doctrine of duress. In *Universe Tankships of Monrovia v International Transport Workers Federation*[61] the House of Lords struck down an agreement relating to seafarers' wages which had been secured through industrial action. It did so on the ground that the agreement had been obtained by means of economic duress. Referring to this decision, Wedderburn (1986: 142) observes:

"The question arises whether an employment on "sweated" terms dictated to a destitute worker by a take-it-or-leave-it employer could ever be seen as one induced by "economic duress". The orthodox answer would appear to be to the contrary, for the judges have always excluded "commercial

---

59   (1983) 151 CLR 447.

60   *Ibid.* at 462.

61   [1983] 1 AC 366.

pressure" and mere "dominant bargaining power". The likelihood of an English court upsetting an individual contract of employment is low".

The caveat entered by Mason J in *Amadio* strongly suggests that the position would not be any different in Australia.

Not only does the common law exhibit minimal concern with the fairness of either the substantive content or manner of performance of a contract of employment, it is also almost entirely indifferent to the circumstances in which the contract is formed (or not formed). In particular, it demonstrates no real preparedness to protect workers against arbitrary exclusion from employment - for example because of their race, gender, trade union activities or political affiliation. A limited exception may be furnished where the rules of sporting or professional bodies are framed, or operate, in such a manner as to deny individual the right to practice their vocation or calling. In some circumstances, the rules of such bodies, or their application, may be adjudged to be in unreasonable restraint of trade.[62]

This non-interventionist stance is entirely consistent with the traditional view that:

"An employer may refuse to employ [a worker] for the most mistaken, capricious, malicious or morally reprehensible motives that can be conceived, but the workman (sic) has no right of action against him...A man (sic) has no right to be employed by any particular employer, and has no right to any particular employment if it depends on the will of another".[63]

Consistent with established principle this may be: but it furnishes yet further proof of the manifest inadequacy of the common law contract of employment as a means of protecting the legitimate interests of employees before, during or after employment. It is not surprising, therefore, that workers in Australia should look for other sources of protection.

---

62   See for example *Eastham v Newcastle United Football Club* [1964] Ch 413; *Nagle v Fielden* [1966] 2 QB 633; *Buckley v Tutty* (1971) 125 CLR 353; *Hall v Victorian Football League* [1982] VR 64.

63   *Allen v Flood* [1898] AC 1 at 172-3 (*per* Lord Davey).

4.   Alternative sources of protection

In 19th century Europe workers increasingly sought to redress the power imbalance between the vendors and the purchasers of labour by combining together for the purpose of negotiating terms and conditions of employment on a collective basis. At first these "combinations" were generally *ad hoc* in nature, but as time went on they increasingly came to be established on a more or less stable basis. Initially, the law reacted with considerable hostility to these developments.[64] Later, however, attempts at outright suppression gave way to a measure of legislative and institutional tolerance, and in some contexts, to positive encouragement of both combination and collective bargaining.[65]

4.1 COLLECTIVE BARGAINING

Australian workers adopted an essentially similar approach. From the 1850s onwards organisations emerged which are recognisably the forbears of modern unions,[66] although there is evidence of attempts at trade union organisation from the 1820s onwards.[67] Like their British counterparts, these early unions had to operate in a hostile legal environment. In particular, the master and servant legislation appears to have been extensively used to make life difficult for unions up to the turn of the century.[68] Collective bargaining at this time appears to have been of a somewhat *ad hoc* character, even where trade union organisation was relatively well established.[69] Nevertheless, as noted earlier, the Australian

---

64   For a most interesting study of attempts at legislative repression in Britain see Orth 1991. See also Hedges & Winterbottom 1930; Phelps Brown 1983; Fox 1985.

65   For an excellent overview of this process see Jacobs 1986. See also Heaton 1963: Chapter XXXI.

66   Often these early organisations operated as branches of British unions. Indeed the principal union in the metal industry severed its formal links with its British counterpart only in the early 1970s.

67   See Quinlan & Gardner 1990: 65-6.

68   They were used in a similar manner in Britain right up to the time of their repeal - see Simon 1954: 168-73.

69   See Creighton et al 1993: 6-7.

unions did secure some significant gains for their members through collective bargaining from the 1850s onwards.

As also noted above, the employers counter-attacked with devastating effect in the first half of the 1890s. This in turn caused the labour movement to look to compulsory conciliation and arbitration as a means of protecting and promoting their organisational interests, and those of their members. These techniques were originally conceived as a kind of default mechanism to be called in aid where collective bargaining was ineffectual: whether through employer intransigence or for some other reason.[70] In practice, however, the tail of conciliation and arbitration came to wag the dog of collective bargaining to such effect that by the 1930s the awards of industrial tribunals were the principal source of the basic terms and conditions of employment of the greater part of the workforce.

It would, however, be quite misleading to suggest that collective bargaining had played no part in the regulation of employment in Australia in the 20th century. On the contrary, it has played an exceedingly important, if often unremarked, role at a number of levels.

In the first place, the outcomes of the system of conciliation and arbitration have always reflected a *form* of collective bargaining. It is true that this bargaining has taken place within the limits imposed by the system itself - for example in terms of permissible wage outcomes. It is also true that this kind of bargaining must inevitably be constrained by the parties' awareness that if they were unable to reach agreement then the tribunal had the capacity to impose a settlement upon them.[71] Nevertheless:

"by the late 1980s around 25 per cent of all federal awards were entirely the product of collective negotiation between the parties, whilst the greater part of the content of the remaining 75 per cent were the product of agreement, with arbitration normally being required only in relation to a small number of outstanding issues".[72]

This suggests that rather than being characterised as a system of "compulsory" conciliation and arbitration, the Australian apporach should be

---

70   See further Deery & Plowman 1991: 274-5; ILO 1930: 310-2.

71   See Sykes & Glasbeek 1972: 369.

72   Creighton et al 1993: 860.

seen as a "hybrid" which "combines arbitration, conciliation and collective bargaining".[73]

Furthermore, there is number of contexts where the parties have traditionally engaged in "true" collective bargaining, in the sense that it was not constrained by the norms of the conciliation and arbitration system. These would include:

(i)   situations where terms and conditions of employment in a particular industry or locality are regulated by negotiation between employers and unions in the industry or area without the involvement of an industrial tribunal. This practice was formerly quite common in remote mining areas, but now appears to be in decline.[74] This can probably be attributed to improvements in communications which mean that tribunal members are now more accessible than would have been the case in the past, and to the shift to enterprise-based negotiation within the formal system of industrial regulation which is discussed below.

(ii)   situations where certain issues were perceived to be outside the jurisdiction of the tribunals - with the consequence that if the parties wished to deal with them in an industrial context it had to be done through collective bargaining. This was a particularly significant factor prior to the decision in the *Social Welfare Case*, due to the fact that the High Court had consistently determined that certain disputes were outside the jurisdiction of the federal tribunal - for example because their subject-matter encroached upon managerial prerogative to an unacceptable degree,[75] or because the workers concerned were not engaged in an industry in the requisite sense.[76]

---

73   Dabscheck 1986: 167.

74   Probably the best-known example was the Barrier Industrial Agreement, which traditionally regulated almost all aspects of economic, and to a considerable extent social, activity in Broken Hill.

75   See now *Re Cram; Ex parte New South Wales Colliery Proprietors' Association* (1987) 163 CLR 117.

76   See now *R v Coldham; Ex parte Australian Social Welfare Union* (1983) 153 CLR 297 (*The Social Welfare Case*).

(iii)   situations where the parties take award entitlements as a starting
point and then negotiate beyond them in order to take account of the
special circumstances of the enterprise or locality. Such "over-award"
bargaining is extremely common - for example the Australian Workplace
Industrial Relations Survey (Callus et al 1991: 42-3) found that at 68 per
cent of workplaces all or part of the workforce were in receipt of over-
award payments.

All of that said, the fact remains that the principal source of protection for
the employment conditions of Australian workers throughout the 20th century
has been conciliation and arbitration. As will appear presently, it is far from
clear that the same will be true for the next century.

4.2 CONCILIATION AND ARBITRATION

Whilst there are many differences as to matters of detail, all of the State and
ederal conciliation and arbitration systems have a number of features in
common.[77] In all cases there is an independent tribunal with power to
exercise powers of conciliation and arbitration in relation to disputes which
are brought before it by the parties, a Minister, or of the tribunal's own
volition.[78] In some States this tribunal also has responsibility for the
interpretation and enforcement of the legislation and of its awards. However

---

77   As will appear presently, Victoria no longer has a conciliation and arbitration system as
     such. However, the system which operated in that jurisdiction prior to its abolition in
     1992 conformed to the model described hereafter. In the interests of clarity and brevity,
     this outline in principally concerned with the Federal system. For more detailed
     descriptions of that system see Creighton et al 1993: Chapters 14-24; Creighton &
     Stewart 1994: Chapters 4-6; McCallum & Pittard 1994: Chapters 5-9 and 12. For a
     brief overview see Mitchell & Scherer 1993.

78   The Federal tribunal is entitled the Australian Industrial Relations Commission - for the
     relevant statutory provision see Part II and ss.170QA-170QG of the *Industrial Relations
     Act* 1988. The State systems generally adopt a similar nomenclature.

in the Federal system, for constitutional reasons,[79] these judicial functions must be vested in a separately constituted court.[80]

The tribunals have very broad discretions as to the manner in which they exercise their functions, and the powers which they may exercise in order to prevent and settle disputes which are brought before them. In the case of the Federal Commission the capacity to take evidence on oath, to make awards or orders, to compelsion they include the attendance of any party, to dismiss or adjourn matters brought before it, and to "generally give all such directions, and do all such things as are necessary or expedient for the speedy and just hearing and determination" of industrial disputes.[81]   The legislation also contains an array of provisions which are ostensibly intended to ensure that disputes are brought before the Commission, and to protect the integrity of the processes of conciliation and arbitration whilst they remain on foot. They are, however, little relied upon in practice.[82] Awards or orders of the Commission have the full force of law, and can be enforced as such by parties to the award or order, individuals to whom the award or order applies or by a labour inspector.[83]

The system accords a very significant role to organisations of workers and (to a lesser extent) employers. It also seeks to exercise what is, in many respects, a quite e traordinary degree of control over the constitution and functioning of organisations which choose to register under the legislation.[84]

There are presently around 900 awards which have been made by the Federal tribunal. Some of these apply to entire industries or occupations.

---

79   See *R v Kirby; Ex parte Boilermakers' Society of Australia* (1956) 94 CLR 254, where the High Court and the Judicial Committee of the Privy Council determined that respect for the principle of separation of powers was an implied   requirement of the Constitution.

80   Presently, the Industrial Relations Court of Australia - see further Part XIV of the *Industrial Relations Act* 1988 (Cth.). For comment see Ludeke 1994.

81   1988 Act, s.111(1)(t). See in general ss.111 and 118.

82   See further Creighton 1991; McCarry 1991; Creighton et al 1993: Chapter 24; Creighton & Stewart 1994: 256-60; McCallum & Pittard: Chapter 16.

83   See for example ss.178 and 179 of the 1988 Act. See further Bennett 1994: 131-64; McCallum 1994a.

84   See 1988 Act, Parts IX and X. For comment see Creighton et al 1993: Chapters 26-31; Creighton & Stewart 1994: Chapter 10; McCallum & Pittard 1994: Chapter 13.

Others apply to particular enterprises or undertakings. Most mirror, with minor adjustment, the provisions of a small number of key, or "parent" awards. In terms of content, they deal with a wide range of matters. In general, however, these provisions fall into one of four categories: (i) those that deal with respondency - that is, with the question of the parties and organisations upon whom the award is to be binding; (ii) those concerning various aspects of the wage/effort exchange, such as wages,[85] hours, leave, termination and suspension of employment;[86] (iii) procedures for settling disputes and resolving grievances; and (iv) trade union security, including preference in employment for union members.[87]

It should be evident from the fore-going that the traditional award system did indeed deal with most key aspects of the employment relationship. In that sense it left relatively little room for the contractual principles to operate. However, it is also important to recall that: (i) the existence of the contract was an essential pre-condition of access to the award system; (ii) award standards frequently mirrored common law principles, especially in relation to discipline and termination, and (iii) it was always open to the parties to

---

85   Over the years the wage fixing process has been dominated by set-piece National Wage Cases. Technically these consisted of periodic (sometimes on as many as three or four occasions per year) applications to vary two or three key Federal awards. In practice they generally consisted of a more or less sophisticated consideration of the capacity of the economy to tolerate wage increases at that point in time. Governments, employer organisations, unions and other interested parties all have an opportunity to make representations to the tribunal. The resultant decision is then "flowed on" to the rest of the economy through award variations and State Wage Cases. This approach is now out of favour. See further Creighton et al: 1993: 709-30; Creighton & Stewart 1994: 37-9; McCallum & Pittard 1994: Chapter 12.

86   On occasion significant new standards were adopted on the basis of test cases in the federal Commission, with the outcome then being flowed-on through the system in the same way as national wage outcomes. See for example *Equal Pay Case 1969* (1969) 127 CAR 1142; *Equal Pay Case 1972* (1972) 147 CAR 172; *Termination, Change and Redundancy Case* (1984) 8 IR 34 and 9 IR 115 (The *TCR Case*). As the title suggests, the first and second of these dealt with the issue of equal pay for work of equal value. The *TCR Case* dealt with minimum notice entitlements, unfair dismissal, consultation in advance of redundancy, and severance pay.

87   Curiously, in the Federal system, it cannot include direct deduction of trade union membership fees - see *R v Portus; Ex parte ANZ Banking Group* (1972) 127 CLR 353 and *Re Alcan Australia Ltd; Ex parte Federation of Industrial, Manufacturing and Engineering Employees* (1994) 123 ALR 193. For more detailed consideration of trade union security within the system see Mitchell 1986; Mitchell 1987; Weeks 1995.

contract up from the award standards - what they could not do was contract down.

4.3 PROTECTIVE LEGISLATION

Workers in Britain and other European countries have long looked to the legislature as a means of securing employment protection. Early examples of such provision can be found in 19th century British factory legislation, which initially sought to protect the health and welfare of children, juveniles and women, but was later extended to deal with the health, safety and welfare of the workforce as a whole.[88] Since the end of World War II there has been increasing emphasis upon legislative protection in relation to issues such as job security, parental leave, income security and protection against discrimination on grounds of gender, race etc.[89]

Australian occupational health and safety legislation can be traced back to the later part of the 19th century, and was closely modelled on then-current British provision.[90] But, traditionally, other forms of employment protection have traditionally largely been the province of the industrial tribunals. In part this may reflect a view that conciliation and arbitration was the most appropriate basis upon which to deal with such issues. But it also reflected a perception that the Commonwealth Parliament lacked legislative power to adopt employment protection legislation of general application.[91] The States laboured under no such disabilities, but in general confined themselves to introducing legislative minima relating to long service[92] or annual leave.[93]

---

88   For an overview of the development of such protections in Europe see Ramm 1986.

89   See for example the standards embodied in the *Employment Protection (Consolidation) Act* 1978 (UK).

90   On the evolution of occupational health and safety legislation in Australia see Gunningham 1984: 65-74. On current provision see Creighton et al 1993: Chapter 40; Creighton & Stewart 1993: Chapter 13; Brooks 1993a; Quinlan & Bohle 1991: Chapter 7; Johnstone & Quinlan 1993.

91   It clearly had the power to introduce such provision for specific groups such as the defence forces (Constitution, s.51(vi)), Commonwealth employees (Constitution, s.52(2)) and workers in the Territories (Constitution, s.122).

92   See for example *Long Service Leave Act* 1955 (NSW) *Employee Relations Act* 1992 (Vic), Part 5, Division 6.

At Federal level, it is certainly true that the conciliation and arbitration power in section 51(xxxv) of the Constitution did not support the adoption of European-style employment protection legislation. However, it has long been clear that there is a number of provisions in the Constitution which *could* be used as a basis for such measures if the Commonwealth were so minded. These would include the trade and commerce (section51(i)), taxation (section 51(ii)), corporations (section 51(xx)), and external affairs (s.51(xxix)) powers.

The point is that, until recently, the Commonwealth has not been "so minded". This can largely be attributed to a combination of indolence and a concern to avoid the inevitable legal and political confrontation with the States in the face of any attempt to extend the influence of the Commonwealth at their expense. However there has been a marked shift of attitude in recent years. In 1992 a conservative government was elected in Victoria with a commitment, *inter alia*, to a radical deregulation of the labour market. It gave effect to this commitment in dramatic fashion by pushing the *Employee Relations Act*, and a number of related measures, through Parliament within weeks of taking office.[94]

The Federal Labor Government reacted to this by introducing a range of provisions which were intended to protect minimum standards relating to minimum wage fixing, equal remuneration for work of equal value, workers with family responsibilities, and termination of employment.[95] These provisions derive their constitutionality from the external affairs power in section 51(xxix) in conjunction with a number of ILO Conventions which had been ratified by Australia.[96] The standards embodied in the legislation are fairly minimal in character. They do, nevertheless, constitute an important development in the evolution of Australian labour law. First, because of the novel use of the external affairs power, and secondly because

---

93   See for example *Annual Leave Act* 1944 (NSW) and *Employee Relations Act* 1992 (Vic), ss.14, 25, 26 and Sch.1 cl 1(a). For an isolated example of employment protection legislation of a more general character see *Employment Protection Act* 1982 (NSW).

94   For further comment on the Victorian Act see Creighton 1993; Mitchell 1993a; Naughton 1993; Pittard 1993; Watson 1993.

95   These provisions were introduced by the *Industrial Relations Reform Act* 1993, and are now to be found in Part VIA of the 1988 Act. For comment see Pittard 1994.

96   On the role of ILO standards in Australia see Creighton & Stewart 1994: Chapter 3.

they are an integral part of the legislative underpinning for the shift towards a more explicitly bargaining-oriented system.

Since 1992 conservative governments in a number of States have radically over-hauled their systems of industrial regulation - although to date only Victoria has gone so far as entirely to abandon the concept of compulsory conciliation and arbitration.[97] The basic purpose of these reforms is to move away from centralised regulation of terms and conditions of employment through industrial tribunals in favour of regulation through negotiation at the level of the workplace. These provisions draw both conceptual and legal inspiration from the *Employment Contracts Act* 1991 (NZ).[98] They are accompanied by a rhetoric which is strongly reminiscent of the 1890s, and all seek to marginalise the role of trade unions in the bargaining process. In order to meet allegations that these new arrangements could severely disadvantage workers who were not in a position effectively to protect and to promote their interests in the bargaining process, the governments concerned have introduced a series of statutory minimum standards in relation to issues such as rates of pay, leave entitlements (annual and parental), and notice of termination. They have also retained existing protections against unfair dismissal.[99] Meanwhile, the Labor State of Queensland has a Labor government has introduced a set of minima which precisely mirror the protections embodied in Part VIA of the Federal Act.[100]

It can be seen, therefore, that formal protective legislation has come to play a much more significant role in Australia in recent years than had been the case in the past. Current attempts to shift the emphasis of the system away from centralised conciliation and arbitration towards enterprise-based negotiation suggest that this trend may well continue, irrespective of what government is in power at State or Federal level. On the other hand, as will appear presently, the present federal Government, and (especially) the trade

---

97   For an overview of these developments see Creighton & Stewart 1994: 122-6.

98   For the conceptual underpinning of this legislation see Brook 1990. For comment see Harbridge 1993; Peetz et al 1993; Ryan & Walsh 1993. See also the decisions of the ILO's Committee on Freedom of Association on a complaint brought against the legislation by the New Zealand Council of Trade Unions - *Case No 1698*, CFA 292nd Report, paras. 675-741 and 295th Report, paras. 132-262.

99   See *Employee Relations Act* 1992 (Vic), s.25(4) and Schedule 1; *Minimum Conditions of Employment Act* 1993 (WA); *Industrial and Employee Relations Act* 1994 (SA).

100 See *Industrial Relations Act* 1990 (Qld), Part 4, Divisions 4-6 and Part 12, Divisions 4 and 5.

union movement, retain a strong commitment to the award system as a safety net to underpin enterprise bargaining.

4.4 THE IMPACT OF PROTACTIVE PROVISION

The combined effect of collective bargaining, conciliation and arbitration and legislative intervention has been largely to marginalise the role of the contract of employment as a protective device for the great majority of Australian workers. However, it is important to appreciate that these techniques have provided a very particular kind of protection.

In general, they have focussed upon the perceived need to *protect* workers against real or imagined threats to their employment interests, rather than looking to protection as an element in developing more productive aspects of the work relationship. Until recently, they have also emphasised the distribution of rewards and benefits as derived from increases in national wealth, rather than looking to improvements in productivity and profitability as sources of improved rewards. Within the employment relationship, they have emphasised substantive issues, rather than process and procedure. For example, the systems have generally concentrated upon the settlement of collective disputes once they have arisen, rather than upon preventing their occurrence in the first place. Similarly, at the individual level, they have concentrated upon securing reinstatement and/or compensation for dismissed workers rather than upon preventing the unfair dismissal through the development and application of appropriate procedures. They have also concentrated upon securing severance pay for redundant workers rather than upon developing techniques for managing change within the enterprise, and within the broader economy.

This emphasis upon protection rather than managing change is also evident in the way in which the systems have tried to discourage overtime or weekend work and the use of part-time or casual workers by imposing additional costs through penalties and loadings, rather than upon trying to develop more flexible kinds of work arrangements which might better suit the needs of both workers and employers.[101]

This is not to suggest that workers are not entitled to adequate and equitable relief when they are unfairly dismissed or made redundant, or to their fair share of the fruits of their labours, or to appropriate remuneration for working at unsocial hours etc. However it *is* to suggest that in the past, the systems and the participants therein, have tended to view these issues

---

101 See further Mitchell & Rimmer 1990.

from a somewhat negative perspective. That is not surprising, given the inherent inequalities in bargaining power which underpin the employment relationship, and the inadequacy of the common law's response to them. But is does raise some difficult issues about the role of both the individual contract and of protective techniques in the future.

5. The Re-Emergence of the Contract of Employment?

Many of the developments outlined in the previous section can be seen as part of global trend towards the "de-collectivisation" of labour law and labour relations.[102] Levels of trade union membership are declining in most developed countries. This almost inevitably carries with it a decline in collective regulation of employment, since in most countries such regulation depends upon the role of unions. To some extent Australia runs counter to this trend. It is true that there has been a marked decline in levels of unionisation since the early 1980s: most recent figures indicate that some 37.6 per cent of the workforce are now union members, compared with 40.5 per cent in 1990 and 49.5 per cent in 1982.[103] However, because the application of industrial awards does not depend upon whether the workers concerned are trade union members, the decline in membership does not necessarily lead to a decline in collective regulation. On the other hand, a continued decline in membership levels in the londer term must inevitably compromise the efficacy of the system as a regulatory mechanism: if only because its effective operation must depend upon the stimulus provided by an active and organisationally secure trade union movement.

The impact of the trend towards decollectivisation is most marked in Victoria and in other States which have quite openly sought to marginalise both standard setting through conciliation and arbitration and trade unions. But it is also reflected in the recent changes to the Federal *Industrial Relations Act* which are intended to promote the development of enterprise level bargaining, with a concomitant shift away from regulation through conciliation and arbitration.[104] However, the Federal provision still

---

102 See further Collins 1989; Ewing 1988; Mitchell 1993b.

103 See ABS 1994: 23. See also the comparative table in Mitchell & Scherer 1993: 89.

104 The relevant provisions are set out in Part VIB of the 1988 Act. For analysis see McCallum 1994; McCarry 1994; Naughton 1994; Creighton & Stewart 1994: Chapter 6.

presupposes a major role for awards as providing a safety net for negotiation at the level of the workplace or the enterprise. It also provides that agreements concluded within the framework of the legislation are to be enforceable as awards,[105] and goes to some lengths to preserve a role for trade unions in the negotiating process. It has, in consequence, been roundly condemned by the advocates of more radical deregulation of the labour market. It does, nevertheless, constitute a profoundly significant shift in the substance and underpinning philosophy of the Federal system.

These developments, national and international, can be attributed to a number of factors, including: (i) the ascendancy of free-market ideologies in many parts of the world;[106] (ii) the adoption of "human resource management" techniques in North America and elsewhere, with their emphasis upon the corporate objectives and the role of the individual in achieving those objectives rather than upon the collective interests of the workforce and resolution of disputes;[107] (iii) the proliferation of small businesses, where the collectivist culture of traditional industrial relations often seems out of place and irrelevant; and (iv) an emerging perception that the "globalisation" of the world economy means that developed countries cannot afford the "luxury" of relatively high levels of employment protection in light of the competition they face from developing economies where workers enjoy much lesser levels of protection.[108]

Self-evidently, all of this has profoundly significant implications for the future role of the contract of employment in Australia, and elsewhere. If the

---

105 Part VIB makes provision for two kinds of agreement: (i) certified agreements, which are really enterprise level collective agreements between trade unions and employers which are formally endorsed by the Commission by reference to the criteria set out in Division 2 of Part VIB, and (ii) enterprise flexibility agreements which are concluded through negotiation between corporate employers and their workforce (Division 3 of Part VIB). Unions may, but do not have to be, party to enterprise flexibility agreements. Division 2 also envisages the certification of agreements which apply to industries or parts of industries, but this is of little practical relevance.

106 See for example the fascinating analysis by Wedderburn (1989) of the impact of the writings of FA Hayek on the industrial relations policies upon the Thatcher Government in Britain. See also Hayek 1960 and Epstein 1983. On New Zealand see Brook 1990, and the analysis in Ryan & Walsh 1993.

107 See further Gardner & Palmer 1992: Chapter 17.

108 On labour relations and employment protection in the South-East Asian region where Australia's trading interests increasingly lie see the national studies collected in Deery & Mitchell 1993.

labour market is indeed to become increasingly individualised, then there clearly needs to be a fundamental re-evaluation of the legal instrument(s) which govern that relationship. The courts, for example, need to adopt a rather more positive and realistic approach to the rights and duties of the parties than has generally been the case in the past. In particular they need to try to come to terms with the social and economic realities which underpin the relationship rather than simply taking refuge in ritualistic incantations about the intentions of the parties and the sanctity of contract. There are some signs that this may be happening - as evidenced, for example, by the apparent emergence of an implied duty to behave reasonably,[109] and a shift in attitude to ordering specific performance of contracts of employment.[110] But there is clearly a long way to go. In particular, the common law needs to develop a meaningful doctrine of unconscionability which can be used to strike down contractual terms which have been obtained on the basis of unfair use of a superior bargaining position. If the courts are unwilling or unable to do this through the development of the common law, then they need to be provided with a legislative basis for doing so. New South Wales already has quite a sophisticated jurisdiction in this regard.[111] Sections 127A-127C of the 1988 Act mark a modest beginning in the Federal sphere, but would clearly need to be extended to contracts of employment as well as to contracts for services as at present.[112]

The nature of employment protection legislation also requires re-assessment. For example, it may be that enhanced standards of job security (perhaps through protection against unfair dismissal or retrenchment, adoption and application of grievance procedures, and provision for job training and career development) need to be off-set by a recognition of greater flexibility in terms of the employee's obligations within the

---

109 See further Creighton et al 1993: 208-10; Creighton & Stewart 1994: 168-70, and the cases cited therein.

110 See further Ewing & Grubb 1987; Furness 1989; Creighton et al 1993: 264-88; Ewing 1993; McCallum & Pittard 1994: Chapter 4.

111 See *Industrial Relations Act* 1991 (NSW), ss.275-8. For comment see Macken et al 1990: 438-80. For examples of the practical application of these provisions in the context of contracts of employment see *Morgan v Coulson* [1981] 2 NSWLR 801 and *Sulkowicz v Parramatta District Rugby League Club* (1983) 4 IR 272. The only other State which makes provision of this kind is Queensland - see *Industrial Relations Act* 1990, s.39.

112 For comment see Brooks 1993b.

parameters of the employment relationship. At the same time there clearly has to be greater recognition of "atypical" work arrangements - both in terms of an acceptance that they perform an important role in the labour market, and that those who enter into such arrangements have legitimate expectations in terms of employment security and other forms of employment protection.[113]   None of this is easy. But an essential starting point is a recognition that, with rare exception, employers and workers do not come to the labour market on equal terms, and that the nature of the power imbalance between them is such that workers must inevitably took to sources beyond their own position in the market in order to protect and to promote their legitimate interests. The nature, and indeed the sources, of that protection may change over time. But the need for protection does not. Current debate, and current legislative provision, in Australia exhibit only a very limited awareness of these imperatives.

---

113 On the position of "atypical" workers in Australia see Bieback 1992; Brooks 1991; Stewart 1992; Owens 1993; Creighton 1995.

Bibliography

- A.B.S. (Australian Bureau of Statistics) (1991) *Award Coverage, Australia*, Catalogue No 6323.0 (A.B.S., Canberra)
- A.B.S. (Australian Bureau of Statistics) (1994) *Working Arrangements, Australia - August 1993*, Catalogue No 6342.0 (A.B.S., Canberra)
- Bennett, L. (1994) *Making Labour Law in Australia: Industrial Relations, Politics and Law* (Law Book Co, Sydney)
- Bieback, K-J. (1992) 'The Protection of Atypical Work in Australian and West German Labour Law' 5 *Australian Journal of Labour Law* 17
- Brook, P. (1990) *Freedom at Work* (OUP, Auckland)
- Brooks, A. (1988) 'Myth and Muddle - An Examination of Contracts for the Performance of Work' 11 *University of New South Wales Law Journal* 48
- Brooks, A. (1991) 'Marginal Workers and the Law' in M Bray and V Taylor (eds), *The Other Side of Flexibility: Unions and Marginal Workers in Australia* (Monograph No 3, ACIRRT, University of Sydney)
- Brooks, A. (1993a) *Occupational Health and Safety Law In Australia* (4th ed, CCH, Sydney)
- Brooks, A. (1993b) 'Federal Industrial Relations Legislation Reform: Independent Contracts and Recovery of Wages' 6 *Australian Journal of Labour Law* 69
- Brooks, A. (1993c) 'The Contract of Employment and Workplace Agreements' in P Ronfeldt and R McCallum (eds), *A New Province for Legalism: Legal Issues and the Deregulation of Industrial Relations* (Monograph No 9, ACIRRT, University of Sydney), Ch 2
- Brooks, A. (1995) 'Damages for Harsh, Unjust or Unreasonable Dismissal: The Implications of *Gorgevski v. Bostik (Australia) Pty Ltd*' in 8 *Australian Journal of Labour Law*, March 1995 (Forthcoming)
- Callus, R., Morehead, A., Cully, M., and Buchanan, J. (1991) *Industrial Relations at Work: The Australian Workplace Industrial Relations Survey* (AGPS, Canberra)
- Collins, H. (1989) 'Labour Law as a Vocation' 105 *Law Quarterly Review* 468
- Creighton, W.B. (1991) 'Enforcement in the Federal Industrial Relations System: an Australian Paradox' 4 *Australian Journal of Labour Law* 197
- Creighton, W.B. (1993) 'Employment Agreements and Conditions of Employment Under the Employee Relations Act 1992 (Vic)' 6 *Australian Journal of Labour Law* 140

- Creighton, W.B. (1995) 'Employment Security and Atypical Work in Australia' 16 *Comparative Labor Law Journal*, Spring 1995 (Forthcoming)
- Creighton, W.B., Ford, W.J., and Mitchell, R.J., (1993) *Labour Law: Text and Materials* (2nd ed, Law Book Co, Sydney)
- Creighton, W.B., and Stewart, A.J. (1994) *Labour Law: An Introduction* (2nd ed, Federation Press, Sydney)
- Dabscheck, B. (1986) 'In Search of the Holy Grail: Proposals for the Reform of Australian Industrial Relations' in R Blandy and J Niland (eds) *Alternatives to Arbitration* (Allen and Unwin, Sydney), Ch. 9.
- Deery, S., and Mitchell, R. (eds) (1993) *Labour Law and Industrial Relations in Asia: Eight Country Studies* (Longman Cheshire, Melbourne)
- de Meyrick, J. (1995) 'The Interaction of Awards and Contracts' in 8 *Australian Journal of Labour Law*, March 1995 (Forthcoming)
- Epstein, R. (1983) 'A Common Law for Labor Relations: A Critique of the New Deal Labor Legislation' 92 *Yale Law Journal* 1357
- Ewing, K.D. (1988) 'The Death of Labour Law' 8 *Oxford Journal of Legal Studies* 293
- Ewing, K.D. (1993) 'Remedies for Breach of the Contract of Employment' 52 *Cambridge Law Journal* 505
- Ewing, K.D., and Grubb, A. (1987) 'The Emergence of a New Labour Injunction?' 16 *Industrial Law Journal* 145
- Forsyth, A. (1994) 'Contractual Incorporation of Award Terms: *Byrne and Frew v. Australian Airlines Limited*' 36 *Journal of Industrial Relations* 417
- Fox, A. (1974) *Beyond Contract: Work, Power and Trust Relations* (Faber and Faber, London)
- Fox, A. (1985) *History and Heritage: The Social Origins of the British Industrial Relations System* (Allen & Unwin, London)
- Freedland, M.R. (1976) *The Contract of Employment* (Clarendon Press, Oxford)
- Furness, G. (1989) 'Injunctions and the Contract of Employment' 2 *Australian Journal of Labour Law* 234
- Gardner, M., and Palmer, G. (1992) *Employment Relations* (MacMillan, Melbourne)
- Gray, P.R.A. (1994) 'Damages for Wrongful Dismissal: Is the Gramophone Record Worn Out?' in R McCallum, G McCarry and P Ronfeldt (eds), *Employment Security* (Federation Press, Sydney), Ch. 3
- Gunningham, N. (1984) *Safeguarding the Worker: Job Hazards and the Role of the Law* (Law Book Co, Sydney)

- Harbridge, R. (ed) (1993) *Employment Contracts: New Zealand Experiences* (Victoria University Press, Wellington)
- Hayek, F.A. (1960) *The Constitution of Liberty* (Routledge & Kegan Paul, London)
- Hedges, R.Y., and Winterbottom, A. (1930) *The Legal History of Trade Unionism* (Longmans, London)
- Heaton, H. (1963) *Economic History of Europe* (3rd ed, Harper & Row, London)
- Hutson, J.H. (1983) *Penal Colony to Penal Powers* (revised ed, Amalgamated Metal Workers and Shipwrights Union, Sydney)
- I.L.O. (1930) *Freedom of Association*, Vol. V, Studies and Reports, Series A (Industrial Relations) No. 32. (I.L.O., Geneva)
- Jacobs, A. (1986) 'Collective Self-Regulation' in B Hepple (ed), *The Making of Labour Law in Europe: A Comparative Study of Nine Countries up to 1945* (Mansell, London), Ch 5
- Johnstone, R. and Quinlan, M. (1993) 'The Origins, Management and Regulation of Occupational Illness: An Overview' in M Quinlan (ed), *Work and Health: The Origins, Management and Regulation of Occupational Illness* (MacMillan, Melbourne), Ch 1
- Kahn-Freund, O. (1954) 'Legal Framework' in A Flanders and H A Clegg (eds), *The System of Industrial Relations in Great Britain* (Blackwell, Oxford), Ch II
- Ludeke, J.T. (1994) 'The Structural Features of the New System' 7 *Australian Journal of Labour Law* 132
- Macintyre, S. (1989) 'Neither Capital Nor Labour: The Politics of the Establishment of Arbitration' in S Macintyre and R Mitchell (eds), *Foundations of Arbitration* (OUP, Melbourne) Ch 8
- Macken, J.J., McCarry, G.J., and Sappideen, C. (1990) *The Law of Employment* (3rd ed, Law Book Co, Sydney)
- Markey, R. (1989) 'Trade Unions, the Labor Party and the Introduction of Arbitration in New South Wales and the Commonwealth' in S Macintyre and R Mitchell (eds), *Foundations of Arbitration* (OUP, Melbourne), Ch 7
- McCallum, R.C. (1994a) ' The Imperfect Safety-Net: The Enforcement of Federal Awards and Agreements' in R McCallum, G McCarry and P Ronfeldt (eds), *Employment Security* (Federation Press, Sydney), Ch 10
- McCallum, R.C. (1994b) 'The Internationalisation of Australian Industrial Law: The *Industrial Relations Reform Act* 1993' 15 *Sydney Law Review* 122
- McCallum, R.C., and Pittard, M.J. (1994) *Australian Labour Law: Cases and Materials* (3rd ed, Butterworths, Sydney)

- McCarry, G.J. (1984) 'The Employee's Duty to Obey Unreasonable Orders' 58 *Australian Law Journal* 327
- McCarry, G.J. (1991) 'Amicable Agreements, Equitable Awards and Industrial Disorder' 13 *Sydney University Law Review* 299
- McCarry, G.J. (1994) 'Sanctions and Industrial Action: the Impact of the Industrial Relations Reform Act' 7 *Australian Journal of Labour Law* 198
- Merritt, A.S. (1982) 'The Historical Role of Law in the Regulation of Employment - Abstentionist or Interventionist?' a *Australian Journal of law and Society* 56
- Mitchell, R.J. (1986) 'The High Court and the Preference Power: Wallis and Findlay in the Context of the 1947 Amendments' 16 *University of Western Australia Law Review* 338
- Mitchell, R.J. (1987) 'The Preference Power and the Practice of the Federal Industrial Tribunal, 1904-1970' 29 *Journal of Industrial Relations* 3
- Mitchell, R.J. (1989) 'State Systems of Conciliation and Arbitration: The Legal Origins of the Australasian Model' in S Macintyre and R Mitchell (eds), *Foundations of Arbitration* (OUP, Melbourne), Ch 4
- Mitchell, R.J. (1993a) 'Notes on the Employee Relations Act 1992 (Victoria)' (Centre For Industrial Relations and Labour Studies, University of Melbourne)
- Mitchell, R.J. (1993b) 'The Deregulation of Industrial Relations Systems and the Rise of the Non-Union Option' in P Ronfeldt and R McCallum (eds), *A New Province for Legalism: Legal Issues and the Deregulation of Industrial Relations* (Monograph No 9, ACIRRT, University of Sydney), Ch 10
- Mitchell, R.J., and Naughton, R.B. (1989) 'Collective Agreements, Industrial Awards and the Contract of Employment' 2 *Australian Journal of Labour Law* 252
- Mitchell, R.J., and Rimmer, M. (1990) 'Labour Law, Deregulation, and Flexibility in Australian Industrial Relations' 12 *Comparative Labour Law Journal* 1
- Mitchell, R.J., and Scherer, P. (1993) 'Australia: The Search for Fair Employment Contracts through Tribunals' in J Hartog and J Theeuwes, *Labour Market Contracts and Institutions: A Cross National Comparison* (North-Holland, The Netherlands), Ch 3
- Mogridge, C. (1981) 'Illegal Employment Contracts: Loss of Statutory Protection' 10 *Industrial Law Journal* 23
- Naughton, R.B. (1993) 'The Institutions Established by the Employee Relations Act 1992' 6 *Australian Journal of Labour Law* 121

- Naughton, R.B. (1994) 'The New Bargaining Regime Under the Industrial Relations Reform Act' 7 *Australian Journal of Labour Law* 147
- Naughton, R.B., and Stewart, A. (1988) 'Breach of Contract Through Unfair Termination: The New Law of Wrongful Dismissal' 1 *Australian Journal of Labour Law* 151
- Orth, J.V. (1991) *Combination and Conspiracy: A Legal History of Trade Unionism 1721-1906* (Clarendon Press, Oxford)
- Owens, R. (1993) 'Women, 'Atypical' Work Relationships and the Law' 19 *Melbourne University Law Review* 399
- Peetz, D., Quinn, D., Edwards, L. and Riedel, P. (1993) 'Workplace Bargaining in New Zealand: Radical Change at Work' in D Peetz, A Preston and J Docherty, *Workplace Bargaining in the International Context* (Industrial Relations Research Monograph No 2, Department of Industrial Relations, Canberra), Ch 4
- Phelps Brown, E.H. (1983) *The Origins of Trade Union Power* (Oxford University Press, Oxford)
- Pittard, M.J. (1993) 'Industrial Conflict and Constraints: Sanctions on Industrial Action in Victoria' 6 *Australian Journal of Labour Law* 159
- Pittard, M.J. (1994) 'International Labour Standards in Australia: Wages, Equal Pay, Leave and Termination of Employment' 7 *Australian Journal of Labour Law* 170
- Quinlan, M. (1986) 'State Regulation of Labour in Australia 1828-1860' (Fourth Australian Law and Society Conference, Brisbane)
- Quinlan, M. (1989) ''Pre-Arbitral' Labour Legislation in Australia and its Implications for the Introduction of Compulsory Arbitration' in S Macintyre and R Mitchell (eds), *Foundations of Arbitration* (OUP, Melbourne), Ch 2
- Quinlan, M., and Bohle, P. (1991) *Managing Health and Safety in Australia: A Multidisciplinary Approach* (MacMillan, Melbourne), Ch 7
- Quinlan, M., and Gardner, M. (1990) 'Researching Australian Industrial Relations in the Nineteenth Century' in G Patmore (ed), *History and Industrial Relations* (ACIRRT, University of Sydney), Ch 5.
- Ramm, T. (1986) '*Laissez-faire* and State Protection of Workers' in B A Hepple (ed), *The Making of Labour Law in Europe* (Mansell, London), Ch 2
- Ryan, R., and Walsh, P. (1993) 'Common Law v Labour Law: The New Zealand Debate' 6 *Australian Journal of Labour Law* 230
- Selznick, P. (1969) *Law, Society and Industrial Justice* (Russell Sage Foundation, New York)
- Simon, D. (1954) 'Master and Servant' in J Saville (ed), *Democracy and the Labour Movement* (Lawrence & Wishart, London), Ch 6

- Stewart, A. (1992) "Atypical' Employment and the Failure of Labour Law' 18 *Australian Bulletin of Labour* 217
- Sykes, E.I., and Glasbeek, H.J. (1972) *Labour Law in Australia* (Butterworths, Sydney)
- Tolhurst, G.J. (1992) 'Contractual Confusion and Industrial Illusion: A Contract Law Perspective on Awards, Collective Agreements and the Contract of Employment' 66 *Australian Law Journal* 705
- Turner, I. (1976) *In Union is Strength* (Nelson, Melbourne)
- Watson, G. (1993) *Guide to Victoria's Employee Relations Law* (CCH Australia, Sydney)
- Wedderburn, K.W. (Lord) (1971) *The Worker and the Law* (2nd ed, Pelican, London)
- Wedderburn, K.W. (Lord) (1986) *The Worker and the Law* (3rd ed, Pelican, London)
- Wedderburn, K.W. (Lord), and Clark, J. (1983) *Labour Law and Industrial Relations* (Clarendon Press, Oxford)
- Weeks, P. (1995) *Trade Union Security Law in Australia* (Federation Press, Sydney) (Forthcoming)

REGULATION OF THE INDIVIDUAL EMPLOYMENT CONTRACT IN THE UNITED STATES

Matthew W. FINKIN

1. Introduction

This paper reviews the law governing the formation and application of the individual (non-unionised) contract of employment in the United States. At the outset, the source of law should be placed in the framework of American federalism in which the power to regulate is apportioned to the Congress and the States respectively. With one ancient exception, federal law has generally rested content with the power of the States to regulate the individual contract of employment *qua* contract. That role fell largely to the state judiciaries application of the common law, in the performance of which an abiding tension has been manifested: Whether the court is only an agent of the contract called upon consequently to apply the intent of the parties even though the terms may have been stated unilaterally and irrespective of what they provide; or whether the court, as a public body, is bound by larger societal values to construe, to limit, or even to nullify contract terms in order to lessen overreaching or an abuse of power, even where expressly reserved. (A variation on the latter has emerged in recent years that conceives of the judicial role as conducing toward more efficient market conditions. By this view a court may limit "opportunistic behaviour" otherwise seemingly allowed under the contract not out of a communal notion of fairness or good faith but to lessen the costs of future contracting.) In the common law system, the tension is even more delicate for it implicates as well the judicial function as gatekeeper of the questions that may be passed upon by a civil jury, that archetypical embodiment of community sentiment. Suffice it to say for introductory purposes, though the tension between positivism and the public function is inevitable and abiding, there is no dispute that the latter is permissibly performed in appropriate cases; the tension lies in deciding what those circumstances are.

Against this historical background, the 1991 decision of the United States Supreme Court in the *Gilmer*[1] case is extraordinary.It bids fair significantly to

---

1   Gilmer v. Interstate/Johnson Lane Corp., 500 United States Reports 20 (1991).

L. Betten (ed.), The Employment Contract in Transforming Labour Relations, 167-185.
© 1995 *Kluwer Law International. Printed in the Netherlands.*

alter the balance of the federal vis-a-vis the state role, and to invite employers to channel all employment disputes, both those founded in federal and state labour protective legislation as well as those of a contractual character, into unilateral employer-promulgated systems of private arbitration. How that has - or might - come about is also explored below.

2.   Federal Deferral to the States

The Constitution gives the federal Congress plenary power over the regulation of foreign and interstate commerce, and one of its earliest enactments in exercise of that power was a labour protective law for seamen. The United States, as a maritime Nation, had particular solicitude for its merchant marine.[2] The evils of legislative concern were the involuntary employment of sailors and the defrauding of them at the conclusion of the voyage. These evils were dealt with in an Act of July 20, 1790.[3] It required that before a voyage be commenced there be an agreement in writing (or in print) with and signed by each mariner specifying the voyage and its "term or time" subject to judicial enforcement and with specified penalties for non-compliance. The law has had many amendments - at one time requiring that the contract be executed before a public officer (who was to keep a copy of it) and further requiring that the discharge of its obligations be similarly witnessed at the conclusion of the voyage.[4] But the essentials of the law remain today: The latest version requires the individual contract to contain provisions specifying *inter alia* the nature and duration of the voyage, wages, the number and disposition of the crew, and the regulations governing conduct on board.[5]

The Seaman's Act remains unique. By the last quarter of the nineteenth century and into the first quarter of the twentieth, two developments in constitutional law eclipsed the power of Congress further to legislate toward the end of labour protection including the regulation of contract. First, the area of interstate commerce over which Congress could exercise control was narrowed by the United States Supreme Court to an irreducible core. Railroad workers

---

2   *See generally*, 3 James Kent, *Commentaries on American Law* 176 (4th ed. 1840).

3   1 Stat. 131 (1st Cong., 2nd Sess.) (1790).

4   The operation of the law is outlined in 1 M. Norris, *The Law of Seamen*, Ch. 6 (4th ed. 1985).

5   46 United States Code § 10302 (1993).

on lines of interstate carriage were obviously engaged in interstate commerce and Congress could exercise legislative power over them. But those employed in the manufacture of goods for shipment in interstate commerce were held not to be so engaged. So in the famous case of *Hammer v. Dagenhart*,[6] the United States Supreme Court struck down a law regulating the interstate shipment of goods produced by child labour. The object of the law, despite the means employed, was directed to the employment of children in factories and mines which, the Court opined, was a matter entirely of State concern. But even when there was no dispute of federal power, for example over railroad workers, the Court held the precise regulation had itself to meet a connection with the regulation of commerce satisfactory to the Court. Thus in *Railroad Retirement Board v. Alton Rr. Co.*,[7] the Court struck down a federally-created pension system for railroad workers in part on the ground that even though the workers were engaged in interstate commerce the pension plan bore no reasonable relationship to the commerce power.[8]

Second, the Court recognised economic liberty - "freedom of contract" - as a constitutionally protected liberty assertable against the federal government under the fifth amendment and against the states under the fourteenth. In *Adair*

---

6   247 United States Reports 251 (1918).

7   298 United States Reports 330 (1935).

8   The decision, by vote of five-to-four, was shortly to be abandoned by the expansion of federal power after 1937. But an excerpt from the Court's explanation powerfully conveys the sense of the time:

The theory [in support of the constitutionality of the law] is that one who has assurance against future dependency will do his work more cheerfully, and therefore more efficiently. The question at once presents itself whether the fostering of a contented mind on the part of an employee by legislation of this type, is in any just sense a regulation of interstate transportation. If that question be answered in the affirmative, obviously there is no limit to the field of so-called regulation. The catalogue of means and actions which might be imposed upon an employer in any business, tending to the satisfaction and comfort of his employees, seems endless. Provision for free medical attendance and nursing, for clothing, for food, for housing, for the education of children, and a hundred other matters, might with equal property be proposed as tending to relieve the employee of mental strain and worry. Can it fairly be said that the power of Congress to regulate interstate commerce extends to the prescription of any or all of these things? Is it not apparent that they are really and essentially related solely to the sound welfare of the worker, and therefore remote from any regulation of commerce as such? We think the answer is plain. *Id.* at 368.

v. United States,[9] for example, the Court struck down a federal statute forbidding railroads from discriminating in employment against union members; and in *Lochner v. New York*,[10] it struck down a state law providing maximum work hours for bakers. In sum, even as the Court ceded power to the states over the employment relationship, it cabined the ability of the states to enact labour protective measures when these were held unduly to infringe upon the liberty of the parties to frame contracts as they chose.

In the late 30's the Court abruptly reversed course, sustaining both the power of Congress to legislate for the establishment of collective bargaining by employees engaged in the production of goods and services and more broadly to permit protective labour legislation. But the legislation sustained by the Court that prefigured the full reach of governmental power over employment, the National Labour Relations Act, may have had the unintended consequence of closing off one avenue of state legislative experiment. It provided for exclusive collective representation by a representative designated by a majority of employees in an appropriate bargaining unit. Though there may be much to be learned for a legislatively mandated system of individual contracting from the Labour Act's experience with collective contracting - dealing with the disclosure of information necessary to bargain over terms and conditions of employment and regulating the "good faith" of the bargaining process - by adopting a principle of exclusive representation by majority rule the Congress exempted any legally enforceable right of individuals or non-majority groups to bargain over contract terms. And, because of the preemptive effect upon state authority of the Congress' having "occupied the field" of employee representation, the Labour Act beclouds any potential role the states might perform even now in experimenting with legislation devised to foster systems of individual or non-majority group representation.

In sum, the use of individual contract *vel non* was left to employers, employees, and the play of market forces. The terms are those expressly negotiated or, more commonly, stated unilaterally by employers as limited, however, by federal or state labour protective law (which would trump any contract to the contrary) and to the state law of contract, to which attention next turns.

---

9   208 United States Reports 161 (1908).

10   198 United States Reports, 45 (1905).

3.   The State Law of Employment Contracts

Putting state labour protective legislation aside, the state approach to the contract of employment has been almost entirely judge-made - that is, in application of the state's common law of contract - in which there are ostensibly no (or almost no) special rules for employment as opposed to other areas of private contracting. The law assumes a market transaction, a buyer and a seller whether of goods or of services; the courts will enforce what they conceive of as a bargained-for exchange - or supply a default rule in appropriate circumstances - subject to common law limits.

One such default rule requires special mention. A critical feature of American law is the widespread judicial adoption after the Civil War of the "at will" rule that presumed, in the absence of express agreement or of surrounding circumstances indicating to the contrary, that the employment was on a moment-to-moment basis - an instantaneous and continuous offer and acceptance - which either party was legally free to terminate at any time for any reason.

The circumstances occasioning the adoption of this rule has been the subject of a good deal of speculation,[11] some of which is bound up in the fact that the latter aspect of the rule - which freed an employer of any legal scrutiny of its reason for exercising its privilege summarily to terminate even, said the courts, for a morally repugnant reason - did not follow from its function as a default rule in the absence of express or implied agreement only as to duration. But a plausible explanation turns to the alternative default rule the "at-will" presumption arguably replaced: A presumption of fixed duration which, if not expressly stated, was governed by the customs of the particular trade or employment.

America of the mid to late nineteenth century was characterised by enormous geographic mobility and job instability. In the railroads of mid-century, less than half the employees tended to stay in employment more than six months.[12] Even in family-style Massachusetts textile mills of the ante-bellum period, annual employee job turnover averaged more than 150%.[13] And these rates of turnover increased dramatically as the century wore on. "Thus it is unsurprising", one observer wrote, that the courts "assumed a relationship of

---

11   Some of these are reviewed critically by Morriss, *Exploding Myths: An Empirical and Economic Reassessment of the Rise of Employment At-Will*, 59 Missouri Law Review p. 679 *et seq.*(1994).

12   W. Licht, *Working for the Railroad,* at p. 73 (1983).

13   J. Prude, *The Coming of Industrial Order,* 1983, at p. 144.

impermanence and instability" because the employment relationship tended in fact to be both impermanent and unstable.[14]

From an ideological perspective, the rule was viewed by the courts at the time as an embodiment of individual liberty: Under a rule that presumed a fixed duration, an employee who quit before the implied duration expired might not be entitled to compensation for the previous services performed - the contract being "entire" - and could be liable as well for breach. The idea of an "entire" contract was well known in the commercial law of the time; and the adoption of an at-will presumption separately for employment may well have contributed to (or drawn from) the regnant idea of "free" labour. In practice, however, those employers who found contracts of stated duration to be of benefit could still demand them - as could employees - subject to market forces.

Because the employment may be held on an "at will" basis, sight is sometimes lost of the fact that the relationship remains nevertheless a contractual one regarding all other terms and conditions of employment. How the law of contract plays out is usefully explored by examining six areas that supply a kind of legal framework of the common law of contract: (1) offer and acceptance; (2) requirement of a writing; (3) consideration; (4) definiteness of terms; (5) "illusory" promises; and, (6) unilateral modification.

3.1   A FRAMEWORK[15]

3.1.1 Offer and Acceptance
Much employment is offered and accepted on an oral basis, the terms are often stated in an interview, sometimes in a manager's more-or-less off-hand reply to a question at the time of hire or later. There is no doubt, however, that a manager's statements made with actual or even only "apparent authority" on the part of the employer and conveying a commitment of sufficient definiteness - most often a concomitant on compensation or, less often, to job security - can supply a term of the employment which, if accepted by the applicant or

---

14   Finkin, *The Bureaucratization of Work: Employer Policies and Contract Law*, 1986 Wisconsin Law Review, p. 733 *et seq.* at p. 739.

15   The following draws from a compilation of the law on point in H. Specter & M. Finkin, *Individual Employment Law and Litigation,* 1989. Some of the texture of the caselaw is supplied where useful.

employee, rises to a contractual commitment.[16] Where, for example, an employer stated rather casually to his employees, "You boys stick with me for five years and I will give you a hundred dollars a year bonus", the statement was held to be an offer.[17] And inasmuch as a contract may be created by conduct as well as by words, even an employer's well established business practice - of severance pay,[18] vacation pay,[19] or bonuses[20] - about which nothing is expressly said, could imply an offer of contractual terms. Acceptance may be manifested by words of assent; but the doing of an act such as commencing upon or remaining in the employment may also constitute acceptance.

3.1.2 Requirement of a Writing

Most states have legislated a statute of frauds that requires a writing, signed by the party to be charged, to evidence any contractual undertaking that cannot be performed within a year of the date of the making. The failure of such written evidence renders the contact unenforceable.

The statute is intended to prevent fraud by preventing a claimant from coming forward years after an ostensible promise had been made and, conceivably, well after the alleged promisor has passed from the scene. This concern is genuine; but in the employment setting, the requirement of a writing places the burden on an applicant or incumbent employee to request and secure a written and signed confirmation of a commitment made at a time when the psychology of the situation arguably would deter that very request from being made: At a moment when an employer has sought to secure the employee's or applicant's trust, the statute of frauds requires the employee to manifest a

---

16   Some companies have attempted to avoid the possibility of being contractually bound by such statements by requiring the execution of an agreement whereby the employee acknowledges that modification of terms may be agreed to only by a designated company officer and only in writing. Inasmuch as a written contract may, in most jurisdictions, be waived or modified orally, the latter limitation is likely to be of no legal effect. But the former has been held to be an effective limitation on an agent's apparent authority to agree. See, *e.g.*, Reid v. Sears, Roebuck & Co., 790 F.2d 453 (6th Cir. 1986).

17   Hartung v. Billmeier, 66 N.W.2d 784 (Minn. 1954).

18   See, *e.g.*, Morschauser v. American News Co., 178 N.Y.S.2d 279 (App. Div. 1958).

19   See, *e.g.*, Spencer v. Burnett, 686 S.W.2d 537 (Mo. App. 1985).

20   See, *e.g.*, Simon v. Riblet Tramway Co., 289 P.2d 1291 (Wash. App. 1973).

modicum of distrust, a lack of complete confidence that the manager will in fact honour the commitment she had just made.

The courts are bound by the legislation and they have, as they must, denied enforcement of oral contracts that are straightforwardly of more than a year's duration. But in the employment setting at least, the courts have tended to read the rule very narrowly: The generally prevailing view, not without dissent or doctrinal criticism, is that a contract of "permanent" employment - a promise of continuing employment subject to termination for cause or other good reason - is capable of being performed within a year; and so an oral commitment of that nature would be enforceable years after it arguably had been made. In one case, this line of reasoning has been followed even as to a promise of employment "until retirement".[21] And where the employment is at will, the statute of frauds is no obstacle to the enforcement of most other terms.

3.1.3 Consideration

This is not the place to explore the metaphysics of the common law requirement of consideration. Suffice it to say, there must be an exchange of promises or the doing of an act - conferring a benefit or sustaining a detriment - to render the obligation enforceable. Under the doctrine of "unilateral" contract, however, the doing of an act in compliance with the offer may constitute at once both acceptance and consideration.

Ordinarily the law does not inquire into the adequacy of consideration; but prior acts done or obligations already assumed - "past consideration" - will not support new obligations. In the employment at-will situation, because either party is free to terminate at any time either may condition future employment upon the extinction of a prior obligation or the assumption of a new one - at least as a matter of doctrine. But the courts have ameliorated the asperities of the doctrine at least in some cases by applying notions of fraud or commercial duress or, more accurately, by allowing juries to apply them.

In two areas, however, rules special to employment have developed. The first concerns an employer's demand that an incumbent employee execute a covenant not to compete. Covenants not to compete, as contracts in restraint of trade, are separately subject to judicial scrutiny as to the reasonableness of their terms. But if otherwise sustainable, there is no doubt that a covenant entered into at the time of initial hire would be enforceable, supported by the offer of the job as consideration. In a number of jurisdictions, however, a covenant required by the employer *after* the employment has commenced requires additional consideration, something more than the employer's forbearance to

---

21   Hodge v. Evans Fin. Corp., 823 F.2d 559 (D.C. Cir. 1987).

discharge, in order to be enforced. The courts have rarely discussed the rationale for this requirement at any length, but the sense of it seems to be that it is permissible for an employee to enter into such an arrangement at the outset, knowing full well that his or her future ability to practice a profession or to utilise special skills or knowledge will be impaired, but quite another to allow an employer to demand agreement by an incumbent employee, who may be a difficult position to refuse, without itself giving something of value in return other than its forbearance to discharge.

The second concerns contracts of "permanent" employment. As noted above, most courts do not read the statute of frauds to require that such commitments be in writing; but by the early twentieth century, many courts did require that such commitments be supported by additional consideration other than the employee's performance of services in order to be enforceable. The rule has been explained as more one of evidence than of substantive law: The courts tended to conceive of "permanent" employment in terms of "lifetime" employment, archtypically a sinecure offered to an injured employee in return for relinquishing a tort claim against the employer. The commitment was thought accordingly to be so "highly improbable", especially where oral and uncorroborated, that the courts were reluctant to enforce it absent some additional circumstance to indicate that such a commitment had indeed been made.[22] "Permanent" employment in the sense of a commitment not to be discharged unless cause is presented or economic considerations would justify it is common today; and a number of courts (but by no means all) have modified the doctrine of "additional" consideration accordingly.

Where consideration is lacking but an employee can show detrimental reliance upon an employer's act or representation, a number of courts have applied a doctrine of "promissory estoppel" to render the representation enforceable. In some cases, the doctrine has been given even broader application than as only a substitute for the lack of legal consideration.[23]

---

22   *See generally*, Littell v. Evening Star Newspaper Co., 120 F.2d 36 (D.C. Cir. 1941); Wolfe v. Graether, 389 N.W.2d 643 (Iowa 1986).

23   In Grouse v. Group Health Plan, 306 N.W.2d 114 (Minn. 1981), for example, an applicant terminated employment with his incumbent employer in reliance upon the defendant's offer of employment, only to be told by the latter that the hire would not be honored. The defendant argued that inasmuch as the offer was for an "at will" job it could not be held liable for any damage; *i.e.*, it could have honored its offer only simultaneously to discharge. The Supreme Court of Minnesota held that the employee "had a right to assume that he would be given a good faith opportunity to perform . . . once he was on the job." The measure of damage was not what he failed to get from his future employer but what he had lost by quitting his prior employer in reliance on

3.1.4 Definiteness of Terms

To be enforceable, the terms of a contract must be "reasonably certain" and the courts, exercising their gatekeeper function over what may and may not go to a determination by a jury, have tended to disallow generalised assurances of good or fair treatment or confident expectations of long duration as being capable of contractual effect. But a number of presumptions or default rules have been brought into play where there was obviously a commitment of some sort that fairness would require be observed; thus, where salary or wages were left unspecified the courts presume that a "reasonable" compensation could be determined from all the surrounding circumstances, as could the precise duties to be performed or the computation of a promised bonus. So, for example, sums "advanced" to a salesman as a "draw" against commissions are not returnable if the commissions fail to materialise unless the contract is explicitly to the contrary. In this as in other cases, the usage of the trade or profession or the employer's own well-established past practice have been held to supply contractual terms.

3.1.5 Illusory Promises

An employer may wish generally to assure a term or condition of employment while reserving to itself an unreviewable power to decide its extent or application. In the matter of job security especially, an employer, while wishing to assure employees of fair treatment, may not wish to have the grounds for its action submitted to a communal assessment. This end is sought to be given legal effect either by expressly reserving unilateral power or by disclaiming a contractual commitment. To some courts such a reservation renders the underlying promise or provision illusory and so no obligation at all; but there is a respectable body of law holding, in essence, that "[A]n employer cannot reserve to itself the power to declare its underlying obligation an illusion".[24]

---

the representation.

24   Finkin, *Commentary on "Arbitration of Employment Disputes Without Unions"*, 66 Chicago-Kent Law Review, pp. 799 *et seq.*, at p. 811 (1992). Some of the law is laid out:

Thus an employer may not enter upon a contract of fixed duration while reserving to itself the power to terminate earlier for no reason. *See, e.g.*, Carter v. Bradlee, 245 A.D. 49, 280 N.Y.S. 368, *aff'd*, 269 N.Y. 664, 200 N.E. 48 (1936), *followed in* Rothenberg v. Lincoln Farm Camp, Inc., 755 F.2d 1017 (2d Cir. 1985). *See also* King v. Control Systematologists, Inc., 479 So.2d 955 (La. App. 1985), *cert. denied*, 482 So.2d 630 (La. 1986); Yazujian v. J. Rich Steers, Inc., 195 Misc. 694, 89 N.Y.S.2d 551 (Sup. Ct. 1949); Dallas Hotel v. Lackey, 203 S.W.2d 557 (Tex. Civ. App. 1947). An employer's reservation of "sole discretion" to pay a

3.1.6 Unilateral Modification

As noted at the outset, where the employment is held at-will either party is free to demand a change in terms on pain of a termination of the relationship. Consequently, where an employer unilaterally changes a term or condition of employment, as a doctrinal matter the prevailing view has been that the employee, who continues thereafter to serve with knowledge of the change, has assented to it: The continuance in service constitutes an "acceptance", and the employer's continuing to employ constitutes consideration. More recently, however, at least some courts have been troubled by that approach, especially where the employment is conditioned upon the relinquishment of a previously earned benefit or job right, and have required a showing of actual consent,[25] or additional consideration other than retention in employment, or have applied notions of fraud or duress[26] to limit the employer's power in that regard.

With the foregoing legal framework in mind, attention next turns to the contemporary contractual status of announced employer policies, rule books, or employee manuals.

---

commission may not defeat an obligation to pay. *See, e.g.*, Spencer v. General Elec. Co., 243 F.2d 934 (8th Cir. 1957); Tymshare, Inc. v. Covell, 727 F.2d 1145 (D.C. Cir. 1984); Allen D. Shadron, Inc. v. Cole, 101 Ariz. 122, 416 P.2d 555, *aff'd*, 101 Ariz. 341, 419 P.2d 520 (1966). Similarly, an employer may not obligate itself to pay a bonus while disclaiming a legal obligation to pay. *See, e.g.*, Cinelli v. American Home Prods. Corp., 785 F.2d 264 (10th Cir. 1986); George A. Fuller Co. v. Brown, 15 F.2d 672 (4th Cir. 1926); Patterson v. Brooks, 285 Ala. 349, 232 So.2d 598 (1970); Ellis v. Emhart Mfg. Co., 150 Conn. 501, 191 A.2d 546 (1963); Wellington v. Con P. Curran Printing Co., 216 Mo. App. 358, 268 S.W.2d 396 (1925); Molbey v. Hunter Hosiery, Inc., 102 N.H. 422, 158 A.2d 288 (1960); Oiler v. Dayton Reliable Tool & Mfg. Co., 42 Ohio App. 2d 26, 326 N.E.2d 692 (1974); Goudie v. HNG Oil Co., 711 S.W.2d 716 (Tex. App. 1986). Nor may it promise benefits while disclaiming a legal obligation to pay. *See, e.g.*, Tilbert v. Eagle Lock Co., 116 Conn. 357, 165 A. 205 (1933); Psutka v. Michigan Alkali Co., 274 Mich. 318, 264 N.W. 385 (1936); Mabley & Carew Co. V. Borden, 129 Ohio St. 375, 195 N.E. 697 (1935); Schofield v. Zion's Co-op Merchantile Ind., 85 Utah 281, 39 P.2d 342 (1934). *Id.* at n. 54.

25   See, *e.g.*, Robinson v. Ada S. McKinley Community Services, 19 F.3d 359 (7th Cir. 1994).

26   See, *e.g.*, Goodwyn v. Sencore, Inc., 389 F. Supp. 824 (D.S.D. 1975).

3.2 EMPLOYER POLICIES AND INDIVIDUAL CONTRACT

Employees and employers have negotiated express, written individual contracts where certainty of terms - and the avoidance of future disputes over exactly what the terms were - has been of importance. In early nineteenth century agricultural employment, for example, individual contracts with farm labourers (hired "hands") were common - specifying duration, rate of pay (whether by the day or the amount of specific work), laundry and mending, and manner of payment including goods provided or a drawing account at the local store.[27] Also common were the use of individual contracts in nineteenth century textile manufacture where skilled labour had been in short supply.[28] These were used to insure the maintenance of a skilled workforce (especially against "enticement" by other mills, which would be an inducement to contract breach) and expressly to incorporate rules governing the withholding of wages and penalties for non-performance - though the latter, too, were subject to judicial scrutiny under a common law that disfavoured forfeiture.[29]

The incorporation of employer rules into individual contracts underlines a key aspect of industrialisation - the division of labour and the growth of large corporate enterprises. Employers adopted rules to enhance their control of the workforce - rules providing for working time, fines for absences or tardiness, prohibitions on leaving the premises, even from engaging in casual conversation; and enforcement of the rules required that they be known. Where written form contracts were not utilised, rules governing such matters were posted, and an employee who had notice of them was charged with their observation as a condition of employment. These rules were intended to be legally binding: As a Pennsylvania legislative committee of the period observed, "Engaging to work in a factory is considered a yielding assent to the laws".[30]

A critical feature of the bureaucratisation of American employment, especially following the Second World War, was the development of internal labour markets by non-unionised firms, often to compete with their unionised competitors. To a considerable extent work was no longer market mediated; the "ports of entry" to the company's workforce were limited, and workers were

---

27   D. Shob, *Hired Hands and Plowboys: Farm Labour in the Midwest 1815-1860,* 1975.

28   C. Ware, *The Early New England Cotton Manufacture,* 1931, at p. 260.

29   *Compare* Schimp v. Tennessee Mfg. Co., 6 S.W. 131 (Tenn. 1887) *with* Tennessee Mfg. Co. v. James, 18 S.W. 262 (Tenn. 1892).

30   *Quoted in* C. Shelton, The Mills of Manayunk, p. 73 (1986).

retained by a commitment to job security, an array of benefits, and internal lines of progression and promotion. These features of late twentieth century employment found expression in the issuance of company policy manuals and employee handbooks. As it has been explained:

> In the nineteenth century, the employer's work rules, if not brutish, were short; as much information as the employee needed to know was ordinarily conveyed by the foreman. As late as 1935, only 13% of industrial firms had adopted company rulebooks. The bureaucratisation of work, however, enmeshes the worker in a "web of rules" and it requires that the rules be known. By 1948, 30% of industrial firms had adopted employee handbooks. A 1979 survey of 6,000 companies revealed that employee handbooks were distributed by approximately 75% of the companies responding.[31]

These documents often contain assurances of job security or contain rules governing probation and progressive discipline. The contractual status of these rules has been widely litigated. A majority of jurisdictions to have considered the issue have held that these documents are capable of supplying contractual terms, but they have differed on the theory involved, on how clear the provision at issue must be, and on whether or not individual knowledge and reliance must be shown as a condition of enforceability; and a minority has rejected contractual status altogether. Even among the majority, the courts have said that a sufficiently clear and conspicuous disclaimer of contractual status should be given effect.

One student of these rules, which he terms "enterprise rights", has opined that until about 1980 the courts had not considered them to be enforceable at all; rather the courts viewed employee handbooks and similar statements of employer policies "both written and oral, as no more than employer benefices . . . and therefore not contractually binding".[32] That is wrong. As noted earlier, employer-promulgated policies (as well as oral assurances) were often held contractually binding; indeed, insofar as they contained rules on work hours, fines, and forfeitures they were intended to be contractually binding. From this perspective, the judicial declination in some jurisdictions to accord contractual status when these rules would seem to contain provisions of job security beneficial to employees is the true anomaly. For the same reason the

---

31   M. Finkin, footnote 14 *supra* at pp. 742-743.

32   R. Edwards, *Rights at Work,* 1933, at p. 157.

prevailing view on the availability of the device of a disclaimer to avoid contractual status of commitments to job security or to progressive discipline seems hard to square with the respectable body of law on illusory promises adverted to earlier; indeed, there seems little doubt that many of these courts would be reluctant to accede to the disclaimer's application to a bonus, commission, vacation, education benefit, or profit-sharing provision contained in the very same manual. Suffice it to say, consistent with the public function of a judicial body, some courts have flatly refused to genuflect to a disclaimer,[33] have read them very narrowly to deny enforcement for want of adequate clarity or conspicuousness,[34] or have avoided the question altogether by holding it one of fact for a jury to decide.[35]

3.3 SUMMARY

Briefly to summarise, and putting the differences between jurisdictions - sometimes sharp, sometimes highly nuanced - aside, if one were to be asked to characterise the law of individual employment contracts in one word, it would be only a slight oversimplification to say that that would be "flexibility". In a great many, perhaps the vast majority of cases, there need be no writing. There need be no express exchange of promises. Most often, the terms are those stated by the employer (or its agent) or, on occasion, as implied from its conduct or surrounding circumstances. And the determination of the actual terms and the extent to which they have been observed is given over to a community judgment via the civil jury, subject to judicial supervision in which the courts have often attempted to strike a sometimes delicate balance between allowing a robust freedom of contract and disallowing an abuse of power.

Apropos the latter, however, it ought be stressed that relief in contract is limited to compensation for the breach - to put the employee in the position she would have occupied had the contract been observed - less mitigation, from which a prevailing plaintiff must pay her attorney fees and costs. Accordingly, it has been observed that contract cases tend to be pursued by the better paid,

---

33 See, *e.g.*, Greene v. Howard Univ., 412 F.2d 1128 (D.C. Cir. 1969).

34 See, *e.g.*, Nicosia v. Wakefield Food Corp., 643 A.2d 554 (N.J. 1994).

35 These cases are catalogued in Befort, *Employee Handbooks and the Legal Effect of Disclaimers*, 13 Industrial Relations Law Journal, 1991-1992, at p. 326.

especially managerial employees, *i.e.* primarily those for whom the sums eventually involved might justify the expense.[36]

4. The Resurgence of Federal Power: Preemption and the Privatisation of Public Law

In 1925, Congress enacted the Federal Arbitration Act (FAA).[37] The Act was intended to facilitate commercial arbitration in the face of the hostility of state judiciaries to agreements to arbitrate future disputes. The Act requires the submission to arbitration where there is a "written provision in . . . a contract evidencing a transaction involving interstate commerce" so providing; but it exempts "contracts of employment of seamen, railroad employees, or any other class of workers engaged in foreign or interstate commerce". The scope of judicial review once an arbitration has been had is extremely narrow.

In recent years, the United States Supreme court had given the FAA a very broad reach, even to sweep into arbitration disputes governed by federal or state commercial law. In *Gilmer v. Interstate/Johnson Lane Corp.*,[38] the United States Supreme Court extended this body of law to a provision in a securities' broker's registration application - under which he agreed to "arbitrate any dispute, claim or controversy" arising out of his employment, pursuant to rules of the relevant stock exchange - to reach the broker's claim that he had been discharged in violation of the federal Age Discrimination in Employment Act.

Professor Robert A. Gorman has characterised *Gilmer* as the beginning of a "vast reallocation of jurisdiction over employment disputes from civil courts and administrative agencies to privately selected arbitrators".[39] And because the private vindiction of public rights are involved attention has quite rightly been placed on the structure of such systems - how arbitrators are to be selected, how individual employees are to be represented, the procedural rights of the parties, and the role of judicial review - on the valid assumption that

---

36   See generally P. Weiler, *Governing the Workplace,* 1990; Summers, *Effective Remedies for Employment Rights: Preliminary Guidelines and Proposals,* 141 University of Pennsylvania Law Review, at p. 457 (1992).

37   9 United States Code, §§ 1 *et seq.*

38   500 United States Reports, 20 (1991).

39   Gorman, *The Gilmer Decision and the Private Arbitration of Public-Law Disputes,* University of Illinois Law Review, 1995 (in press).

because public rights are to be submitted to a private forum there must be a public determination of the fairness of the procedures, the accuracy of the results, and the degree of faithfulness to the statute at hand.[40]

Less commented upon thus far are the implications of *Gilmer* for the vindication of private contract claims of the sort reviewed here; nor is it at all obvious why that should be of particular concern. A great many states have adopted arbitration statutes that in general track the federal Act - that channel contract claims to agreed-upon arbitral mechanisms and that narrow judicial review. And employers were free prior to *Gilmer* to bring themselves under these laws for contract claims, though they may have been reluctant to have done so for fear of encouraging the claim to be brought.[41]

Moreover, if employers were to avail themselves of the Court's invitation in *Gilmer* to submit public protective law claims to private arbitration, they would be likely as well to include any purely private contract claims in the same procedure, for the sake of convenience and cost. If so, employees might be afforded more rigorous procedures than the employer otherwise might be required to observe for contract claims standing alone. Apropos of that, Professor Samuel Estreicher has argued that insofar as the source of the claims asserted arise under employer policies, there is no reason why the employee should not be bound by the procedure provided under that policy to vindicate

---

40   The final report of the Commission on the Future of Worker-Management Relations, appointed by the Secretaries of Labor and Commerce, laid out seven requirements for such systems. They must provide:
      a neutral arbitrator who knows the laws in question and understands the concerns of the parties;
      - a fair and simple method by which the employee can secure the necessary information to present his or her claim;
      - a fair method of cost-sharing between the employer and employee to ensure affordable access to the system for all employees;
      - the right to independent representation if the employee wants it;
      - a range of remedies equal to those available through ligitation;
      - a written opinion by the arbitrator explaining the rationale for the result; and
      - sufficient judicial review to ensure that the result is consistent with the governing laws.
      Report and Recommendations of the Commission on the Future of Worker Management Relations, p. 31 (Jan. 9, 1995). Evenso, the Commission recommended, pending the developed experience under such systems, that they not be considered as enforceable conditions of employment. *Id.* at p. 33.

41   One attorney representing management was reported as observing that some companies were concerned lest arbitration become "too accessible". *BNA Daily Labor Report,* No. 34 at A-9 (Feb. 21, 1995).

the claim *whatever* it may be; that in such a case the employee has to take the "bitter" with the "sweet".[42] Thus, it is possible that non-highly compensated employees will be better off under *Gilmer* vis-a-vis their contract claims if a swift, inexpensive, and fair forum is now made available - the latter assuming that the same procedural standards of fairness adopted to control the arbitration of public claims will extend to private ones.

Without denying the force of the above, one may nevertheless entertain some nagging second thoughts. An arbitrator, we have often been reminded, is a creature of the contract whose authority can rise no higher than its source. He dispenses what the contract says and is worthy of deference only to the extent he has been faithful - however badly or however much in error - to that task. He does not dispense a sense of justice external to the contract. A judge is a civil officer who is expected to apply larger societal values even to the task of reading a private contract, as some of the cases previously noted, *e.g.* on illusory promises, duress, and covenants not to compete, evidence. This is not to gainsay that a body of arbitral "common lore" might not develop in this setting, as it has under union-management grievance arbitration, to temper the ostensible positivism of arbitration.[43] But it is to observe a significant difference at the outset in the role to be performed; and to suggest that it is unlikely that the courts, however deeply they examine the arbitral treatment of

---

42   Estreicher, *Arbitration of Employment Disputes Without Unions*, 66 Chicago-Kent Law Review, p. 753 *et seq.*, n.53 at 771 (1992). The thrust of Estreicher's positivism would deny any public scrutiny of the procedure adopted by an employer for the determination of its own contractual obligations, even a reservation of final disposition to management or to a body controlled by it. Contrary to this view, there is a respectable body of state decisional law that considers the fairness of the procedure for the violation of even purely private contract rights a proper question of public concern. See Renny v. Port Huron Hosp., 398 N.W.2d 327 (Mich. 1986); see also Cross & Brown Co. v. Nelson, 167 N.Y.S.2d 573 (App. Div. 1957); Burger v. Jan Garment Co., 52 Luz L. Reg. 33 (Pa. Com. Plas 1962); McConnell v. Howard University, 818 F.2d 58 (D.C. Cir. 1987); Manes v. Dallas Baptist College, 638 S.W.2d 143 (Tex. App. 1982) (writ of error refused, no reversible error). But see Suburban Hospital v. Dwiggins, 596 A.2d 1069 (Md. 1991).

43   See, *e.g.*, Paine Webber In. v. Argon, -F.3d.- (8th Cir. 1995) reported in BNA DAILY LABOR REPORT No. 45 at A-2 (March 8, 1995), where an arbitration panel in the securities industry awarded a remedy for a broker, discharged for signing the client's name to an account transfer with the client's permission, despite a company rule prohibiting signing the client's name under any circumstance. The court held, under the scope of review of the FAA, that it may not upset the arbitral judgment "no matter how wrong" they believe it to be.

public law questions, will subject the purely private contract claim to any more exacting examination than the FAA contemplates..

Moreover, even if a number of states had adopted statutes similar to the FAA, some have excluded individual contract claims; and in any event, the degree of deference on the facts in any one case would present a question of state law. From this perspective it is difficult to discern precisely what the *federal* interest is that requires claims not only under state labour protective legislation but also arising under the state law of contract (or tort) to be governed by federal law. The only answer is to the commerce clause; but this returns analysis to the fact that the FAA exempts contracts of employment of "seamen, railroad employees, or any other class of workers engaged in foreign or interstate commerce". The *Gilmer* court expressly declined to reach the application of this exemption, relying instead upon the employee's registration statement as the writing evidencing a transaction in interstate commerce.[44] It is, then, at least theoretically possible for the Court to apply the exemption, just as it reads, to exclude from the FAA contracts of individual employment. As Archibald Cox has pointed out, the language of the FAA was chosen at a time when the commerce power extended to the employment of seamen and railroad workers but not to most other employments.[45] Putting the FAA in historical context, Congress would seem to have exempted all those employments over which it could have exercised jurisdiction, and as that class expanded so would the reach of the exemption. If this were so, whether or not an employee's claim should be referred at the outset to a greivance or grievance-arbitration procedure promulgated unilaterally by an employer, and whether or not the product of that procedure should be deferred to thereafter, would be governed by state law in the disposition of which the state's public policy might potentially be implicated.

Contrary to this view, Professor Estreicher reads the legislative history of the FAA to indicate that the exemption was intended to preclude the submission to arbitration of "interest" disputes, disputes over future terms and conditions of employment, there being at the time very little arbitration of "rights" disputes, disputes arising under existing collective bargaining agreements.[46] He points out that organised labour strongly opposed an earlier draft of the FAA that lacked the later-adopted exemption, and that one of labour's voices raised

---

44   Justice Stevens dissented on the ground of the Act's inapplicability to individual employment disputes.

45   Cox, *Grievance Arbitration in the Federal Courts*, 67 Harvard Law Review, 1954, pp. 591 *et seq.*, at p. 598.

46   Estreicher, footnore 42 *supra,* at n.25 p. 761.

in opposition was Andrew Furuseth, President of the International Seamen's Union.[47]

If interest arbitration were the gravamen of the exemption, Congress chose very odd language to achieve it. More important, it is well to remember that under the Act of 1790, seamen were the only employees who were required by law to have individual contracts of employment, even if on terms stated (in writing or in print) unilaterally by the employer. The application of the FAA to them would allow an employer to bring itself out of a judicial determination of its obligations merely by the insertion of a boilerplate arbitration provision in such a form contract;[48] and long after the protections of the National Labour Relations Act were extended to seamen, the United States Supreme Court rejected the argument that these individual contract claims should be subject to the arbitration provision of an applicable collective bargaining agreement even as to a wage provision set by the collective bargaining agreement.[49] To the Court's plurality, requiring submission of the individual contract claim to arbitration would be antithetical to the role of the courts as an important component of a protective scheme. From this perspective, the extension of the FAA to unilaterally promulgated employer arbitration systems for all other (non-transportation) employees, not only as to public law claims but even as to claims arising under individual contract, would appear difficult to defend.

In the event, it remains to be seen what the content of these unilaterally promulgated arbitration systems will be, how faithful to the public purpose their dispositions are, and of the extent to which their approach to the contractual content of employer policies will contain a concern for fairness or an abuse of power. In other words, it remains to be seen whether the heightened access to a forum for the vindication of contract rights made available by *Gilmer* will be worth the preclusion of a public function in the process.

---

47   *Id.*

48   Accordingly, Furuseth's objection might well be better understood in that context. I am indebted to Professor David E. Feller of the Law School (Boalt Hall) of the University of California at Berkeley for bringing this explanation of the legislative history to my attention. These remarks were penned, however, while in residence at the University of Konstanz whose resources in American history, while altogether admirable, did not allow research to test the suggestion.

49   U.S. Bulk Carriers v. Arguelles, 400 U.S. 351 (1971).

LIST OF AUTHORS

Lammy BETTEN was Associate Professor of Labour Law at the University of Utrecht; from 1996 onwards she is Professor of European Law at the University of Exeter.

Marco BIAGI is Professor of Labour Law and Industrial Relations at the University of Modena.

Breen CREIGHTON is Professor of Law at the School of Law and Legal Studies, La Trobe University, Melbourne.

Reinhold FAHLBECK is Professor of Labour Law at the University of Lund.

Matthew FINKIN is Albert J. Harno Professor of Law and Professor in the Institute of Labor and Industrial Relations at the University of Illinois.

Mark FREEDLAND is Reader in Law at St. John's College, Oxford.

Richard MITCHELL is Professor of Law at the Centre for Employment and Labour Relations Law, University of Melbourne.

Manfred WEISS is Professor of Labour Law at the Wolfgang Goethe University, Frankfurt.

Ryuichi YAMAKAWA is Associate Professor of Law at the Musashi University, Tokyo.